YOUTH IN FIJI AND SOLOMON ISLANDS

LIVELIHOODS, LEADERSHIP AND CIVIC ENGAGEMENT

YOUTH IN FIJI AND SOLOMON ISLANDS

LIVELIHOODS, LEADERSHIP AND CIVIC ENGAGEMENT

AIDAN CRANEY

Australian
National
University

ANU PRESS

PACIFIC SERIES

For Kiri

Australian
National
University

ANU PRESS

Published by ANU Press
The Australian National University
Canberra ACT 2600, Australia
Email: anupress@anu.edu.au

Available to download for free at press.anu.edu.au

ISBN (print): 9781760465148
ISBN (online): 9781760465155

WorldCat (print): 1309098982
WorldCat (online): 1309098948

DOI: 10.22459/YFSI.2022

Cover design and layout by ANU Press. Cover artwork by John Pettitt.

This book is published under the aegis of the Pacific Editorial Board of ANU Press.

Contents

Abbreviations

FSII	Forum Solomon Islands International
GDP	gross domestic product
HDI	Human Development Index
ICT	information and communication technology
ILO	International Labour Organization
NEC	National Employment Centre (Fiji)
NGO	nongovernmental organisation
OECD	Organisation for Economic Co-operation and Development
PIFS	Pacific Islands Forum Secretariat
REP	Rapid Employment Project
SINU	Solomon Islands National University
SPC	Secretariat of the Pacific Community
TVET	technical and vocational education and training
TWP	Thinking and Working Politically
UN	United Nations
UNDP	United Nations Development Programme
US	United States

Acknowledgements

I would like to acknowledge that the research and writing of this book took place on the lands of the Wurundjeri people of the Kulin nation in Australia, the people of Rewa and Naitasiri in Fiji, and the people of Guadalcanal in Solomon Islands. I extend my thanks to these peoples and their elders and leaders, past and present. As an Irish-born Australian, I am eternally grateful to be able to work in these spaces.

My utmost gratitude goes to my research participants, both the communities with whom I engaged and the key informants who shared with me their wisdom and experiences. I also could not have completed this research if not for the help of some incredible research assistants: Viola Lesi, Sina Suliano, Loqi Tawaivuna and Litea Bola in Fiji, and Fredrick Watson Vava and Eddie Pii in Solomon Islands.

There are an incredible number of people at La Trobe University who have been of invaluable support to me. Principally, Helen Lee, who has been an incredible supervisor, mentor and friend, whose continued generosity is a genuine gift. As an interdisciplinary researcher, I have been helped by many others in my intellectual journey and so my thanks goes to: Chris Roche, Wendy Mee, Michael O'Keefe, Yeshe Smith, Jack Taylor, Natalie Araujo, Makiko Nishitani, Tarryn Phillips, Tait Brimacombe, Nicks (Barry, Herriman and Smith), Raul Sanchez-Urribarri, Julie Rudner, Ray Madden, Brooke Wilmsen, Tom McNamara, Rae Wilding, Sue Davies, Linda Kelly, Eileen Christou, John Cox, Lis Jackson, Lisa Denney, Ujjwal Krishna, Chris Adams, Allan Mua Illingworth, Tim Thornton, Dan Bray, Ben Habib, Dominic Kelly, Gijs Verbossen, Kirsty MacFarlane, Mia Hansen, Alex Cosma, Karen Strojek, Chris Trinh, Julie Blythe and, more generally, the Department of Social Inquiry, Institute for Human Security and Social Change, and the Department of Politics, Media and Philosophy. Apologies to anyone I have overlooked.

Thanks also to David Hudson and the team at the Developmental Leadership Program, Patrick Vakaoti, Matthew Allen, the staff of the Pacific Leadership Program, members of the Green Growth Leaders' Coalition, and colleagues from the Australia Pacific Training Coalition and The Asia Foundation.

The greatest thanks of all go to my amazing family and friends. I would love to name them all individually, but there are too many, and I fear missing someone. For broad-stroke purposes, this includes my high school (and adjacent) mates, my Fiji family, those who supported me in Honiara, Curtin drinking buddies (and the John Curtin Hotel for providing a wonderful alternative classroom) and a host of wonderful individuals whom I have met across the globe.

To my parents, Deirdre and Brendan, who took the greatest of risks in uprooting their family and moving to the other side of the world, my eternal thanks. Thank you to my brothers, Colin and Evin, their partners, Margeaux and Melissa, and the tykes, Aisling, Torin, Liam and growing. Henry Dale and Dorothy Marie, thanks for being excellent study buddies.

For funding assistance, I acknowledge the generous support of a La Trobe University Postgraduate Research Scholarship and Internal Research Grant that supported the research process for the thesis from which this book is derived. I also acknowledge the support of the La Trobe University Social Research Platform Grant in funding the copyediting of this book. I also thank ANU Press for their ongoing commitment to open-access publication, which helps to make works such as this readily accessible in the Pacific. I particularly extend this thanks to Pacific series editor Stewart Firth, and the two anonymous reviewers of my draft.

A special thank you goes to John Pettitt for his wonderful cover art.

Finally, to Kiri, words will never express how thankful I am for your love and support.

Extracts of some of the data and discussion in this book have previously been published elsewhere. This includes chapters in Helen Lee's edited volume *Pacific Youth: Local and Global Futures* (see Lee and Craney 2019; Craney 2019) and articles in *Asia Pacific Viewpoint* (Craney 2021a) and *The Contemporary Pacific* (Craney 2021b).

Prologue

The research presented in this book unofficially commenced on 3 August 2012. On that day, I arrived in Suva, Fiji, for a 10-month stint working for the local office of an international nongovernmental organisation (NGO). Through the Australian Youth Ambassadors for Development program, I was employed in a research, training and evaluation capacity on a project that aimed to improve the livelihood opportunities for peri-urban and rural youth who were unemployed and had varying levels of education. During this period, I not only worked on the particulars of the project but also was exposed to a network of youth activists and advocates attempting to address a range of issues that young people faced in Fiji and throughout the Pacific region.

Through my work, I became aware of the multiple and compounding issues that young people in the Pacific face to actualise their livelihood, leadership and civic engagement potential. The challenges these young people faced were typically siloed and essentialised: unemployment, idleness, teenage pregnancy, and so on—each a genuine issue to confront. The more knowledgeable I became about these issues, the more it appeared to me that there was a pattern in how these problems were identified and how it was proposed they should be addressed. Policy papers were written and development projects were funded.

The quality of these interventions and the extent to which there was genuine commitment to their success varied. When each intervention resulted in less-than-perfect outcomes, they were discontinued or reframed. There is nothing new or unusual about this; it is common practice in public policy and the development sector (Andrews et al. 2015; Cornwall and Rivas 2015; Wong 2003). Rather than reflecting on how challenging it is to address youth livelihood and development issues, however, I began to consider that the reasons the same issues were discussed decade on decade and interventions did not achieve their intended goals were the essentialisation of each issue and the failure of interventions to go beyond paper commitments. This was how the seeds were planted for my decision to formally research youth livelihoods, leadership and civic engagement in Oceania. It was also where I first began to form my conceptual framework for understanding these issues through a 'holistic livelihoods' approach and to develop the contention that young Pacific peoples' lives are marked by their 'structural minimisation'—two concepts that I discuss further in the book proper.

Introduction

With roughly one-third of their populations aged 15–34, both Fiji and Solomon Islands are experiencing what is referred to in the social sciences as a 'youth bulge'. Expanded to include those aged 0–14, these population percentages increase to more than 60 per cent and almost 75 per cent, respectively (FBoS 2018; SINSO 2011).[1] As with all countries, the future prosperity of the Great Ocean States of the Pacific (Naupa 2016)[2] is inherently linked with the capacities of their young people to become full, active and positive participants in all facets of society. Based on the large population of young people in these states, the development of such capacities is pertinent. Despite this, there remains a significant shortage of literature related to the opportunities for Pacific youth to develop their individual potential, engage in prosocial behaviours and decision-making processes, and contribute to discourse about the developmental futures of their communities, countries and cultures.

This book addresses these issues. Through a combination of case studies and conversations with youth advocates and young people, particularly in activist spaces, I explore the concerns young people in Fiji and Solomon Islands face regarding the daily provision of needs, engaging with their

---

1   The population breakdown by age demographics from the 2019 census is yet to be released.
2   Throughout this book, I employ interchangeable terminology to refer to the region consisting of Pacific island countries and territories—specifically 'Pacific', 'Oceania' and the 'Great Ocean States of the Pacific'. This reflects current debates within Pacific studies from both established and emerging scholars about the elasticity of such terms and which is/are most appropriate (McGavin 2014: 134), supported by personal communication with various Pacific studies scholars. The terminology 'Great Ocean States'—or sometimes Large Ocean States (Jumeau 2013) or Big Ocean States (Sogavare 2016)—is designed to contrast with the established development parlance of 'Small Island Developing States'. The rationale for this terminology is twofold: the first is to recognise that many Pacific cultures identify the Pacific Ocean as part of their spiritual and ancestral homeland—that is, their borders do not cease at their shorelines; the second is to challenge notions that may equate smallness in land size with inferiority in terms of intellectual or cultural capacity. The adoption of this term has been heavily influenced by Epeli Hau`ofa's essays 'Our Sea of Islands' (1994) and 'The Ocean in Us' (1998), both of which discuss these issues even if not the specific terminology.

communities as active citizens, and their opportunities to achieve self-actualisation. This includes an examination of some of the formal and informal structures—such as education, employment and civil society—that are intended to assist young people in reaching their potential and becoming productive members of their communities to see the extent to which they are promoting or inhibiting young people to achieve that potential.

The framing of youth issues all too often applies a pejorative lens that assumes youth deviancy (Protzko and Schooler 2019; Pruitt 2020). I do not engage with this subject through a security-focused risk-management lens, however (Goldstone 2002; Moller 1968; Urdal 2006). Rather, my research acknowledges the capabilities of youth to have both positive and negative impacts on their societies, with a focus on identifying where their positive potentials can be and are being nurtured. This perspective also allows for the recognition that most of the everyday practices in which young people engage in any location are neither objectively positive nor objectively negative. Like any other demographic, young people have the capacity for good and ill but most generally display a neutral disposition and engagement with their societies.

Field sites

Outsiders often wrongly impose assumptions about cultural homogeneity across Oceania as well as within states. This is despite the Pacific Ocean occupying roughly one-third of the world's surface and recognition that Oceania is home to great cultural and linguistic diversity (Tryon 2009). In an attempt to acknowledge the cultural heterogeneity across and within states, this book examines Pacific youthhood at three intersecting levels: the experiences of youth within Fiji and Solomon Islands, the experiences of youth in these states in comparison with one another, and the experiences of Pacific youth more broadly.

The selection of Fiji and Solomon Islands for comparison was due to similarities and differences across the two that provided insights at subnational, national and regional levels. They are, respectively, the second and third most populous Oceanic states. Fiji's population was recorded in 2017 as 884,887 people spread across its 332 islands (FBoS 2018). More than three-quarters of these people live on the largest island of Viti Levu, with most of the rest of the population living on the second-largest island of Vanua Levu. The most recent Solomon Islands census provisionally approximated a population of 721,455, in 2019 (SINSO 2020: 1). Though Solomon Islands comprises more than 900 individual islands, most are uninhabited. Six island groups hold most of the population, with Guadalcanal and Malaita the most populous.

Both Fiji and Solomon Islands have experienced civil unrest since the late twentieth century. Fiji has experienced four attempted coups d'état since 1987, with the first three represented by the perpetrators as rooted in tensions between the iTaukei and Indo-Fijian populations (Fraenkel and Firth 2009a: 3; Lal 2009: 36).[3] The two coups in 1987 were conducted by the armed forces, resulting in military-led government, and stimulated by fears in the iTaukei community about the increased political influence of the Indo-Fijian community following elections that resulted in an Indo-Fijian majority-led government (Ravuvu 1991: 79–81, 97). The 2000 coup, backed by businessman George Speight and similarly represented as motivated by fears of Indo-Fijian political influence, was unsuccessful and led to the peculiar situation of parliament being dissolved and then reinstituted by the High Court (Fraenkel and Firth 2009b: 453; Lal 2002). The 2006 coup—the 'coup to end all coups' (Fraenkel and Firth 2009a: 4)—was described by its leaders as intended to unite a divided nation (p. 7). Though the role of ethnic tensions should not be understated and continues to be acknowledged by scholars as an underlying cause of unrest (Tarte 2009), studies by scholars such as Fijian sociologist Vijay Naidu (2013) and development historian Robbie Robertson (2012) suggest that issues of land rights, economic opportunity and political power were more salient factors.

Solomon Islands was the site of civil conflict between 1998 and 2003, which is known locally as 'the Tensions' (Bennett 2002; Liloqula 2000; Vella 2014). The conflict required foreign security and governance intervention to stabilise the country (Dinnen 2012). Similar to the first three coups d'état in Fiji, the cause of the conflict in Solomon Islands

---

3   iTaukei is the term used for all ethnically indigenous Fijians, other than those from the island of Rotuma. Usage of the term 'Indo-Fijian' to refer to Fijians of Indian ethnicity is employed in this book to reflect its common usage by people of all ethnicities in Fiji. With continuing social and political discussions regarding who can and should be able to refer to themselves as 'Fijian' (for example, Lal 2016: 74; Narsey 2012), this should not be read as a commentary of my personal beliefs regarding this debate. To avoid confusion, 'Fijian' is used in this book to represent all Fijians regardless of ethnicity, 'Indo-Fijian' to represent Fijians of Indian ethnic descent, and 'iTaukei' to refer to indigenous Fijians.

appears on the surface to have been ethnic friction between the Guale of Guadalcanal island[4]—which is home to the nation's parliament and major trading industries—and the Malaitans of Malaita, who have migrated to Guadalcanal in large numbers since the end of World War II. Ostensibly sparked by a document produced by the Guadalcanal Revolutionary Army in 1988 and again in 1999, 'Demands by the Bona Fide and Indigenous People of Guadalcanal', the conflict has been positioned by numerous scholars as rooted more precisely in issues of poor livelihood opportunities, land rights and concerns about institutional legitimacy (Allen 2005; Hameiri 2007; Kabutaulaka 2001; Wainwright 2003). Though I do not offer a thorough evaluation of the Tensions (see Allen 2013; Hameiri 2007; Wainwright 2003), the role of youth during and after the conflict needs to be addressed. As a vulnerable population at the time of the Tensions and the generation whose formative years were most shaped by the conflict, these youth have experienced acute personal suffering and have been subjected to the effects of the erosion of social capital. Evaluations of the conflict—including by the official Solomon Islands Truth and Reconciliation Commission (2012)—have found that young people's role in the conflict was significant and they were overrepresented as both victims and perpetrators (Noble et al. 2011).

Significant differences between the two nations also need to be noted. With reference to their conflicts, Fiji's have been far less violent and its politics since gaining independence in 1970 has been marked by strong political parties (Fraenkel 2015; Madraiwiwi 2015; Ravuvu 1991: 74). Solomon Islands politics has been more fragmented, relying on loose coalitions to form and maintain government (Alasia 1997; Firth 2018; Wood 2014).

Beyond these measures, greater developmental differences are present across the two states. Fiji, for example, is considered by the United Nations Development Programme (UNDP 2020) to experience high human development according to the Human Development Index (HDI), while Solomon Islands is the lowest-ranked of all countries assessed as experiencing medium human development by this measure. The most recently published HDI table ranks Fiji 93 of 189 countries, with Solomon Islands ranked 151—ranking four places above Papua New Guinea to

---

4   Guale is the term used for all indigenous people of the island of Guadalcanal; Malaitans refers to all indigenous people of the island of Malaita. Each island is home to multiple ethnolinguistic groups (Reilly 2004).

be the second-least developed country in Oceania (UNDP 2020). Fiji is the regional hub for most development and multilateral organisations (Schmaljohann and Prizzon 2014: 6) and a site of considerably more international trade and diplomacy than Solomon Islands. Fiji's greater connection to global markets is also evident in its annual tourist numbers compared with Solomon Islands; they attracted 792,230 and 23,192 foreign visitors in 2016, respectively (SPTO 2017: 6). Further differences include the cultural diversity within each country, with Fiji's multiethnic population mainly comprising those who identify as iTaukei and as Indo-Fijian,[5] while in Solomon Islands, the diversity of indigenous cultures represents considerably more linguistic and kinship identities (Firth 2018: 3).

As well as recognising differences between Fiji and Solomon Islands, it is important to acknowledge differences within each country, particularly those marking urban and rural locations. Looking at multiple sites in multiple countries minimises the risks associated with what Pacific historian Kerry Howe referred to as 'monographic myopia'. Howe's (1979: 81) primary concern regarded the lack of relativity and connectedness in much academic writing on Pacific history that has led to our knowing 'more and more about less and less' because of research being conducted in very localised contexts. By looking at the issues of youth livelihoods and development across multiple communities, I hope to avoid the risk not only of the research being too location-specific, but also of what I see as an equal threat: the conflation of information from one Pacific site as being representative of all Pacific locations and cultures—something expressed by anthropologist Michael Herzfeld (2001: 18) as the 'myth of the homogenous Other'. In this way, I seek to highlight the heterogeneity of experiences across and within Fiji, Solomon Islands and other Pacific locations.

The heterogeneity of youth experiences is explored in this book through engaging the perspectives of a wide range of young people and those who work with them. The voices consulted and represented in this book include youth activists and advocates with varied backgrounds and interests according to indicators of age, gender, ethnicity, sexuality, education and disability, among others. Focus groups with youth and village communities

---

5   Fiji's ethnic population was recorded as 57 per cent iTaukei, 37 per cent Indo-Fijian and 6 per cent 'other' in the 2007 census (FBoS 2021a). Figures regarding ethnic demographics were not released following the 2017 census—to some controversy (Narayan 2018).

also occurred in urban, peri-urban and rural settings in each country. Most discussion relates to data drawn from fieldwork in Fiji—due to my previous experiences working and living in the country, as well as its position as the regional development hub, making it a more appropriate space in which to engage in discussions about regional issues with professionals working in multilateral organisations. This is complemented, compared and contrasted with data gathered in Solomon Islands, which at times magnify differences between the states, at others indicate similarity and, importantly, provide insight into similarities and differences across both countries according to demographic and geographical indicators. That is, sometimes the two sites offer broad similarities and differences from one another, but sometimes the experiences of young people living in rural areas of each country may have more alignment than with the experiences of urban youth in their respective countries. The value of investigating a multiplicity of perspectives was captured by Kris Prasad, an activist for LGBTIQ+[6] rights from Fiji, who said to me: 'If we just look at the mainstream and not the margins, we're not going to get anywhere.'

The inclusion of diverse voices is also an attempt to mitigate as best as possible my limitations as an outsider. Having experience working with and alongside Fijian youth of various ethnicities,[7] education levels and life experiences, I was exposed to different responses to and forms of engagement with my position as a white *kai valagi*,[8] including situations where my own biases were highlighted and exposed. My history of living and working in Fiji reinforced my theoretical knowledge of the principles of research based in participant-observation and exposure to practical limitations as, prior to commencing research, I had already lived the experiences that anthropologist Ray Madden outlines as central to ethnography:

> It is a practice which values the idea that to know other humans the ethnographer must do as others do, live with others, eat, work and experience the same daily patterns as others. (2017: 16)

---

6   LGBTIQ+ represents Lesbian, Gay, Bisexual, Transgender, Intersex, Queer, and others who do not identify as heterosexual and/or cisgender.
7   iTaukei, Indo-Fijian, Fijians of European and Chinese descent and *kai loma* (Fijians of mixed descent/ethnicity).
8   Fijian, meaning 'foreigner'.

Advancing my own reflexive ethnographic experience, this book champions the experiences and knowledge of my informants. Although the findings discussed are my interpretations of the information provided to me through interviews, focus groups and participant-observation, I am explicitly aware that this knowledge has been co-created alongside those I engaged as research informants as well as innumerable contacts who have shaped my understanding of the livelihood and development issues facing the Fijian and Solomon Islander youth represented in these pages. The work presented intends to represent the experiences and expectations of youthhood in Fiji and Solomon Islands from those who work with and for these young people, including youth themselves. This is why my research primarily engages with the voices of youth activists and advocates.

The research approach

Most of the discussion within this book was produced during my PhD candidature at La Trobe University from 2014 to 2018. Fieldwork was conducted during two periods in 2015. From March through May of that year, inclusive, I was based in Suva, with travel around the greater metropolitan area and into the highlands of Naitasiri. For six weeks during July and August, I was based in Honiara, with travel extending to the Visale region. That I spent a greater amount of time in Fiji, both for fieldwork and for employment (prior to, during and following the formal research period), is reflected in the contents. As much as I am aware that the ethnographic detail in this book is much more robust in relation to Fiji than to Solomon Islands—and as much as I sincerely wish it was more balanced—I am heartened to know of multiple emerging scholars focusing on the experiences of young Solomon Islanders whose work will fill this gap in coming years (see Evans 2019; Oakeshott 2021; Ride 2019). The experiences and evidence of Fijian youth activists and advocates are complemented with information received in Solomon Islands and with reference to the wider Oceania region through informants whose work has a broader regional focus.

I conducted 37 interviews with a total of 43 informants. In Fiji, I interviewed 28 people in 23 discrete interviews, with two interviews involving two informants and one involving four. In Solomon Islands, I interviewed 15 people in 14 discrete interviews, with only one involving multiple people. My interviews were focused on activist youth and professionals working in sectors relevant to youth livelihoods, leadership and civic engagement.

The informants interviewed were drawn from a wide range of areas of expertise. The cross-section of those with whom I consulted included academics, bureaucrats, civil society actors and activists, disability workers, economists, multilateral development program staff, NGO staff, religious leaders, youth activists and youth group representatives, with multiple informants representing multiple roles. Informants have consented to all quotations attributed to them. References to their employment or work in civil society are accurate as at the time of data collection. Informants are referred to by their first names throughout the book to delineate informant responses from the literature as several informants have also published material relevant to the research.

The informants quoted should not be read as representative of all those in their area of expertise or demographic. Though they were engaged as experts, their responses must be understood as representing their individual experiences. My rationale for engaging with people representing broad communities and interests was affirmed by several informants, particularly those from communities that are regularly excluded from discussions of mainstream approaches to social issues yet who have experience in research and development programming related specifically to the interest group they represented.

Prior to each interview, I emailed participants a list of themes about which I was interested in speaking. I opened interviews with a variation of the question, 'What is the current state of youth in X location?' according to the specific demographic being discussed. Once the interviews began, I was guided by the informants as to the information they thought was relevant, only occasionally guiding the discussion if I felt it had moved significantly from the core issues of youth, livelihood and development issues. Only one informant wished not to have their thoughts officially audio recorded, or their name attached to their statements. This informant did, however, clarify that they wished to speak about the issues affecting their community and have their experiences inform and be represented in the research findings.

Focus groups were also undertaken with seven discrete communities—four in Fiji and three in Solomon Islands. In each country, one urban, one peri-urban and one rural community were selected to discuss livelihood and development issues as experienced and understood by their young people. Each focus group lasted approximately two hours during daytrips to the sites, with the peri-urban and rural communities each visited twice at intervals at least one week apart. These focus groups primarily engaged local youth, only allowing adults into the space to be informed of the purpose of the research and segregating youth and adults when communities requested adults be allowed to contribute to the conversations. An extra focus group was conducted in Fiji with a work-based collective, the Suva Crime-Free Wheelbarrow Association.

All focus groups were conducted in a combination of English and local languages (Fijian/Vosa Vakaviti[9] in Fiji and Solomon Islands Pijin[10] in Solomon Islands) with support from local research assistants. The initial intention was to run the consultations in a manner akin to *talanoa* or *tok stori*, which is designed to replicate loosely structured conversations that are commonplace in communities throughout both countries (Burns McGrath and Ka`ili 2010; Halapua 2000, 2013; Sanga et al. 2018; Tagicakiverata and Nilan 2018; Vaioleti 2006). Although I had an initial list of questions to guide the discussions, the focus groups were designed to be quite iterative and responsive to the wishes of the youth communities and how they wished to engage. Instead, all communities except the Suva Crime-Free Wheelbarrow Association requested that they respond to my questions using butcher's paper I provided, engaging in limited discussion to elaborate on their written responses. Community definitions of youth, discussed below, proved interesting, though it was the discussion of examples of youth leadership that was particularly insightful (covered in Chapter Four). I was also particularly entertained by the honest response from a group of young men from the peri-urban Fijian community I consulted, who wrote that alongside completing household chores, engaging in informal economic activities and playing, their days were marked by a practice to 'roam around aimlessly looking for girls'.

---

9   Fiji is home to hundreds of dialects (Geraghty 1983). The most widely recognised indigenous language is based on that of the high chiefly island of Bau (Geraghty 2005).
10   The lingua franca of Solomon Islands.

The focus groups held with urban communities provided opportunities to see how other communities worked in different contexts. For the urban Fijian community, a lengthy *talanoa* was held that incorporated both youth and adults alike. All the youth in this group were aged at least 18 years and kava was consumed during the process. This conversation was highly enlightening for understanding the livelihood struggles this community faced, but there was minimal input from young people and discussion regularly strayed from youth-specific issues.

The urban group I engaged in Solomon Islands operated differently from all other communities consulted. The group was based at a church in central Honiara and met weekly to discuss social justice and religious matters. Led by John Firibo, a young Solomon Islander whom I later interviewed and whose thoughts are represented at times in this book, this group chose to respond to the questions using butcher's paper, as did their peers in the focus groups. This group, however, engaged in deep discussion with one another, without the need for facilitation, and elaborated to me on the answers they provided on paper.

The focus group with the Suva Crime-Free Wheelbarrow Association arose as a response to an interview conducted with a Fijian youth development activist, Usaia Moli. He informed me of the existence of the association and the work they were doing to act collectively to improve the livelihoods of 'bara boys'—informal wheelbarrow porters in and around the central Suva marketplace whose livelihoods are precarious and who hold little social status. Most bara boys are young men, many of whom are or have been street-frequenters. I chose to meet with them to hear their stories of self-driven collective action. This discussion is captured in a case study presented in Chapter Three.

As with my informant interviews, in the focus groups, I intended to gather information from a wide range of young people in these communities. Despite attempts to engage Indo-Fijians—particularly in the peri-urban settlement where a significant community existed—I was unable to engage representatives in any of the communities I consulted. Multiple Indo-Fijian interviewees explained to me that Indo-Fijian communities were less inclined to be involved in social research projects than other ethnic groups and that the voice of young Indo-Fijian women is particularly difficult to engage. This is a problem that has been experienced by others. Barrington et al. (2016: 92), writing of their experience working with communities on participatory projects related to water, sanitation and hygiene, said: 'In Fiji, we struggled to engage community members of Indo-Fijian ethnicity.' Urban geographer Luke Kiddle (2011) suggests this may be a hangover effect from Indo-Fijian indentured labour practices of the late nineteenth and early twentieth centuries. He posits that the physical isolation that came from living and working on large tracts of land as individuals and families both limited informal contact between Indo-Fijians and iTaukei and emboldened concepts of individual identity within Indo-Fijian communities, in contrast to the sociocentrism of iTaukei *mataqali* (clan, landowning unit) (Kiddle 2011: 53).

With this in mind, it is important to recognise that the experiences captured in this book do not reflect the universal experiences of all Fijian and Solomon Islander youth. Drawing on concepts for the teaching and understanding of Oceanic cultures by Pacific studies scholar Teresia Teaiwa (2005), the information in this book should be read as an interpretation of knowledge collected during the research process. What I hope emerges in these pages is a picture of the diversity of ways in which young people in Fiji, Solomon Islands and throughout the Great Ocean States of the Pacific experience issues related to their livelihoods, leadership and civic engagement.

An outline of the themes explored

In this book, I explore the impacts of complex and intersecting cultural, structural and institutional stimuli on youth livelihoods, leadership and civic engagement from multiple angles to provide a holistic understanding of the challenges and opportunities faced by youth in Fiji, Solomon Islands and the wider Pacific. I commence with framings that situate the text. These explore definitions of youthhood, the contemporary resonance of studying Pacific youth during this period when the region is experiencing a 'youth bulge' and my theoretical conceptualisation of development at individual and collective levels. This is followed by an analysis of the formal education systems of Fiji and Solomon Islands in Chapter Two, with significant overlap in the discussion about the real and desired livelihood opportunities for young people that occurs in the exploration of employment realities in Chapter Three.

Chapter Four moves away from formal pathways and indicators of good citizenship, investigating how young Fijians and Solomon Islanders are expected to engage as social citizens. I explore these ideas further through case studies of positive deviance (Hummelbrunner and Jones 2013) in Chapter Five, looking at examples of young people creating new opportunities to be critically engaged citizens in prosocial ways. This is followed in Chapter Six with a discussion of the challenges of maintaining and reimagining cultural values and traditions in an ever-globalising world.

I conclude by drawing these discussions together not only to demonstrate that Pacific youth should be seen both as partners for today and as leaders of tomorrow, but also to highlight that, in many ways, they already are.

1

Youth and development

The projected youth population in the [2018] elections is 47 per cent, so we hold the highest majority of the mandate, so to speak.
— Jope Tarai, Fiji

This comment by Jope Tarai, a young Fijian academic and social commentator, highlights the significance of Fiji's youth population and its potential power as a political bloc. If this 47 per cent of eligible young voters took a consensus position on any political issue—social, economic, environmental or other—it would be difficult to conceive of their will not being met. To assume that these young people can exercise their will in such a manner, however, overlooks the social structures that influence young people's political participation in Pacific countries such as Fiji. Although youth are numerically significant, the power they exercise and the extent to which their civic engagement is encouraged are extremely limited. Analysing youth populations in Fiji and Solomon Islands, this book discusses where and how young people practise civic engagement and leadership, the concerns they espouse for their current and future livelihood opportunities, and the structures that work to assist and/or impede their positive potentialities.

A note on youthhood

Defining youthhood in the Pacific island region is not a straightforward exercise. Understandings of who and what are 'youth' in Solomon Islands and Fiji are somewhat fluid. The Solomon Islands Government notes in its National Youth Policy that 'youth in Solomon Islands is now defined as *"persons between 15 and 34 years of age, inclusive"'* (Government of Solomon Islands 2017: 14, emphasis in original)—a slight amendment from previously identifying youth as ranging from 14 to 29 years of age (Government of Solomon Islands 2010: 4). The Fijian Government (2012: 3) defines youth as 'those between the ages of 15 to 35 years', but acknowledges in working documents that this definition is flexible according to community values. Perhaps most comprehensively, Pacific youth experts Richard Curtain and Patrick Vakaoti note in the 2011 version of *The State of Pacific Youth* report:

> The age span covering youth, as a stage in the lifecycle moving from dependence to independence, varies. It can range from as young as age ten years to as old as mid-thirties, depending on the age at which some children have to start to fend for themselves and what society deems to be the end point of the transition. (2011: 8)

Both the 2011 and the 2017 versions of *The State of Pacific Youth* report note significant age definitions of 'youth' across multiple Pacific states. Curtain and Vakaoti (2011: 8) note that while 'the age group 15–24 years is often used', common usage in the region ranges from 12 up to 34 years of age. Similarly, Clarke and Azzopardi (2017: 4) write: 'Definitions of the youth period vary in terms of its duration in the Pacific region.'

In each of the interviews I conducted with youth activists and professionals working in youth development fields, I asked how 'youth' was defined in their culture. The responses varied significantly, ranging from strict age parameters to working definitions used for engaging young people in youth-targeted programs, and cultural norms that informed practical applied definitions. Typical responses stayed within the age distinctions of 14 at the lower end and 35 at the upper end. Within these parameters, there was no consensus that these were fixed ages, with multiple respondents stating that the upper age limit for youth was 25 while others disclosed that cultural factors could see people as old as 50 still being considered as youth.

A sample of interviewee responses reflecting the lack of an agreed definition of 'youth' according to age included the following:

> The categorisation of youth [is] from 18–35 generally in the Pacific.
>
> — Emily Hazelman, regional development worker, Fiji

Youth in the Pacific is defined up to 35.

— Salote Kaimacuata, regional development worker, Fiji

Some [NGOs] focus on youth from 14 to 27 … but the National Youth Policy has a sentence that opens it up for young people to be [understood] in cultural situations and circumstances.

— Harry Olikwailafa, youth activist, Solomon Islands

Some are saying 14 [year olds] are considered youth. Some are saying 18. Some are saying the cut-off age is 25. Some feel that they are still youth into their mid-thirties.

— Joshko Wakaniyasi, disability advocate, Fiji

Rather than age, culture appears to be the dominant determinant of who is or is not considered a youth. Taking on adult responsibilities and characteristics—marriage, having children, employment and/or positions of authority—provides more workable boundaries for categorisation of a transition out of youthhood. Tura Lewai, a civil society activist from Fiji who has worked with rural and urban communities across Oceania for various development organisations, positioned this in relation to young people marrying in Fiji:

You can be part of the youth group in the village, even if you are 50 or 45, as long as you're not married. Once you are married, you are no longer a young person.

Sandra Bartlett, a youth development worker from Solomon Islands, echoed this cultural conception in her country of graduating from youthhood through marriage or becoming a parent:

Society looks at it as married or not married. You just hear it being said in the language: '*Hem woman nao*'—she's had a kid, so she is a woman now.

Sandra added that 'student' has entered the local lexicon in recent years as shorthand for young people in Solomon Islands Pijin, with 'youth' still used as a term but increasingly being associated with more formal definitions for policy and programming purposes. She explained that student is a value-neutral term applied to children and young people that simply recognises them as yet to achieve the abovementioned status markers. More interestingly, Sandra disputed the notion that young people are regularly referred to by, or even necessarily associated with, the term *masta liu*, which she referenced as derogatory, and which is discussed further in Chapter Three.

In Indo-Fijian communities, social justice activist Roshika Deo explained, there are no pure translations for 'youth' between English and Fiji Hindi.[1] The closest comparisons are the relational terms *larkan* and *jawan larkan*, which translate roughly as 'child' and 'mature child', respectively. Roshika explained that these terms can be used to refer to any person younger than the speaker, although they are more likely to be used to refer to children, youths and where there is a clear generational gap.

Indigenous definitions of youthhood become a little more complicated in iTaukei communities. As Vakaoti (2018: 13) has discussed, terminology for young people in Fijian is delineated by gender, with young women referred to as *goneyalewa* and young men as *cauravou*. Development industry professional Peni Tawake explained that these terms inform how notions of 'youth' are conceptualised by iTaukei people, with both being predicated on the notion of young people existing as 'developing individuals' (Vakaoti 2018: 13). Supporting Tura's comments above, Peni added that *goneyalewa* and *cauravou* are most precisely used to refer to people who have not realised status markers such as marriage and parenthood in a manner that is 'open ended' and only loosely connected with age. Peni also spoke of alternative local terminology for formal youth spaces, such as how Methodist Church youth groups at the congregation or parish level are called *mataveitokani*—directly translated as 'friendship group' but used almost exclusively to refer to Methodist Church youth groups. Subtle differences abound between the social understandings of *goneyalewa* and *cauravou*, the use of 'youth' as a primary category in policy and programming, and spaces created specifically for young people in localised settings, such as *mataveitokani*. These multiple, complementary terminologies demonstrate how local and foreign discourses shape and reshape how youthhood is conceptualised at the local level in different contexts.

The common thread between conceptions of youth across the languages and cultures of Fiji and Solomon Islands is that they position youth in relation to a transition beyond that stage of life. As multiple writers have described, young people are regularly considered to be adults-in-waiting, rather than people with full functionality, both in the Pacific (Baba 2014; Bacalzo 2019; Good 2012; Mitchell 2011) and beyond (Caputo 1995; Golombeck 2006; Honwana 2014; White and Wyn 2013; Wyn 1995).

---

1   Also known as Fiji Baat (Willans and Prasad 2021).

Akuila Sovanivalu, a bureaucrat with Fiji's Ministry of Youth and Sports, more explicitly stated: 'Youth is a transition point for children way up to adulthood.'

Jope Tarai mentioned shifts in familial responsibility, but also explained that employment acts to mark the social evolution from youth to adult, including the status and respect afforded to such a transition. When I asked him how young people became adults, he explained:

> It's typically them having a family and a job … Because they are able to contribute to the obligations of the community and in having to contribute, they get to have a say in how things are done. In that regard, they are no longer seen as young. Once you are able to contribute to social functions [and] family obligations, you are taken more seriously. You are seen as a person who is of particular status and, ultimately, part of the authority.

Some interviewees even expressed frustration with what they saw as a social-structural category inflated to be so inclusive as to render meaningless usage of the term 'youth' in the Pacific. Jope stated:

> Our national youth age is projected to be 18 to 35. Then it became 15 to 35. Then the Provincial Youth Council wanted it to be 15 to 45. It is embarrassing. Even that is questionable, because the World Bank statistics represent [youth as those aged] 18 to 24.

Elisha Bano is a youth activist from Fiji who resigned her position on the Fiji National Youth Council at the age of 28 as she felt she was becoming too old for the role and wanted to create an opportunity for younger leaders. She offered similar concerns to Jope, pointing out that the large age range could include people across multiple generations:

> UN-wise, we usually consider 18 to 24. When I started doing work with the National Youth Council, it's from 15 to 35, which I think is ridiculous … I cannot say my parents are youth, so I started struggling with that from day one.

The fluidity of youth definitions was evident when meeting with urban, peri-urban and rural communities in both Fiji and Solomon Islands. In each focus group, I asked participants to assemble into smaller groups to answer some questions about their lived experiences. When I asked how 'youth' was defined, it was regularly reflected that the starting point was turning 15, with no group offering a younger age. This was despite multiple young people between the ages of 12 and 14 attending two of the focus groups. When I inquired with the larger groups if these young people were considered youths, I was told they were. When I followed up on the discrepancy between what had been stated as the base age range for youth and the inclusion of the 12–14-year-olds, neither group could explain the disconnection between definitions and application, though they were able to acknowledge its presence.

It is evident from these examples that the definition of youth in the Pacific is fluid and contested. My own working definition of youth includes those aged 15–35 years who are socially recognised as such. This reflects the most common range of ages used in Pacific youth organisations and as expressed by my informants.

The youth bulge

Although I do not approach this research through a security-focused framework that problematises youth civic activity, I acknowledge that such approaches have been the foremost prism through which such issues have been investigated in the international development literature and that they do offer significant insights. The most common framing of this perspective is through the 'youth bulge' terminology (Urdal 2006). In its simplest terms, youth bulge refers to populations where the youth cohort is particularly large in comparison with other age ranges. Population geographers Gary Fuller and Forrest Pitts (1990: 9–10) state that a youth bulge is reached when the proportion of people aged 15–24 in a country exceeds 20 per cent of the total population, though they note this figure is 'somewhat arbitrary'. Youth bulge theory, however, goes further to link such population bubbles with an increased risk of civil unrest. The exact origins of 'youth bulge' as a term and as an identified social issue are unclear. For example, development practitioner Anne Hendrixson (2004: 2) claims that Fuller coined the term in the 1980s, while political scientist Lionel Beehner (2007) attributes it to social scientist Gunnar Heinsohn in the 1990s. Regardless, discussions of a link between a significant youth population and an increased risk of violence date at least as far back as Herbert Moller's 1968 paper 'Youth as a Force in the Modern World', which noted that youth populations can act to promote either progress or insecurity. As Moller wrote:

The presence of a large contingent of young people in a population may make for a cumulative process of innovation and social and cultural growth; it may lead to elemental, directionless acting-out behavior; it may destroy old institutions and elevate new elites to power; and the unemployed energies of the young may be organized and directed by totalitarian rulers. (1968: 260)

There are significant and legitimate data to support claims connecting a youth bulge with an increased risk of civil unrest. Both Moller (1968) and Jack Goldstone (2002), a political scientist with expertise in revolutionary movements, have written about the impact of youth as drivers of historical movements dating back centuries. Examples they provide include the French Revolution in the eighteenth century, the civil rights movement in the United States (Moller 1968) and 'most twentieth-century revolutions in developing countries' (Goldstone 2002: 10). More recently, young people have been involved in social protest movements in cities and countries with significant youth populations such as Burkina Faso (Harsch 2016), Jakarta, Tehran, Belgrade and Harare (Urdal 2004: 4), and in the Middle East and North African states that were involved in the Arab Spring (Al-Momani 2011; Anderson 2011; Herd 2011; Moghadam 2013).

The Pacific region also has experienced multiple instances of civil unrest in the past two decades, partially marked by the involvement of youth. Conflicts of varying scale have taken place in Fiji, Kanaky/New Caledonia, Papua New Guinea, Solomon Islands, Tonga and Vanuatu. It must be noted that the intent and level of unrest have varied significantly across these states, as has the extent to which young people have been drivers of, or responders to, conflicts and demonstrations. In 2003 and 2005, Tongan commoners took to the streets to protest in support of greater democracy and against media censorship (Singh and Prakash 2006). They also caused widespread damage to the capital, Nuku`alofa, in riots in 2006 prompted by the stalling progress of democracy and perceptions of dishonest governance processes regarding trade and business dealings that favoured the nobility (Campbell 2008; van Fossen 2018). In the early years of the twenty-first century, civil conflicts engulfed parts of Kanaky/New Caledonia, Papua New Guinea, Solomon Islands and Vanuatu, and were attributed to a combination of poor livelihood opportunities, urban migration squeezes and ethnic tensions (Storey 2005; Wainwright 2003). Unrest was also sparked in Papua New Guinea in 2016 as student demonstrators called for the resignation of then Prime Minister Peter

O'Neill following allegations of corruption (Connors and Barker 2016). Similarly, riots took place in Honiara in 2019 linked to issues of poor livelihood opportunities and concerns about government corruption, with youths identified as a core cohort of demonstrators (Fraenkel 2019a; Ride 2019), although the extent of their involvement is unclear. Meanwhile, Fiji has experienced recurrent issues related to political legitimacy since 1987, with roots in issues of livelihood opportunities, land rights disputes and hostility between ethnicities (Firth 2012; Naidu 2013). In all instances, the involvement of youth has been reported.

Rather than proving that disproportionately high youth populations necessitate civil unrest, these global examples arguably speak to a peaceful status quo being held by youth in each of these societies, which is demonstrated by the rarity and notability with which protest movements and revolutions occur in specific settings. The foremost thinker on youth bulge issues of this century, political scientist and peace researcher Henrik Urdal (2006: 617), notes that a high youth population does not necessitate or even greatly increase the risk of conflict: 'An increase of one percentage point in youth bulges is associated with an increased likelihood of conflict of more than 4%.' Yet he also identifies that this is only a marginal increase on a minimal risk base (Urdal 2006: 619, 620). Urdal argues that a youth bulge is just one of a combination of factors that increase the risk of civil unrest and must be understood in relation to many corollary and compounding factors. Primary among these are poor livelihood opportunities (Urdal 2006: 609, 619–24; see also Thomas 2001: 6; Ware 2004: 2; Sukarieh and Tannock 2017: 858), particularly for well-educated youth generations (Urdal 2004: 4) in countries with populations in the tens of millions (Urdal 2006: 619; see also Fearon and Laitin 2003: 85). This is just as true at the local level. As Imelda Ambelye reports of youth antisocial behaviour in two rural communities in Papua New Guinea:

> The antisocial behaviour and other problems that youths face are a result of many factors. Displaced aggression is the result of youths looking for opportunities to release their frustrations as victims of structural deprivation. (2019: 198)

Thus, we can see that large youth populations do not, by themselves, necessitate social upheaval. Instead, as with the conflicts experienced in Oceania this century already discussed, the provision—or the possibility for provision—of livelihoods offers a more salient explanation for instances where young people rupture the peaceful status quo. As Urdal (2004: 2) states: 'It is clear that if large youth bulges that hold a common generational consciousness would always produce conflict, we would have seen a lot more violent youth revolts.'

Critical youth scholar Lesley Pruitt (2020) has written that uncritically framing youth development issues through the prism of the youth bulge risks assuming youth deviancy in the design of policy and program documents. She argues that discussions of the youth bulge essentialise violent and problematic outbursts by young people—predominantly males—marginalising female perspectives, without giving due consideration to the diverse demographics within youth populations or examining the social factors contributing to violence. Pruitt writes:

> [R]esearch must acknowledge that young people may take on a range of roles, not only as perpetrators or victims, but also as peacebuilders, and this evidence base should be used to inform future policy-making. (2020: 728)

With youth bulge framing that positions youth as a security risk gaining credence in the Pacific (Clarke and Azzopardi 2017), it is important that the behaviours of youth in countries such as Fiji and Solomon Islands are kept in perspective.

Considering this literature and my own experiences, I believe it is more prudent to focus on the skills young people have and can be reasonably expected to develop, their capabilities to exercise these skills, the formal and informal structures that promote or inhibit these, and how they are currently engaging as active citizens of their communities. Rather than viewing youth as a potentially problematic generation, I view them as a generation whose positive potentialities, if realised, can result in their individual benefit, as well as the collective benefit of their communities and cultures. Examples throughout this book demonstrate that cohorts of youth are eager to be engaged in decision-making processes regarding the developmental futures of their communities and have significant skills in exercising developmental leadership.

Although young people should be recognised for their positive potential, it is important this is not framed in terms of an assumed duty of youth to serve their societies. My research approach looks at youth not as a subservient demographic obliged to perpetuate contemporary social ideals of what is good and valuable, but as active citizens capable of positively challenging and reshaping their communities. In this way, I see a link between individual and communal capabilities because a failure to provide young people with opportunities to achieve their individual potential will limit their ability to engage critically and positively with and shape their societies. As Curtain and Vakaoti state:

> Without a major investment in young people, they may well flounder as a generation, undermining the capacity of Pacific Island countries and territories to escape aid dependence, develop economically and, in some cases, even survive as viable societies. (2011: 5)

Viewing young people as a human and social resource in which to invest is not a new approach to matters of youth livelihoods in developing contexts, yet it is one that has significantly less traction with governments and developmental donor agencies. Curtain wrote in 2006 of a global tendency to not acknowledge the positive possibilities of youth and instead view young people as an issue through a security lens:

> The view of young people as critical assets for lifting economies and societies out of poverty offers the most potential for change, yet it has gained the least attention. Governments, international agencies, and donors could harness far better the capacities of young people. (Curtain 2006: 440)

Similarly, the World Bank's 2007 *World Development Report*—which was notable for its focus on youth[2]—identified a window of opportunity in which to utilise youth bulge populations to drive developmental advances, if properly supported, which is estimated to be between 10 and 40 years, varying by country (World Bank 2007: 4). It is theorised that investing in youth during this period holds significant promise of reaping developmental dividends due to factors including a general increase in the formal education of these youth and a gradual general decline in fertility rates. Failing to do so risks stalling economic and developmental growth, with possible intergenerational impacts of minimised opportunities for growth and development. Combined, these factors suggest increased possibilities for young people to invest more of their own time and resources in formal and informal livelihood activities, which will likely

---

2   Annual *World Development Reports* investigate global development issues with specific attention to one area of opportunity or concern. Though there are significant overlaps between some of the reports, none has yet duplicated a previous focus. As such, there has been no similar youth focus since the 2007 report.

lead to social and economic benefits (World Bank 2007). Projections of average annual growth in the youth population in the Pacific island region of 2.2 per cent (Maebiru 2013: 148) and census statistics showing higher childhood five-year indices than for youth (FBoS 2018; SINSO 2011) indicate that the window will likely remain open in the Pacific for many decades.

The demographics of the Great Ocean States of the Pacific mean they are primed to take advantage of the potential of their youth populations. Regional youth development policy and program expert Rose Maebiru (2013: 148) notes: 'With a mean age of 21 years for most Pacific island countries, the region has a huge resource at its disposal to address national and regional issues.' Critical youth scholars Mayssoun Sukarieh and Stuart Tannock (2017) argue through their research into the framing of youth as a peace and security concern that while youth are the most likely generational cohort to push for social change through civil disobedience, this can be mitigated by providing livelihood opportunities for them. Like Pruitt (2020), they also caution that it is equally problematic to view youth through myopic lenses as either potential troublemakers or developmental saviours:

> Youth has always had a double-sided aspect, such that for every stereotypical representation of youth as problem and pathology there exists an inverse idealisation of youth as possibility and panacea. (Sukarieh and Tannock 2017: 855)

The strengths perspective I take is not intended to suggest that these youth populations hold the answers to questions of sustainable positive development, that they should be appreciated only for their working-age potential, nor that increased employment and ever-expanding economies are necessarily the best or most appropriate forms of development for these countries. Rather, my approach helps to better understand the opportunities that currently exist for young people to engage in activities that will enhance their opportunities for prosperous livelihoods, to engage with their communities as prosocial active citizens and to achieve their own full potential regarding agency and identity. It aligns with rights-based approaches to youth development that recognise the structural issues impeding individual and collective youth development, advocate for the active engagement of young people in identifying and addressing such issues and oblige those in decision-making spaces to act to address these issues (UNFPA 2005: 11).

Structural minimisation

A central and recurrent theme in the literature and discovered through my own research is the concept that youth are to be seen but not heard. Passivity is considered a desirable trait of youth in Oceania (Baba 2014; Good 2019; Lee 2019a; McMurray 2006; Vakaoti 2012)—something that is steeped in concepts of tradition and signifying respect. Young people are not encouraged to be outspoken or to ask questions; their role is to learn from observation and example, and to do as they are instructed. These views are held at family and village levels, and permeate to higher decision-making levels with deleterious results, producing what I label as the structural minimisation of youth experiences and perspectives. These negative effects manifest in multiple ways.

First, the customary silences of youth translate into a lack of advocacy for young people during policymaking processes. As leaders age, they are influenced by their peers and by those who can communicate with them on a relatively level platform. As youth are largely denied access to decision-making processes at the institutional level, their potential input is largely ignored. Further, if their needs are considered but not met, youth represent a subsection of society with little power to challenge such decisions. Cameron Noble, Natalia Pereira and Nanise Saune (2011) provide a prime example of this silencing of youth issues in their report on urban youth pacification approaches for UNDP Pacific. They note that '[y]outh are not mentioned in the *Pacific Plan Annual Progress Reports* from 2008 and 2009' (Noble et al. 2011: 16) and 'there are only limited opportunities for young men and women to participate in national and regional decision-making processes in the Pacific' (p. 19). This issue was again reflected in the lack of action on youth matters in the 2013 *Pacific Plan Annual Progress Report* (PIFS 2013), despite the 2012 version discussing the need to 'mainstream' youth development matters throughout policy processes (PIFS 2012). Notably, the page dedicated to youth development issues on the website of the Pacific Islands Forum Secretariat (PIFS)—the body responsible for the Pacific Plan and its successor, the Framework for Pacific Regionalism—has variously shown as being 'under construction' or, worse, displaying an 'Error 404'[3] message between 2015 and 2021 (PIFS n.d.), except for a brief period in 2018 when a post was uploaded

---

3   A standard response displayed on websites when a specific location is erroneous or not being actively maintained.

with a tangential appeal to young people to 'actively pursue a healthier ocean' (Taylor 2018). These issues of youth minimisation at the highest levels of decision-making are further reinforced by the lack of formal opportunities given to youth to discuss development issues with their peers. For example, this book draws repeatedly on the Suva Declaration created by the more than 300 youths who attended the second Pacific Youth Festival in 2009 (SPC 2009b) as an example of regional youth priorities, although I am acutely aware that this document is more than a decade old. This is because although two regional youth festivals were held, one in 2006 and one in 2009, a third has not eventuated.

Second, denying youth the opportunity to engage in decision-making processes and share opinions creates an environment that implicitly discourages critical thinking. When young people are aware that their opinion counts for little, they may be less likely to engage in thinking about how situations could be improved or upheld. Democratic theorist and economist Anthony Downs (1957) coined the term 'rational ignorance' in relation to this process when writing about the limits of democratic engagement, positing that humans regularly choose—consciously or unconsciously—to not engage with the development of a skill for which the time and energy costs are unlikely to result in equivalent benefit to the individual. Downs related this specifically to levels of engaging with political and policy ideas, arguing that to consider issues on which one's thoughts and feelings are unlikely to bear any impact is a waste of energy. He concludes that this results in a lack of capacity for critical thought in affected areas (Downs 1957).

The effects of not valuing the participation of youth are many, particularly in relation to the themes of agency, civic engagement and the roles young people are expected and allowed to play in their communities. For example, discussion of the lack of opportunities for youth participation and visibility of youth leaders as role models, which I examine in Chapter Four, prompts reflection: if young people are considered only as the leaders of tomorrow but are not engaged in leadership processes today, what purpose do they serve as individuals and as a collective? Mereia Carling (2009) addressed this conundrum in her master's thesis on youth citizenship in Fiji, referencing a shift in thinking around the role of youth in international development policy and practice in recent decades, away from a conception of them as passive citizens-in-waiting to one in which youth are more active and engaged. She writes that this change in approach moves forward from the popular adage, '*children and young people are the leaders of tomorrow*', towards the notion that children have a vital role to play in the present—'*children, young people and leaders are partners today*'. (Carling 2009: 26; emphasis in original)

Many people with whom I spoke described the expectation of adult villagers, teachers and leaders that young people would engage in society only in prescribed and acceptable ways and that when they ran afoul of these expectations their contributions would largely be ignored. Salote Kaimacuata, a child protection specialist at UNICEF Pacific and former magistrate in the Fijian judiciary who oversaw juvenile hearings, expressed how young people are denied opportunities to actively participate in decision-making processes throughout the Pacific:

I know that in each of the countries [of Oceania] their youths have been struggling but they are not getting the door to open so that they can be included. We leaders are really good at talking the talk but not really following up with the actions promised our youth.

Reflecting on how youth minimisation is built into the structure of Pacific societies, Luisa Senibulu, a regional development worker from Fiji, discussed how such marginalisation is couched in justifications of culture and tradition:

The culture of Pacific island countries is such that it limits a lot of young people's potential in being engaged in a lot of issues because of the structures of our cultures and our traditions. It places a lot of limits on the ability of young people to freely express themselves.

Benjamin Afuga, a civil society activist from Solomon Islands who helped to create an online space for Solomon Islanders to engage in civic discourse (discussed in more detail in Chapter Five), articulated a desire to see increased youth participation in decision-making processes. His experiences have led him to believe that this silencing of youth voices does not benefit the people of Solomon Islands:

Youth in this country, in comparison to other countries, they have been disengaged in many things. Decision-making, I believe, is important when it comes to consultation and ideas. Youth must always be part of it.

Usaia Moli has worked with Fijian youth for more than a decade, including as an outreach worker for at-risk and street-frequenting youth, as former chair of the Fiji National Youth Council and as a political candidate in the 2014 national election, in which he campaigned on a youth platform. He expressed the frustration that youth activists feel through such exclusionary practices:

> Throughout our lives, when we grow up, when we tried to do things, they'd say, 'Grow up', so we grew up and now you're telling us, 'Go back and be children'. We come up willing to take responsibility, we have proven ourselves, but they say it is still not enough. When will it be our time?

This marginalisation of the youth voice described by many of my interviewees cannot be seen in isolation as a problem of youth engagement. Rather, the cultural context that informs this disregard for youth voices and the wider impact it has on local, national and regional scales need to be understood. When examining youth livelihood and development issues across the societies of Oceania, it is imperative to examine the current state of affairs. Equally, how access and agency for young people are promoted or inhibited on an institutional level, both formally and informally, must be interrogated. Youth make up a vast cross-section of the greater population of Oceania, so to understand the issues they face and project how their futures, and those of their communities, may look require a holistic examination of the roles youth play across the gamut of civil society. Youth issues cannot be quarantined. In the Great Ocean States of the Pacific, as elsewhere, it is not that youth are an issue, but that youth issues are representative of wider cultural, social, economic and political issues.

Holistic livelihoods: A framework

Truly reflexive engagement with a subject requires an understanding of how the subject is theorised. This book analyses concepts of livelihoods and how young people in Pacific societies achieve their full potential, as individuals and as part of their communities, as well as how they engage with their societies as active citizens. My view of livelihoods goes beyond the practical ability of providing for oneself, incorporating notions of how people can explore and achieve their potential. As is discussed below, this incorporates aspects of historically influential as well as more contemporary critical social and international development theories. Historically influential approaches include Abraham Maslow's (1943) hierarchy of needs, the sustainable livelihoods approach of Robert

Chambers and Graham Conway (1991), and the capabilities approach to development created by Amartya Sen (1999, 2003). Contemporary critical approaches informing this research are drawn largely from the alternative development school (for example, Berner and Phillips 2003; Nederveen Pieterse 1998) and adaptive development school (for example, Andrews et al. 2012; Leftwich 2011; ODI 2014; TWP Community 2016). Informed by what I label a holistic livelihoods approach, my research approach views livelihoods as being rooted in the capacity to secure the provision of goods, whether through subsistence agriculture, the formal market or alternative measures, and further incorporates notions of wellbeing, including how individuals and communities are able to engage with their societies as full and active citizens.

As this book deals with discourse regarding 'development', it is vital this is somewhat defined. As development scholar Dorothea Kleine (2010: 675) writes: 'Research positioned in the contested space that is "development" needs to be able to answer the fundamental question of what is understood as development.' My approach is informed by the literature related to matters of international development, Pacific epistemologies and reflections on the impacts of development, anthropological texts on cultural identity and cultural expression, analysis of data from my fieldwork, and my own experiences working in international development programs in Oceania. Together, these factors have highlighted to me that development operates at two complementary levels. At a societal level, it is about freedoms and capabilities, while at the household experiential level, it is about food and security. As a concept and a discipline, development is about creating conditions that will ultimately allow the opportunity for all individuals and communities to fully determine and achieve their future trajectories, with reasonable caveats regarding how these trajectories impact on others' rights to their own developmental opportunities.[4] For the most disadvantaged and marginalised members of any society, it still must be acknowledged that such lofty ideals are inconsequential in relation to immediate concerns regarding how they feed themselves and their loved ones, their access to adequate physical shelter and security, and their ability to access opportunities regardless of factors such as their gender, sexuality, ability or ethnicity. Though these two understandings of development may appear to be contradictory, they are contingent on one

---

4   Comprehensively detailing such caveats is not possible due to differences in cultures and the fact that cultures themselves are constantly evolving (for example, Good 2012; Pigg 1996; Sahlins 2005). As guiding principles, they are best articulated in the *Universal Declaration of Human Rights* (UN 1948).

another: freedoms and capabilities are moot if basic needs cannot be met; and, as is discussed below with relation to Maslow (1943), basic needs can only be met when the possibility for the satisfaction of higher-order needs is present.

This understanding of development is influenced by discourse about rights-based approaches to development. There has been a broad global acceptance of the notion that all people are entitled to the provision of basic rights and freedoms since the adoption of the Universal Declaration of Human Rights in 1948, at least at the level of public discourse. If we accept that Maslow's (1943) basic safety and psychological needs can act as effective proxies for foundational rights, the poverty-reduction focus of much development policy and programming (Nankani et al. 2005)— that is, those interventions that seek to secure the ability of people to put food on the table—can be recognised equally as a human rights initiative. The rights discourse in development moves beyond these foundational considerations, however, to advocate for the economic and social conditions in which people can thrive as full and active citizens as an ethical imperative (Nelson and Dorsey 2003; Sen 2001: 229–30; Uvin 2007). The principal ethic that young people should be recognised as active citizens while their societies provide the conditions by which they can develop their individual potential provides an overarching framework for the holistic livelihoods approach.

The holistic livelihoods approach is applicable to understanding development that is both 'intentional' and 'immanent'. As described by economist Michael Cowen and historian Robert Shenton (1996), intentional development is that which is targeted, follows a strategy and is generally represented through economic-focused policies and programs. Immanent development describes development that occurs as a more natural process even though influenced by social, political and economic ideas and policies. As the holistic livelihoods approach is concerned with issues of access to basic needs and the potential for individual and community advancement, it is equally applicable to both intentional and immanent forms of development, noting that each is concerned with 'human improvement' (Cowen and Shenton 1996: 54).

The need to acknowledge the basic needs concerns of disadvantaged and marginalised people was expressed to me by multiple informants. Usaia Moli, from Fiji, told me:

> In the end, it comes down to the food that you put on the table. It's always been about that. At the end of the day, with everything else that comes in—there is a lot of talk of climate change, there is a lot of talk on unemployment—but in the end, it comes down to that. It is food on the table: 'How can I support my family?'

The pre-eminence of basic needs for poor, disadvantaged and marginalised people was echoed by Rosie Catherine, a mental health and women's rights activist, also from Fiji, who said: 'People are concerned about their basic needs; if I have food and I have a job, that's more important to me than all these [employment and development] policies and legislation.'

The holistic livelihoods approach that I apply is strongly informed by Maslow's view of basic needs outlined in his seminal article 'A Theory of Human Motivation' (1943), in which he first presented his theory of a hierarchy of basic human needs. This is complemented by Sen's (1999, 2003) capabilities approach, which is grounded in how development is experienced through the opportunities available to the most disadvantaged and marginalised. Maslow (1943: 383) argued that basic needs could not be appreciated in isolation from other needs and that the realisation of basic needs was only possible when the opportunity for the realisation of higher-order needs was also present. The capabilities approach to development builds on this base, advocating that opportunities for the individual enabled by society are a more appropriate prism through which to explore developmental advances than conventional indicators such as gross domestic product (GDP) per capita (Hicks and Streeten 1979; Sumner and Tezanos Vazquez 2014), which can hide significant variations in how development is being experienced by and within different communities.

One of the strengths of the capabilities approach is that it does not limit its assessment of how communities can achieve their potential to the provision of goods or the capital accumulated. All forms of capital— human, social, political, economic, and so on—can be built on, but all are useless without the capability to be expended. For example, providing a university education to a young person may provide them the skills to be a lawyer, but if there are no employment opportunities for lawyers then the capabilities do not necessarily result in a significant increase in the human capital an individual can exercise. Such issues are discussed in Chapters Two and Three in relation to the education and employment preferences of Pacific youth as well as mismatches between formal education and employment sectors.

Communications and international development scholar Thomas Jacobson (2016), writing about the applicability of the capabilities approach to development communication programs, explains the need to connect capabilities with opportunities through the prism of 'functionings'. Unless resources match opportunities, they have little utility:

> The concept of functioning is paired with that of *capabilities*. Capabilities refer to real opportunities citizens have to enjoy a functioning rather than to the actual enjoyment of the functioning. This pairing of functionings with capabilities is important because for Sen development refers principally to the availability of choices, and the ability to make choices, about whether to enjoy particular functionings. (Jacobson 2016: 794; emphasis in original)

This is what Sen is referring to when he proposes that development is about freedom: the freedom to access institutions of development; the freedom to participate in society; and the freedom to choose livelihood courses (Sen 1999: 3; 2003: 5).

Building on concepts of complexity—explored below—within capabilities, I do not view livelihoods as being connected solely to provisions. As Chambers and Conway (1991: 5) note: 'A livelihood in its simplest sense is a means of gaining a living.' Instead, I understand livelihoods as being holistically connected with personal ambition, social capital and the structures that allow for or impede these. In this way, my holistic livelihoods approach incorporates aspects of Chambers and Conway's (1991) sustainable livelihoods approach, as this is concerned with existing in an environment that allows for the ongoing realisation of needs. For a livelihood to be considered sustainable, it needs to be able to

> cope with and recover from stress and shocks, maintain or enhance its capabilities and assets, and provide sustainable livelihood opportunities for the next generation; and … [contribute] net benefits to other livelihoods at the local and global levels and in the short and long term. (Chambers and Conway 1991: 6)

The value of the sustainable livelihoods approach is that it locates individual livelihood needs and capabilities in the context of the needs and capabilities not only of other disadvantaged and marginalised peoples, but also of future generations. It understands that capacities to meet basic needs must be met with the complementary, continuing capabilities to utilise them to their fullest potential.

The paradox of the sustainable livelihoods approach is that while it addresses the need for livelihood opportunities to be available to all on an ongoing basis, it offers no clear purpose for development beyond the realisation of making a living. Its focuses of poverty eradication (Krantz 2001: 6) and social equity (Chambers and Conway 1991: 22–23) are certainly worthy causes and benefit from being approached in a manner that acknowledges the diversity of factors that can lead to and perpetuate poverty. The sustainable livelihoods approach does not, however, address concerns about the purpose of development as connected to concepts of wellbeing, happiness and opportunities for self or community-advancement (Hopwood et al. 2005). Nor does it engage with questions of politics and power imbalances that may impinge on the ability of certain individuals and groups to access livelihood opportunities (de Haan and Zoomers 2005; Scoones 2009). Though Chambers and Conway (1991: i) expressly challenge the reader to 'examine this paper from the perspective of a person alive in a hundred years' time, and then to do better than the authors have done', there is no clear picture of the kind of societies they envisage existing at the end of that time frame, other than that all people will have the capacity to make a living. This overlooks Maslow's (1943: 382) conception of needs as both a continuum and a web that allow individuals to achieve self-actualisation—the realisation of one's full potential—within the cultural and social relations that make human action meaningful.

The holistic livelihoods approach offers a way of understanding the aims of international development policy and practice that better marries the concepts of basic needs and capabilities. I recognise that while the provision of food and physiological security needs provides the most rudimentary platform for development, they are limited in their scope to promote sustainable developmental change, even at the individual level. To be developed at an individual level requires being granted the ability to seek meaning and self-actualisation. For this to be achieved, structures need to exist that promote the potential proliferation of people's capacities and capabilities. For citizen-led social change to occur, the possibility to develop individual capabilities must be available.

Thus, when speaking of holistic livelihoods, I speak of the needs and opportunities afforded to individuals and communities not only to provide for themselves, but also to envision change at individual and collective levels and to have the opportunities to achieve such change. Youth livelihoods are about more than education, employment or subsistence; they are also about agency, identity and opportunity. This is why this book not only looks at the structures of formal education and employment that are commonly understood to promote people's capabilities, but also analyses how young people in Fiji and Solomon Islands actively participate in their societies.

It is important to note that although this approach may appear to favour the needs and capacities of the individual, this is not at the expense of the needs of communities. The holistic livelihoods approach is interested as much in the structures that promote or inhibit capabilities as it is with the practicalities of who achieves such capabilities and how. In this way, this approach addresses needs at both the individual and the community levels. Though such connections may not always be self-evident, this is an inevitable consequence of ever-changing cultural attitudes and practices, as well as the shape and function of the formal and informal structures of politics, society and the economy. These problems have been addressed in critical development theories, as mentioned below, and are discussed in greater detail in Chapter Four in relation to young people's engagement in civil society in Fiji and Solomon Islands, and in Chapter Six with reference to the influence of social constructs of 'tradition' and 'modernity'.

Critical and reflexive engagement

While the holistic livelihoods approach is utilised as an applied vision of development, it is strongly informed by critical development theories, including the writing of Pacific scholars who did not work specifically in the development studies space. Pacific writers such as Wendt (1976), Hau`ofa (1983, 1985) and Ravuvu (1988) have long engaged in debates about issues of dependency, neocolonialism and alternative visions of development that are the hallmarks of critical theories in the schools of alternative development, adaptive development and related concepts of intersectionality and complex adaptive systems. While the majority of my informants did not describe their approach to change with reference to specific development theories, their ideas about the ideal processes informing social change accorded with the key approaches on which I have drawn, and this influenced my development of the holistic livelihoods lens. These discussions and my reading of critical development texts by Pacific writers have forced me to constantly revisit my position as an outsider to the region while conducting this research.

Critical development theories challenge the notion that to be 'developed' requires economic growth and material gain. Post-development theorists such as Arturo Escobar (1992) and Gustavo Esteva (2010) specifically dispute the terminology and practice of international development, arguing that the industry and the discipline entrench power imbalances by defining who is 'developed' and who is 'developing' or 'underdeveloped'. Recognising issues of power imbalances, alternative development perspectives propose approaching development theory and practice from a values base that emphasises the agency of beneficiary communities. Alternative development approaches place emphasis on the wellbeing of individuals and communities in terms relevant to them (Berner and Phillips 2003; Nederveen Pieterse 1998). They seek to avoid the paternalism of the donor-directed modes of development that may assume linearity and impose ethnocentric beliefs about the desires of the recipient populations (cf. Rostow 1971). Alternative development is underpinned by the belief that disadvantaged and marginalised peoples are the experts on their own situation and that any developmental interventions should be grounded in the values of the communities they seek to impact (Berner and Phillips 2003).

Like alternative development, adaptive approaches to development specifically acknowledge the lack of universality around developmental goals and interventions, harshly critiquing interventions that seek to transpose 'working' policies, projects and programs from one context to another (Andrews et al. 2012). Adaptive approaches are largely informed by complex adaptive systems thinking, which argues that systems made up of multiple and independent parts are inherently unpredictable as any interaction between two or more parts can have unforeseen ramifications on other parts (Gell-Mann 1992; Rittel and Webber 1973). Rittel and Webber (1973: 160) write of social issues as 'wicked problems' for which interventions responding to individual stimulus cannot reasonably anticipate the corollary affects they may have without understanding the often unknown—and sometimes unknowable—other stimuli affecting the problem. When interviewed, Jack Maebuta, a peace and education studies scholar from Solomon Islands, succinctly connected this notion to the need to holistically understand and address issues of Pacific youth livelihoods. Speaking of unemployment, Jack noted that '[u]nemployment gives birth to other livelihood issues'.

Critical approaches to development have evolved in recent years through conversations and debates among development practitioners, organisations and academics—mostly Western-based—that have furthered the ideas of alternative development to champion adaptive, context-relevant development interventions. Approaches such as Doing Development Differently (DDD), Problem-Driven Iterative Adaptation (PDIA) and Thinking and Working Politically (TWP), which belong to an emerging adaptive school of development, are prime examples of this. DDD is defined as an approach to development that is 'problem-driven; iterative with lots of learning; and engaging teams and coalitions, often producing hybrid solutions that are "fit to context" and politically smart' (ODI 2014). TWP understands all social interactions as political (Leftwich 2011: 2) and thus seeks to promote social change that acknowledges local histories, etiquettes and power relations and attempts to drive interventions with the support of local individuals or coalitions with influence (TWP Community 2016). Further, by explicitly exploring the impacts of power and networks on social change, TWP offers a framework by which to explain how immanent social changes occur (Hudson et al. 2018). PDIA places an emphasis on addressing development problems as they are understood by those affected by them, emphasising a need to 'generate, test and refine context-specific solutions in response to locally nominated and prioritised problems' and to 'tolerate (even encourage) failure as the necessary price of success' (Andrews et al. 2015: 125). By advocating for development problems and solutions to be identified by those experiencing them and for development organisations to play a supportive role with respect to local initiatives, each of these approaches builds on alternative development ideas.

Though not explicitly using the language of adaptive development, Jack Maebuta discussed the need for development interventions to be context specific. Jack shared a story of his experience working as consultant to development organisations, including helping to design the Rapid Employment Project (REP) in Solomon Islands, which will be discussed in Chapter Three. Echoing adaptive development concerns about the transposition of development interventions that work in one environment to another without considering context, he discussed how he was consulted about expanding REP to Papua New Guinea following its perceived success in Solomon Islands:

> Even though PNG and Solomon Islands are both Melanesian, the dynamics of the development work on the ground is totally different. We ended up trying to work with these locals in order for them to understand that they have a different ball game altogether. We were trying to get everything off the ground as we did it here, but we found that it didn't work for them. We may say that success breeds another success but when you look at transferability from one country to another, even in the Pacific, I still doubt that it would work. It will come down to those people who are on the ground … to make it work because they don't keep to one thing.

What the theories that make up the adaptive school of development have in common is that each rejects universality in development approaches and outcomes, values research that acknowledges failure and sees developmental reform as possible only through interventions that appreciate local context. These concepts are not new. Indeed, they reflect and build on arguments made through approaches such as capabilities and alternative development. As development economist Sakiko Fukuda-Parr writes:

> Sen's ideas [on capabilities] provide the core principles of a development approach whose flexible framework allows policy-makers to analyse diverse challenges that poor people and poor countries face, rather than imposing a rigid orthodoxy with a set of policy prescriptions. (2003: 302)

The value of the critical development approaches to my own understanding and practice of development lies in the onus they place on development practitioners to justify their engagement in a field or with a project. They force outsiders to be continuously reflexive and critical of their own practice; assumptions must be checked and positions of privilege acknowledged and mitigated, where possible. More so, the value of the outsider needs to be considered with relation both to the history of international development practitioners positioning themselves as experts and saviours (Escobar 2000; Esteva and Prakash 1998; see also Easterly 2006) and to the evidence that social change most often occurs through immanent social, political and economic processes (Ferguson 1994).

Just as dependency theorists like Frantz Fanon (1967) and Andre Gunder Frank (1970, 1972) claimed that the involvement of Western donors cemented power imbalances between the international haves and have-nots, leading to a loss of autonomy, Pacific peoples have also decried the dependency created through development interventions. Fijian social commentator Jone Dakuvula wrote more than four decades ago:

> Alien religious systems have been one of the influences that have had the most profound influence on Pacific peoples in the past and continue to do so … One of the least noticed religions that has been here for some time is 'Development Planning'. (1975: 15)

Hau`ofa discussed the potentially insidious side-effects of development assistance in his fictional novel *Tales of the Tikongs* (1983), referencing the allure of prestige and material gain that may occur because of engagement with well-resourced organisations and large sums of money. At one point in the novel—a satirical look at development practices in the Pacific— one character comments to another about altering development project ambitions to suit the donor: '[Y]ou're set to sell your soul no less. Do it and you'll never get it back because you will not want to' (Hau`ofa 1983: 88).

Hau`ofa's words regarding the seductive nature of development benefits highlight the issue at the heart of dependency critiques in the Pacific. Improvements in basic-needs indicators are an undoubted positive, but the greatest risk of accepting development aid dictated by the terms of donors is that it may lead to the gradual surrender of culture and identity. Ravuvu noted this as a trend in Fiji in the 1980s, writing:

> In this process of 'development', urban and rural proletarians have emerged: people who can neither return to a rural self-sufficient, need-fulfilling community, nor to a situation over which they have ultimate control. The country is witnessing the emergence of a new breed of people who are like Zombies or puppets. They cannot return to their local way of living and have no influence over their future. They are a new breed of *tamata vakararavi*— dependent persons. They have become greatly confused by indiscriminately involving themselves in the foreign development process of modernism, individualism and multiracialism, which allowed others to undermine their beliefs and values and the respect for their way of life. (1988: 187; emphasis in original)

These challenges are particularly pertinent given the amount of aid funding received by Oceanic states. As Matthew Dornan and Jonathan Pryke (2017: 386) note: 'Official development assistance is higher in the Pacific than in any other region on a per capita basis.' Since the movements for sovereignty and regional cooperation boomed in the 1960s and

1970s (Fraenkel 2019b; Fry 1981; Ratuva 2019), critical development thinkers in the Pacific have espoused the need to be actively engaged in development planning in their communities and countries, as well as to remain vigilant of the risk of cultural loss. Samoan philosopher and writer Albert Wendt wrote of the need for Pacific peoples to determine their own destinies, by envisioning their own image of development of the region. In 'Towards a New Oceania', he writes:

> [W]e must rediscover and reaffirm our faith in the vitality of our past, our cultures, our dead, so that we may develop our own unique eyes, voices, muscles, and imagination. (Wendt 1976: 51)

At a similar time, former Fijian prime minister and later president Ratu Sir Kamisese Mara (1997: xvi) coined the term 'the Pacific Way', which Ron Crocombe (1975: 1), the founding Professor of Pacific Studies at the University of the South Pacific, once explained as being based on the recognition that knowledge is not monopolised by the West, that Oceania is heterogeneous and, most critically, that 'Pacific people are not only entitled to, but obliged to, be actively involved to the fullest possible extent in shaping their own future'. Hau`ofa similarly wrote in his seminal essay 'Our Sea of Islands':

> [The] future lies in the hands of our own people, not of those who would prescribe for us, get us dependent and indebted because they can see no way out. (1994: 159)

These visions did not involve the isolation of Oceania from globalisation and modernisation through advancements in education, medicine, technology or social change. Acknowledging the impacts of colonialism, globalisation and the international development industry, and the fact that cultures are in a constant state of evolution, Wendt wrote:

> I do not advocate a return to an imaginary pre-papalagi[5] Golden Age or utopian womb. Physically, we are too corrupted for such a re-entry! Our quest should not be for a revival of our past cultures but for the creation of new cultures which are free of the taint of colonialism and based firmly on our own pasts. The quest should be for a new Oceania. (1976: 53)

---

5   Samoan, meaning 'foreigners'.

The capacity for outsiders to misinterpret and understate the histories they carry into Pacific contexts was a key motivation for my engagement with youth activists and advocates who could, in the words of Ivan Illich (1968), a key figure in post-development, 'tell … [me] to go to hell'. The value of engaging these communities was reinforced through their criticism of well-intentioned outsiders. Tura Lewai, who has significant experience working on development interventions with professionals and volunteers across the globe, expressed to me:

> A lot of people from the outside are well-meaning, they come in with good intentions, but they are not informed about what is going on on the ground, about what the real situations are.

Rosie Catherine, of Fiji, specifically discussed the challenges of having outsiders documenting the experience of Pacific peoples. She lamented the fact that there are a limited number of local Pacific peoples representing their own communities in academia:

> People complain that other people from Australia and New Zealand or from Canada and America come and write about our stories and why aren't we writing our own stories? Why are we depending on other people to write our stories?

Tura and Rosie shared with me that they did not have a problem with people from beyond the Pacific engaging in the region as academics and development workers, but such outsiders needed to appreciate local context and ensure their work was provided for the benefit of the communities with which they worked, not just for their own professional advancement.

This ability to consider community needs is crucial in affecting change in Oceania. Sociocentric, sustainable lifestyles are at the heart of Pacific village ways of life (Brison 2001). Imposing developmental ambitions that favour the individual and the market may be alluring on some levels, but they are less likely to lead to significant improvements in the lived experience of those most in need of development assistance than interventions aimed at increasing access to developmental goods and services for a broader population spectrum (Birdsall et al. 1995; Bradshaw 2007). Engaging these people and communities in the means through which they can exert a level of control is critical to the chances of any intervention not only being successful, but also not undermining their cultural and economic values through the imposition of foreign ideologies.

This is not to ignore the influence of institutions of power and authority. The evidence of successful developmental states (Johnson 1982, 1999; Leftwich 1994, 1995; Nem Singh and Ovadia 2018; Thurbon and Weiss 2016) proves the need to understand that positive reforms are more likely to come about if driven collectively both from the grassroots and from structures of influence. This is particularly important in Pacific cultures, where challenging leadership is culturally discouraged. Appreciating how power works to promote or inhibit participation and opportunity is a vital step in developing and implementing appropriate development interventions.

The value of the holistic livelihoods approach is that it eschews assumptions of universality, acknowledges that social structures are complex and adaptive, and allows for both the aims and the ends of development practices to be determined by those directly affected—including the disadvantaged and the marginalised. This is not a new concept, but rather an evolution of previous critical approaches to development—and is one that seeks to equally privilege the individual and the community, and that understands that the prospects for individuals to improve their livelihoods and wellbeing are connected to how communities work to improve the freedoms and opportunities of all. It is also one that advocates for the currently minimised voice of youth to be involved in determining purposes and pathways of development for the Great Ocean States of the Pacific.

Due to the population significance of youth in the Pacific, this is a role that cannot be overlooked, and youth activists are acutely aware of this. As Usaia Moli told me: 'Every issue in the country—if it's climate change, teenage pregnancy and all these things—young people are at the forefront.' Taking a broader, Pacific-wide view, Tura Lewai expressed that: 'We need to be able to realise that the future of the Pacific, the future of Fiji, the future of any Pacific island lies in its young people.'

Conclusion

This chapter has discussed the influences that have informed my approach to this research. Following Kleine's (2013) exhortation that development commentators need to make clear how they envisage development, I have outlined how I conceive of international development in theory and in practice. I note that while the ultimate ambition of development should be creating opportunities for people to realise and actualise their individual capabilities, this lofty aspiration should not overlook the basic needs of the disadvantaged and marginalised. It is from this basis that my holistic livelihoods approach seeks to address the immediate concerns of marginalised peoples while creating and supporting social, economic and political structures that provide access for all to achieve their potential.

This perspective has been built from both theoretical and practical bases. International development theories belonging to the alternative and adaptive development schools have shaped my understanding of how context dictates development outcomes and the need to view local development beneficiaries and partners as the experts in their own situation. This is demonstrated throughout this book through the voices of my informants, primarily the activist youth and professionals working on youth issues whom I interviewed during my fieldwork.

It is my use of informants' voices that connects this book to debates about the purpose of development in the Pacific region. As an outsider to the region, I have had to comprehend the cultural values that inform concepts of what is good and desirable at a societal level in Pacific communities. The holistic livelihoods lens is intended not to be superimposed on to Pacific development debates and practices, but to engage with how these have evolved. In this way, I discuss how concepts of what is 'traditional' and what is 'modern' shape culture and development to impact on youth livelihoods and development in Fiji and Solomon Islands.

2

Education as an enabler and a barrier

Our education system … fails our young people. There is not a link between the government development plans, doing an assessment of what the needs are in five years' time so that we can prepare our labour forecast now, so that we influence our education system.

— Salote Kaimacuata, Fiji

Like many people with whom I spoke in both Fiji and Solomon Islands, Fijian Salote Kaimacuata reflected on the failures of formal education to prepare young people to be active, engaged citizens, to secure their individual livelihoods and to contribute to economic growth and social capital. This is not to say that Salote or others saw little value in education. Indeed, those with whom I spoke regarded education as one of the most fundamental social structures that could help to improve livelihoods and lead to self-directed development. This aligns with regular portrayals of education globally as the closest thing to a panacea for poverty that exists.

This belief is not entirely unfounded. Educational psychologists Bradford Brown and Reed Larson (2002: 7) note, for example, that 'expansion of educational opportunities for youth in Japan, Korea, and China helped to propel these nations into strong positions in the world economy'. The belief stands that a better educated populace will result in societies with improved health, innovation, resilience and civic engagement (Curtain and Vakaoti 2011: 7). With the examples set by increased investment in education in East Asia after World War II, the need for a robust, adaptive education system is apparent. T.S. Saraswathi and Larson write:

> The most dramatic improvement in the circumstances of youth in the last half century has been in Japan and in the other countries known as 'Asian Tigers', where deliberate government infusion of money into education have [sic] greatly increased the capabilities of youth. As they reached adulthood this education permitted young people to make valuable contributions to society, which have lifted these nations from the ranks of 'developing' to 'developed' nations. (2002: 346)

The experiences of these developmental states resulted in a direct correlation being seen between educational investment and economic growth, through the middle points of increased employment and enterprise. Across Oceania, the espousal of education as the key to individual and community improvement has been heeded to the extent of significant government investment in formal education, targeted particularly at children at primary education levels, with a tapering of resources as young people become teenagers (Curtain and Vakaoti 2011: 5).

Current evidence paints an unclear picture as to how education systems throughout the Pacific region are improving individual livelihoods or leading to economic growth. In Solomon Islands, for example, only one in every six school leavers finds employment (Holmberg 2016). Encouragingly, the World Bank (2011: 21) has found in Fiji that increased educational qualifications for heads of households lead to a decreased likelihood of the household being classified as impoverished, though the benefits gradually lessen with each year of post-secondary education qualification—although this may bring into question findings by the International Labour Organization (ILO 2016a) that the risk of youth unemployment in Fiji increases for those with higher education qualifications. Based on 2016 statistics, the ILO (2016a: 3) notes that this figure may be inflated by highly educated youth 'holding out in hopes that they land a higher paid job that meets their aspirations'.[1]

---

1   In Fiji, primary and secondary education are legislated as free for all children and young people (The Fijian Government 2015), while in Solomon Islands, this applies throughout primary until senior secondary education (Honiara City Council n.d.; Solomon Times 2009). These policies relate mainly to teaching fees, with citizens still responsible for associated costs such as clothing, daily meals and some personal resources. Further, many remote communities do not have their own school and students' transport and accommodation costs are not subsidised by either government. For these reasons, education in Solomon Islands remains non-compulsory (Binns 2015). Tertiary education is not universally subsidised in either country.

The lack of clarity around the impacts of education in Pacific societies is evidence of the need for wider research investigating the societal pressures on youth and the impediments these place on developing human capital.

The urgency of this problem was noted to me by Isimeli Tagicakiverata, the President of the Pacific Association of Technical and Vocational Education and Training and an educator at Fiji National University. He has been researching tertiary education in the Pacific for more than a decade, during which he has witnessed a continued struggle for graduates to secure employment. He told me:

> The Fiji school system produces about 16,000 school leavers every year, according to government data, and 8,000 are able to find further education or employment,[2] so the remaining 8,000 … they're the biggest question. In five years, that's 40,000 young people, school leavers. Where are we going to channel them? How? Those are some of the questions that the government needs to provide answers for.

This chapter explores issues related to the education systems of Fiji and Solomon Islands and how they are operating to promote or inhibit the potential of the countries' youth populations. Throughout, it is clear there is a lack of direction and willingness to adapt education provision to livelihood realities. White-collar training and employment are valued despite the lack of livelihood opportunities they present (UNICEF Pacific et al. 2005). This issue speaks to a wider structural problem related to cultural expectations of youth to learn through passive observation, which informs an education environment that does not strongly promote critical inquiry. This reinforces the subordinate status of youth in Fijian and Solomon Islander societies and results in young people having limited influence in determining their own livelihood trajectories in relation to education ambitions and employment opportunities.

The purpose of education

The purpose of education is an area of inquiry that has long been overlooked in practical terms in the Pacific. The dominance of capitalist approaches to social and economic policies in developing countries over the past century has led to education being understood implicitly as

---

2   These figures are indicative only and are explored in more depth in the next chapter.

connected to the formal economy through its creation and re-creation of persons able to work. Asesela Ravuvu's (1988: 168) treatise on Fiji's negotiation of sovereignty and dependency as a developing state noted the problematic disconnection between the processes of formal education and the needs of the community: 'The school system in Fiji has long been so narrowly academic that it has become increasingly irrelevant to the cultural, social, economic and political development in the country.' Here, Ravuvu is not only referencing the lack of connection between the outputs of the Fijian formal education system and the needs of the state, but also questioning the utility and purpose of the system.

This is a critical issue. As education philosopher Gert Biesta noted when discussing the lack of reflexivity in the design of formal education systems throughout the world:

> [T]he absence of explicit attention for the aims and ends of education is the effect of often implicit reliance on a particular 'common sense' view of what education is for. (2009: 37)

The concept that education is a tool for ongoing economic growth has taken hold across both developed and developing countries (MacFarlane 2018: 771).

An increased reliance on standardised testing and viewing educational qualifications as status symbols and signifiers of one's competency to undertake certain tasks at certain levels (Biesta 2009: 39–40) speak to the wider issue of education as primarily a vehicle for increased economic output. The World Bank admits it paid scant attention to education as a developmental input or output until it recognised that educational outcomes could be tied to economic growth (Psacharopoulos and Woodhall 1985: 3). Whether or not such attitudes are politically motivated and even whether such attitudes are widespread are beyond the scope of this book. However, it does bear considering what other purposes education may serve.

One idealistic vision is that education is about creating a base of knowledge for perpetual learning. This view takes as its starting point the idea that curiosity is natural and good for the individual and the community. In this context, education is about the pursuit of learning first and foremost, with tangible gains, such as those to the economy, understood to flow from thought and discovery. This approach to education seems to be out of favour and yet it still bears consideration. As Biesta (2009: 37) states, 'at least in democratic societies there ought to be an ongoing discussion about the aims and ends of (public) education'.

From an international development perspective, numerous social benefits flow from high rates of engagement in formal education. Numerous studies globally have identified that growth in the percentage of the population completing formal education—ideally, beyond primary level— is positively associated with reductions in poverty and livelihood stress (Cremin and Nakabugo 2012).[3] This is particularly true of educating girls, with development economists Stephan Klasen and Francesca Lamanna (2009) finding significant links between female education and economic growth across the Middle East, North Africa, East Asia and South Asia. Though there are variances across the studies, the evidence clearly points to gains in human capital and social capital because of formal schooling. Related to these gains is the common association between increased education levels and improved economic growth in developing countries (Benos and Zotou 2014). Correlations have even been made between increased education and disaster preparedness in at-risk communities (Muttarak and Lutz 2014).

Crucial to achieving the benefits of high levels of formal schooling in developing countries is that the quality of education is high. Unless education leads to improved cognitive skills across a wide cohort of the population, simply attending and being assessed to have completed levels of schooling will not be related to positive development outcomes (Hanushek 2016; Hanushek and Woessmann 2007). In fact, differing levels of education quality within both developed and developing states can result in greater inequality, as a group of South African economists discovered when synthesising results from several studies of the quality of education offered in various locations across South Africa (van der Berg et al. 2011). Further, as will be discussed in the following chapter, widespread increases in education that are not met with commensurate employment and other livelihood opportunities can also lead to social unrest. Recent global examples include the Arab Spring (Kuhn 2012) and the Occupy movement (Milkman et al. 2013).

---

3   For case studies, see Awan et al. (2011) and Ncube et al. (2013), writing about the Middle East and North Africa; and Zhang and Minxia (2006), writing about China.

These potential social impacts relating to matters of access to and the quality of education should not be overlooked when considering the purpose of formal education. Contemporary approaches to education understand its provision to be a public good, with Biesta (2006: 169) writing that 'today lifelong learning is increasingly understood in terms of the formation of human capital and as an investment in economic development'. How education acts to benefit the public good and to what ends need consideration, though. At the most basic level, this means that the quality of formal education should be high enough to equip students with adequate literacy skills and general knowledge to successfully transition into their adult roles. At a societal level, this raises questions about the type of society that is desired by a state or community. Tensions between individualistic and sociocentric conceptions of self, exacerbated by globalisation, are present in formal education systems. This has been noted beyond the Pacific, also, with youth studies researchers Anita Harris, Johanna Wyn and Salem Younes (2010: 12) noting in their discussion of active youth citizenship in Australia that 'individualization within education and work has led to weaker mechanisms of political socialization, and … job insecurity and neo-liberal ideology alienate young people from the political system'.

Case study: Opinions of the education system held by civically engaged Pacific youth

Though the positive impacts of formal education on driving economic growth, reducing inequality and even promoting disaster resilience are well established, it is vital that such education is of a high quality. Numerous young informants with whom I spoke in both Fiji and Solomon Islands told of deficiencies within the formal education systems of each country. The core issue raised by these informants related to a standardised approach to teaching that assumed homogeneity in how the curriculum should be provided to and accepted by students. They saw this as limiting the space for young people to realise their potential, with correlated consequences of diminishing critical thinking development, minimising the active citizenship of youth and failing to prepare young people for appropriate employment or other livelihood opportunities.

Roshika Deo and Tura Lewai, from Fiji, expressed frustration at the rote dictation that they see as the most common teaching method in Fijian schools. Roshika told me: 'One of the … big problems with the education sector is that it doesn't recognise multiple intelligence.' Roshika elaborated that this had the impact of marginalising at the individual level students who did not respond well to the established paradigm:

> A lot of the time you have dropouts because they have some kind of reading disability, or they don't respond to the current design of the education curriculum, but they may be highly intelligent people.

Tura added that, at a broader level, the lack of conversational and experiential learning resulted in critical thinking deficits in Fijian students:

> Young people are taught, if you listen, you will succeed, but there is no encouragement to listen and critically analyse [and ask,] 'Why do you think that happens?' People that ask that in class are often shunned because they are told to shut up by their teachers.

For Tura, this reflects the structural minimisation Fijian youth experience throughout social interactions: 'Even outside school, they have family, they have church and the church is one [institution] where it is "up-down", "down-up", "listen" [and] "You are a sinner".'

The discouragement of young people from forming and articulating opinions was also expressed by youth informants in Solomon Islands John Firibo and Harry Olikwailafa. They described the lack of connectivity between learning and livelihoods, as well as the discouragement of critical thinking in young people. John echoed Tura's comments regarding the wider impacts this has on the youth voice, saying: 'Here in Solomon Islands, once you start expressing yourself, the elders say that it's no good. To them, their word is the law.' Harry told me: 'What I see from the curriculum is not empowering young people. It's just numeracy and literacy and not giving young people an understanding of "this is the world".'

Beyond this, Elisha Bano, from Fiji, discussed with me how formal education could act to inhibit livelihood opportunities for some young people. With specific reference to rural Fijians, she spoke of the research of Vanisha Mishra-Vakaoti (2013) into why children and young people drop out of school. She explained how some see formal schooling as a barrier to providing for their livelihoods:

> There were children she [Mishra-Vakaoti] met who were school dropouts and they'd been farming and earning more than some of us graduates. They are saying they only want maths and English or maybe they only want agriculture, but they have to go to a school from 8 to 3, which is affecting their farming time.

All these civically active young people argue that the education systems of their countries are not appropriately adaptive, making them ill-suited to the learning needs of some students. Moreover, they express the view that the social and institutional structures surrounding how education is delivered in Fiji and Solomon Islands reinforce the repression of the development of individual skills, intellect and cognition in children and youth.

The inefficiencies of education systems

Within Oceania, evidence suggests the island nations are not utilising their education systems to maximise the potential of their significant youth populations. Demographer Chris McMurray observed more than a decade ago that the education systems of many Pacific states fail to acknowledge local needs and work to create a class of skilled underemployed:

> Dropping out of school and high rates of unemployment are interrelated symptoms of two underlying problems: inflexible education systems geared mainly towards white-collar work and distorted economies that do not provide enough employment opportunities for young people. (McMurray 2006: 8)

The longstanding nature of this issue is reflected in the statistics previously presented for education and employment in Fiji and Solomon Islands. These figures mirror the assertion from Pacific development policy experts David Abbott and Steve Pollard (2004: 54) that, across Oceania, 'in general only around one fourth to one third of all those finishing school will likely be able to find regular work in the formal sector'.

Unfortunately, the veracity of these statistics is hard to establish. Figures related to employment and education in the Pacific are not reported regularly and are often disputed. Taking Fiji as an example, the Fiji Bureau of Statistics (2020) has not included figures for levels of unemployment, let alone disaggregated to reflect graduate pathways, in its latest report on employment statistics. Meanwhile, the country's unemployment rate—

which Education Minister Jone Usamate claimed was 4.5 per cent in 2018 (Kumar 2018)—is reported so intermittently by the Fijian Government that it is difficult to identify irregularities and is viewed by some as an inaccurate representation of the figures for political purposes (Australia Network News 2013).

One reason for the inefficiencies in Pacific education systems that is regularly acknowledged in the literature, and was repeatedly highlighted by those I interviewed, relates to the functional design of formal education systems throughout the region and how this has been influenced directly and indirectly by non-Oceanic cultures. This began with colonial European governments, in concert with Christian churches, and the creation of an education system that reflected those of industrial-age Europe, which were designed to inculcate European customs and approaches to logic in the upper classes (Corcoran and Koshy 2010; Oakeshott and Allen 2015: 7; Watson-Gegeo and Gegeo 1992: 15) as well as to create a disciplined working class (Coleman 1968). In an article on the continuing influence of traditional and colonial stereotypes on iTaukei women's education and career paths, youth sociologist Pam Nilan quotes Katarina Tuinamuana to argue that:

> The early model of education for Fijian children was one that would 'prepare a workforce that would occupy subordinate positions in factories and offices'—one that indicated low academic expectations. (Nilan 2009: 33)

This system managed to not only serve colonial plantation interests, but also create an understanding that Western approaches to education were of the highest possible standard.

Though direct colonial influences on education policy have long subsided, interviewees believed the influence of Western models remains. Roshika Deo is a feminist activist whose social justice advocacy led her to run for Fiji's parliament in 2014 (which is detailed in a case study in Chapter Five). She explained that even though the occupying forces of European colonialism have departed most Pacific states, their ideas remain: 'The education system is really archaic and, to a certain extent, is very colonial.'

This was a view shared by Viliame Cagilaba. Viliame is the Director of Fiji's National Employment Centre, working at the nexus of policies and projects designed to create employment opportunities for citizens, with one focus being the employment prospects of new graduates. Viliame told me:

> Information is popping up that our education system should be overhauled. There should be a match between our education system and the supply of labour, so they connect. Our education system is still driven by [the influences of] colonial law … This is our challenge. That is why there are a lot of youth in unemployment. When they graduate, they have nowhere to go.

In the postcolonial period, Western influence on Fiji's education system was expressed through its orientation to producing potential employees for white-collar and service-economy roles (for example, Cavu et al. 2009: 611; McMurray 2006: 8; Nilan 2009; Nilan et al. 2006). The focus on providing students with requisite skills for white-collar careers reflects similar progressions in Organisation for Economic Co-operation and Development (OECD), post-industrial societies where transferable service skills, with a focus on critical thinking, shape curricula and the mindsets with which students approach their education in relation to future employment. Across Oceania, where the economies are neither industrial nor post-industrial, yet exhibit aspects of each, the ambition to instil critical thinking capabilities and prepare youth for the workforce seems to be failing.

Rather than this reflecting poor delivery of curriculum across the Pacific region—though this is an issue (Government of Solomon Islands 2002; Naidu 2003; Woo and Corea 2009) and will be discussed later in this chapter—these failures are created through curriculum design. Indeed, the structure of the education system seems to not only fail to adequately link with employment ambitions, but also pushes young people away from fully engaging with and completing formal education. As Woo and Corea write in their review of the literature related to youth livelihood opportunities in the Pacific, commissioned by the Pacific Community:

> As both parents and youth are aware of the dearth of jobs in that sector and the fact that, consequently, their education does not provide them with much advantage after graduation, there is little motivation to remain in school. (Woo and Corea 2009: 8)

Isimeli Tagicakiverata similarly expressed to me:

> Our secondary and primary school system is designed in such a way that it encourages young people to pursue white-collar careers and there are very good reasons for that. If you go back to

our history, our postcolonial heritage, when the British colonised Fiji, they built these flagship schools in Fiji: Queen Victoria School; Adi Cakobau School …

This issue of a mismatch between education system outputs and livelihood opportunities again cuts to the very purpose of formal education, as discussed earlier. In turn, this raises several critical questions. Should education provide skills for work? Should it focus on critical thinking to enable people to make appropriate career, life and societal choices? Should the system develop entrepreneurial traits to create future-ready generations? Should its primary aim be to encourage and reward intellectual curiosity? Or should the ambition be some combination of these four areas, as well as others?

While it is beyond the scope of this book to suggest a definitive answer, it is important to acknowledge that it is not easy to respond to these questions. I contend that the issue of shaping an education system that meets local Pacific needs is reflective of deeper and more general developmental challenges facing the states and peoples of the Pacific. Where *kastom*[4] clashes with foreign hegemonic structures—whether European colonial histories, capitalist international trade or others—it is incumbent on the people of the Great Ocean States of the Pacific to consciously determine their vision of an ideal future and establish solutions to the developmental problems they face in ways that are most appropriate for them.

This is a debate that influential Pacific thinkers have articulated since the independence movement of the 1960s and 1970s (for example, Crocombe 1975; Hau`ofa 1994; Puna 2015; Wendt 1976). Even Australian international development scholar Helen Hughes (2003: 25) declared:

---

4   *Kastom* is a word common in Melanesian pidgin languages that is used at times in this book to denote cultural norms and concepts of traditional ways of living. Researchers have found it difficult to provide a clear or concise definition of how *kastom* can be understood outside the communities where it is practised. Anthropologist Roger Keesing (1982: 360) explains: '*Kastom* does not correspond neatly to English "custom" or to anthropological usages of "culture". *Kastom* canonically denotes ancestrally enjoined rules for life: pollution taboos, rules about cursing and swearing, about the purity of women, and procedures for sacrifices and purification. Genealogies, lands, and shrines, all closely associated with ancestors, are *kastom*.' Michael Goddard (2010: 12) helpfully asserts that '*kastom* meant a set of rules imposed by ancestors, as distinct from everyday customary behaviour', clarifying its fluid nature by stating that '*kastom* can be an edited, idealized, mythicized version of the past' (p. 18). As a word with etymological roots in Melanesian pidgin languages, *kastom* is used much more regularly in Solomon Islands than in Fiji, where there is no direct equivalent. Despite this, I employ the terminology of *kastom* at times in this book to represent the culturally understood meanings behind it, which can cross cultures. Similarly, I utilise various Fijian terms and phrases throughout this book where appropriate.

'Change can only come in the Pacific from Pacific initiatives.' It is an issue that is pertinent when examining current education paradigms that appear to reflect isomorphic mimicry[5] of institutions as they operate in Western, developed states (Tuinamuana 2007), rather than being driven by endogenously determined ideas of the purpose of education as applicable to local needs. This is just one example of how local institutions can reflect foreign conceptions of how development should look as a process and an end, with formal education structures theoretically the ideal locations for the production and support of the human and social capital requisite in the self-determination of Pacific developmental futures.

Informants in Solomon Islands were particularly concerned about the disconnection between the structures of education and employment systems. Julianne Oge is a youth development worker with a Honiara-based NGO, involved in projects to assist young people to find work. She spoke to me of how the problem of youth unemployment begins with deficits in the resources available in the education system, manifesting in overcrowding of classrooms and a lack of appropriately skilled staff:

> With our education system, it fails us in some ways. There are all these dropouts. It is not enough to cater for the population. Right from the start, the population size is problematic. The government cannot keep up with the population size. Then with the economy there is just not the employment market there for us to put enough youth into employment. In the formal sector, there is not enough opportunity for young people.

The difficulties related to issues of limited resources, staffing and overpopulation are compounded by the nature of communities in Fiji and Solomon Islands being widely geographically dispersed. The Government of Solomon Islands (2002: 51) identifies physical resources including infrastructure, water and toilets as inadequate in many schools, on top of human resource issues of untrained teachers, inadequate curriculums and irregular hours of operation (pp. 51–52; see also Oakeshott and Allen 2015: 9). Until appropriate infrastructure, curriculums and training are supplied and schools are inspected for quality assurance more than 'once a year or not at all' (Government of Solomon Islands 2002: 50),

---

5   Isomorphic mimicry refers to practices of transposing policies and programs from foreign contexts into developing countries, either to give the appearance of reform or to try to re-create positive results identified in the original location without consideration of the wider social, cultural, political and economic factors that influenced these (Andrews et al. 2012).

it is hard to picture an improvement in formal education in such states, particularly for marginalised groups, including girls. Though Solomon Islands development researchers Matthew Allen and Sinclair Dinnen (2015: 386) argue that the delivery of education to isolated communities has improved in this century, Allen has also identified, with David Oakeshott, that inequities in the delivery of quality formal education across Solomon Islands have been a causal factor in limiting a sense of national unity in Solomon Islanders (Oakeshott and Allen 2015).

It appears that the fissure between the goals and the design of the education systems across Oceania when compared with the needs of the employment sector is a leading cause of youth disengagement. The education systems favour academic achievement—even going so far in Solomon Islands as to force students from school who fare poorly in end-of-year exams (Allen 2013; Evans 2016; Jourdan 1995)—streamlining students for employment in the service economy even though jobs are quite limited in that space (Curtain and Vakaoti 2011: 5; Tagicakiverata 2012; Woo and Corea 2009: 8). This disconnection is highlighted by the Pacific Community as the premium concern for youth capacity development and civic engagement in their exploration of the participation and livelihood challenges facing Pacific youth:

> The unavailability of jobs and inadequate training and preparation of young people for employment are the major contributing factors [to youth unemployment]. Self-employment is another option; however, resources and skills to generate and implement these ideas are not available. Training programmes to equip young people with employable skills are limited and the number of young people coming out of education systems is far greater than the number of available jobs in the market. (SPC 2009a: 9)

In a discussion with Salote Kaimacuata, of Fiji, she echoed this sentiment. Following comments about the lack of connection between education curriculums, employment opportunities and development planning, as quoted at the beginning of this chapter, she remarked on the feast-or-famine characteristics of Fijian employment opportunities: 'We are still bringing engineers from New Zealand and Australia. [Meanwhile,] we have an oversupply of lawyers: big deal!'

In their examination of the career ambitions of Fijian final-year secondary school students, Nilan et al. (2006: 897) comment in relation to Fiji that 'there seems to be little present alignment of the education system with manpower needs'. Quoting a secondary school principal, they write:

> This is what happens when you take people through a system that is targeting white collar jobs—that job market. It takes young people through that kind of tunnel kind of preparation. So if the job's available they will be able to get those jobs. But if the jobs are not available, those young people just stay ... in towns. (Nilan et al. 2006: 900)

This is pertinent as, indeed, those jobs appear not to be available, suggesting the focus of the education system may be a significant contributing factor to the high rates of youth joblessness. Similarly, in Solomon Islands, youth unemployment runs high while there is a 'strong demand for skilled labor in specific occupational areas in both the private and public sector' (Woo and Corea 2009: 9). Again, this reflects debates spanning decades, with these issues discussed by Francis Bugotu (1986) in Solomon Islands in the mid-1980s. In conversation with me, Biman Prasad, one of Fiji's leading economists and a prominent nongovernment Member of Parliament since 2014, appealed that:

> [What] we need to do is align our education system, our training programs for the young and youth, so that we can match some of the skills that are demanded in the different sectors of the economy.

Quality of formal education

Exacerbating the problems in the education systems of Fiji and Solomon Islands is the lack of access to high-quality formal education in numerous areas. Geographic obstacles to access to schools, poor facilities and inadequate training of teachers contribute to a disturbing picture that access to quality education in these countries is sorely lacking for many.

While urban areas, and particularly the capital cities of Suva and Honiara, are home to primary, secondary and tertiary institutions, rural areas and outlying islands are significantly disadvantaged in regard to access to such institutions (Oakeshott and Allen 2015: 15). Though it may not be economically feasible to host schools in every village and on every island, this does not diminish the problem that many families are left to decide whether to send their children away for education or to keep them at home and, thus, without access to formalised systems. With limits to access seen as a primary deterrent to the engagement of children and youth in formal education (SPC 2009a: 9), the further social issue of rural–urban migration is intensified (Phillips and Keen 2016), as discussed in the following chapter.

The evidence of access to education as a wicked problem plays out as youth discover that the skills and education that were held in esteem in their rural societies are either undervalued or unhelpful in the competition with the masses of other youth for income-generation and other livelihood opportunities when they relocate to urban areas. Writing of opportunity deficits that operate alongside real and perceived increased livelihood possibilities for youth in Tonga, Good (2012: 25) argues that this mismatch 'has opened them up to new insecurities about their status within the rest of the world'. Again, this issue is not new, with anthropologist Christine Jourdan highlighting in her 1995 study of street-frequenting youth in Honiara:

> Very many of the young people who reach Honiara nowadays have had some schooling, however minimal. They were sent to school by their parents with the expectation that education would make them employable at good salaries. When they come to town with a Standard 6 year of education or a Form 3, they quickly realize that the level of education and training they have obtained is not sufficient to give them access to the good job they expected to find. Education has let them down. (Jourdan 1995: 209–10)

Even in areas where there are physical schools, their existence can at times be more symbolic than functional. Not only may these schools lack adequate facilities—noted by the Government of Solomon Islands (2002: 51) to include 'water, toilets, reading rooms, security'—they also may lack active and regular engagement from teaching staff. Isimeli Tagicakiverata informed me that the lack of monitoring of rural Fijian schools results in many operating only irregularly and on an ad hoc basis:

> If you have a school in a remote rural area and the committee is not active, whoa, the teachers are going to have a good time! I've heard of teachers who spend more time fishing and farming than with their students in the classroom.

This attitude among some teachers may reflect the lack of skills held by many working outside urban areas. While multiple interviewees in Fiji informed me that the country has an abundance of unemployed qualified teachers, problems with teacher qualifications remain an issue throughout both Fiji and Solomon Islands. In 2002, the Government of Solomon Islands noted a problem with teacher qualifications and class regularity (2002: 51–52). In 2004, Abbott and Pollard (2004: 38) reported that in Fiji 'only about 4% [of teachers] had degree or diploma qualifications while 16% had not even completed Form 5', though this was partially tempered by the finding that '99% had some formal training'. They also noted that more than 80 per cent of teachers in Solomon Islands had 'no more than a Form 3 (Grade 9) education' (Abbott and Pollard 2004: 38).

While the figures for Solomon Islands were identified as dating from 1996, the depth of the continuing issue of teacher training remains. This struck me when talking with a former secondary schoolteacher completing an undergraduate degree in education in Solomon Islands with the aim of becoming a school principal. When I asked what his previous teaching qualifications were, he responded, matter-of-factly: 'I almost finished High School.'

Naidu (2003) frames this problem in Fiji and Solomon Islands as being indicative of Melanesian approaches to education. He writes that in comparison with Polynesia, where 'education was especially valued and literacy rates are generally above 80%' (Naidu 2003: 23), Melanesian states have not held education in the same esteem for as long. Noting that core reasons for this relate to the greater cultural and linguistic heterogeneity of Melanesian states, together with geographic isolation within these countries and the later adoption of systemised formal education than in Polynesian states, Naidu (2003: 23) also observes that a cycle exists of poorly trained teachers resulting in part from the deficits of the formal system, which results in high rates of premature dropout (p. 24). This is no doubt compounded in Solomon Islands by the competitive nature of securing secondary school places, based on end-of-year exam results that eliminate from the system those who do not pass (Braithwaite et al. 2010: 99). Further limiting the equitable access to quality education are the histories of the education systems of Fiji and Solomon Islands, where elites were segregated into exclusive schools designed to train them for leadership roles (Oakeshott and Allen 2015; White 2007: 55) and in colonial forms of thinking (Tavola 1991: 12; Watson-Gegeo and Gegeo 1992).

Access to and esteem for formal education are issues not only for young people living in remote communities. For example, Solomon Islands disability worker Davis Ladofoa explained to me how these challenges are compounded for people experiencing multiple forms of marginalisation. On educating young people with disabilities, he said:

> Because people with disabilities are often viewed by their families as not capable of doing anything, they are often not even sent to school and then not encouraged to do anything for their future. At schools across the country, it is rare to see children with disabilities.

Coupled with the lack of facilities designed specifically for, or friendly to, persons with disabilities, it is understandable how

> [p]eople with disabilities are seen as the poorest and most marginalized members of Pacific island societies with an estimate of less than 10% of children/youth with disability having access to any form of education. (Sharma et al. 2016: 2)

Of the flow-on effects, Davis explained to me:

> If a child grows up with a disability and they don't attend school then that's it. They cannot do anything more in life, whether it be further education or whatever. When that happens, you will see that a child with a disability as they grow older, they can't do things like get a job or get further training.

Technical and vocational education and training

The biggest divergence between educational outcomes and opportunities in the employment sector appears to sit with the lack of Pacific youth attaining skills for vocational employment. Despite multiple informants discussing how opportunities currently exist for skilled labourers in Pacific states—supported by recent research conducted by Tagicakiverata and Nilan (2018: 553)—there remains a view that vocational training centres are a significantly poorer option for students. In Fiji, such centres are colloquially referred to as 'dropout schools', as 'those who perform poorly in secondary school are directed to technical and vocational education' (Woo and Corea 2009: 9; see also Tagicakiverata and Nilan 2018: 551). As Nilan et al. (2006: 896) point out, such views significantly curtail the potential beneficial impacts of the education sector on employment and state economies as they discourage youth from pursuing these opportunities regardless of whether they are better suited to their abilities or more likely to result in the provision of a secure livelihood.

These problems are evident both in Fiji and in Solomon Islands. According to education experts, their impact is persistent despite efforts to make technical and vocational education and training (TVET) options more appealing. Jai Narayan, Director of Secondary Education at Fiji's Ministry of Education, Heritage and Arts, said:

> Previously we were providing vocational education [only] to those children who may have dropped out from the mainstream academia. For too long, we focused only on academics and then we found that there was a gap.

Similarly, Jack Maebuta, lecturer in education at the University of the South Pacific (USP) campus in Honiara and consultant on youth livelihoods to development agencies, told me: 'The stigma around that is that it is a second chance kind of education for youths who are not able to make it through the formal system.'

Despite issues of stigma, there remain calls for a boost to vocational training opportunities for youth across Oceania. Rather than a centralised institution offering such training or a collection of dispersed schools already tainted by the stigma of the 'dropout school' labelling, Curtain and Vakaoti (2011: 904) suggest vocational training should instead be incorporated into mainstream curriculums, representing the needs of the community—'not only because they are sorely needed, but because there is some evidence that the very presence of these programs in schools expands future career awareness for all pupils'. This is a recommendation accepted—on paper at least—by the Government of Solomon Islands in its *National Education Action Plan 2016–2020* (2016). Inserting vocational training into mainstream curriculums—if monitored and reviewed appropriately—would allow for such training to be responsive to community needs and market opportunities, including on-the-job work experience. It would also avoid what development economists Michael Clemens, Colum Graham and Stephen Howes (2014: 15) identify as the risk of 'creating excess supply of any particular skills in which a course can run'. This has the potential to improve the links between formal education and livelihood practices.

Jack Maebuta emphasised to me how appeals to boost the value and appeal of vocational training in Solomon Islands repeat patterns dating back decades, which have had limited impact. He displayed frustration born of decades of watching well-intentioned education and employment plans fail to be implemented or to shift social perceptions:

> There needs to be an overhaul of the system to really focus the entire system of education in the Solomons on vocational skills. These are currently in the curriculum but are not given a strong emphasis. That needs to be really looked into, and the government needs to show strong leadership in that area. The idea of vocational education has been around for some time and was a big focus in the 1970s, even the early 1960s in the White Paper called 'Education for What?', and the idea has been coming every now and again, but every time it is considered to be reintroduced, things tend to go back into the academic stream.

As with many other developmental efforts in the region, the accessibility of TVET for Pacific youth is disproportionately weighted to urban areas. The lack of technical and vocational training in rural areas has wideranging consequences in terms of rural–urban migration and rural employment. Furthermore, rural–urban migration for education will only benefit rural communities when the skills gained from that education have a direct and beneficial impact on rural areas. This benefit may be material, such as remittances, or in kind, where the person who has gained the skills is able to share their knowledge with their peers. In many village communities, this knowledge transfer is reliant on the newly skilled returning to their village—an expectation based on one of at least three suppositions: that there are livelihood benefits to be gained from returning to the village; that these benefits outweigh the potential livelihood benefits of remaining in proximity to urban hubs; and that they wish to return to the village.

Providing skills training in rural locations may assist to alleviate concerns about the urban bias in training opportunities. Sina Suliano has managed youth livelihoods and other development programs in Fiji. She suggested how greater access to vocational education in rural areas may minimise the push factor of migrating to urban areas:

> With the vocational centres, most are based in the urban areas. Having it accessible and taking it out there to the community level [would be beneficial], where they don't have to break an arm and a leg just to come to work or to come to school, where they don't have to live with relatives to be able to access that kind of service.

One strategy to minimise the dual problems of rural–urban migration for education and lack of human capacity in rural areas is the introduction of outreach training in Fiji. Since 2012, Fiji National University has operated the Sustainable Livelihood Program with the aim to provide skills training in rural communities to, first, improve self-sufficiency and, second, create greater economic opportunities, whether through formal or informal wage employment or microenterprise. Isimeli Tagicakiverata informed me in an interview about Fiji National University's efforts:

> We've trained more than 3,000 people in rural areas in the 14 different provinces free of charge, fully funded by the government … [in] 20 different skills that they can choose from.

A similar program is the Fiji School of the Air, a radio and internet-based correspondence school for children and youth who have no physical access to formal education (Bole 2009). These examples speak to some of the creative options educators, institutions and governments can apply to making appropriate education accessible beyond urban hubs.

Beyond these, a potential option discussed with me by multiple people was to mandate that recent teaching graduates spend a defined period at a rural or island school after they complete their degrees, such as five years. Models already exist in Fiji that could serve as the foundation for such a policy, including a 'rural service' scheme that offers urban transfers to teachers who have taught in rural areas (Mishra-Vakaoti 2013: 81). Similarly, in the medical profession, graduates are required to spend two years serving in a remote location as a way of consolidating their skills and providing access to quality health care for remote villages and islands. Following such a model would also help to alleviate concerns about appropriate professional development for early-career teachers, based on lessons learned from the medical model, which could be applied to ensure that teachers are appropriately skilled in a practical sense and offering quality education to their students. This would have the added bonus of encouraging youth to remain in rural locations for longer as they are engaged in active citizenship in their home areas—a theme central to the previously discussed Sustainable Livelihood Program—and potentially encouraging youth from these locations to aspire to be teachers so they can remain connected with their community.

All such measures will be limited in their impact, however, if the issue of child and youth engagement in critical thinking in the classroom is not addressed. As critical thought can be viewed culturally as undermining accepted authority, any reform measure of this nature would need to be culturally sensitive and, arguably, promoted through top-down modifications to the curriculum. Innovative approaches to teaching techniques beyond a lecture and dictation format would be needed and teachers would have to be convinced of the value of such approaches.

Adapting to local needs

Exposing youth to training that reflects local market needs may address a further issue impacting on the ability of young people to enter career-based livelihoods—the issue of choice and understanding one's options. This requires an awareness of market opportunities and the ability to critically appraise these livelihood opportunities, as well as those that may be unforeseeable. These conditions seem remote, however, with the career-path choices of Fijian students displaying remarkably little diversity (Nilan et al. 2006) and a continued preference for white-collar qualifications regardless of employment opportunities.

Nilan attributes this to the influence of older relatives and the institutionalised lack of agency encultured in Pacific youth, citing the modelling influence of relatives in professions such as nursing and law:

> [I]n Fijian culture children still play a relatively small role in family decision-making. A child who does well at primary school becomes a topic of debate and decision-making for adults at the family, extended family, community and church level. (2007: 5)

This assertion is echoed by Vakaoti (2014: 7), who, in his study of how to promote active citizenship in Fijian youth, writes that 'young people's participation in Fiji is generally influenced by adult views and structures that govern young people–adult relationships'. Similarly in Solomon Islands, Oakeshott and Allen (2015: 4) have pointed to evidence that it is parental preference for academic education that limits opportunities for youth to engage with alternative livelihood options.

If the issue of the mismatch between education design and employment opportunities is to be addressed appropriately, any intervention must be cognisant of contributing factors across all levels of society. Government interventions would be required to identify failures of the education system and gaps in the employment sector and develop strategies to address each. Further needed would be evidence of social attitudes to preferred forms of education delivery and livelihood provision, as discussed below. Commitment to these interventions would require them to be based on the best available evidence with the ability to alter inputs in real time to achieve the desired ends.

There is considerable room for change without any of the extensive reforms that may be required by swinging too far in either direction towards decentralisation or a centralised vision of education in a Western image. A concerted effort to remove the stigma that currently surrounds TVET provides an obvious, and often repeated, starting point (Abbott and Pollard 2004: 54; Brown and Larson 2002: 7; Jayaweera and Morioka 2008: 31; Nilan et al. 2006). This could be expanded to link education to existing livelihood opportunities, such as in agriculture, tourism (Abbott and Pollard 2004: 54) and public works. Crucially, any response requires viewing young people as contributing to shaping the future of their societies and listening to their voices. To that end, it should be noted that the more than 300 youth delegates who participated in drafting the Suva Declaration from the second Pacific Youth Festival in 2009 called for, among other things, greater investment in 'young people and their capacities to assist with national development' (SPC 2009b: 5), 'gender equality in male dominated professions including the political and leadership arena', and 'civic education for young people including their rights and citizenship responsibilities' (p. 7). These aims suggest young people do not wish to obtain a generic education with few prospects for engagement in their communities, but want to be endowed with the critical thinking capacities required to construct their own futures.

Critical thinking and rational ignorance

The social attitudinal barriers to education reform in both Fiji and Solomon Islands cannot be overstated. Mindsets that prioritise white-collar careers and associated skill sets make it difficult to justify educational reform to the public and limit the likelihood of behaviour change if reforms are implemented. If status is connected to socially ascribed roles of more or lesser worth, an understanding of this is required, including how it is enacted and why. If the community values the qualifications of an unemployed lawyer or accountant more highly than a tradesperson who is not only successful financially but also can offer practical and material assistance to their community, it becomes apparent why white-collar skills and careers are so sought after and TVET is treated as a last resort for the unworthy. By this reckoning, thousands of educated unemployed can be viewed as problematic only if they engage in antisocial behaviours.

This disjuncture between socially valued education markers and their utility in society symbolises a concerning deficit in critical thinking around and among Pacific youth. This problem was identified in 16 of the 37 interviews I conducted as being a cultural issue where young people are discouraged from holding an opinion that may run counter to the status quo. This is primarily displayed in the dissuasion of youth from voicing their opinions.

John Firibo leads a youth group in Honiara with which I consulted during my time in Solomon Islands. Struck by his immediate openness in expressing his frustration at the social and economic inequalities present in Solomon Islands, I invited him to be interviewed as a key informant. He told me that the discouragement of critical thinking in youth was reinforced through the functioning of his strongly Christian society:

> Most of us, especially our local priests, don't encourage us to express ourselves. We are not free to do that. Even in the confessional, we are not allowed to do that.

His was certainly not an isolated opinion. Mereia Carling, regional youth advisor for development organisation the Pacific Community, connected this lack of free expression to the influence of the society in family, village and school settings:

> Our traditional parenting and the school systems don't naturally encourage expression and reflection and creativity. I think that inhibits a lot of growth in young people and a lot of growth of life skills and protection capabilities as well, particularly for girls.

Likewise, Fijian civil society activist Tura Lewai summarised: 'Education here is very linear. It is basically A to B; 1, 2, 3. There is no questioning … there is no sense of critical thinking.'

These issues are intimately connected with social values of hierarchy. Jope Tarai is a postgraduate civil society activist and university educator. Further, he is developing a strong public profile in Fiji as a social commentator through formats including a TEDxSuva talk (Tarai 2016) challenging social concepts of what masculinity should look like in Fiji, which had been viewed more than 45,000 times by September 2021, and a

June 2018 podcast interview in which he commented in relation to citizen leadership: 'We are the leaders. We elect our representatives' (cited in Two Fishes 2018). Despite his growing profile as a public intellectual, he noted to me his diminishing status when he returns to his village community:

> When I step out of the urban area and put on my culturally conservative, good, obedient, Christian boy mask, so to speak, you walk into the village and you know your place and you have to maintain that place or else you will be called *susu madrai*.[6]

President of the Honiara Youth Council, Harry Olikwailafa, is a prominent youth activist in Solomon Islands. He sees how the notion of being 'seen but not heard' extends the limitation of critical thinking from the home to the classroom. Harry told me:

> 'This is the answer' is what they do here. Our cultural environment was one of the suppressive factors in learning and education. If your parents are having a discussion and you want to give your opinion, you are told, 'You're too little. Get out.' So sometimes young people see that in their teachers. Even at university level in Solomon Islands, go into classrooms and ask if anyone has any questions. In Solomon Islands, the silence is something that is carried over from their families because their families don't allow them to raise their opinions and it restricts their learning.

The role of universities in the Pacific also needs to be looked at when discussing the preference for white-collar training and the dearth of critical thinking. The presence of universities, both physically and intellectually, is quite limited in Solomon Islands, with Honiara hosting the only two active campuses: the Solomon Islands National University (SINU) and the USP Solomon Islands campus. Neither campus has a strong culture of research and inquiry, with SINU focused on teaching undergraduate diplomas and certificates, with four streams of bachelor's degrees (SINU 2021). USP offers a more diverse range of undergraduate and postgraduate opportunities, though its staff presence is small and primarily focused on training. Students at USP's Honiara campus informed me that their primary motivation for studying was to gain employment. This is presumably no different from cohorts of students across the globe and is consistent with the notion that learning constitutes an individual and public good (Biesta 2006). However, given issues of small staff and student

---

6   'Raised on bread': a city slicker.

cohorts and the quality of formal education at lower levels, as discussed previously, it is understandable that tertiary education has limited social influence in Solomon Islands.

The university sector has a significantly greater presence in Fiji. There are three multidisciplinary universities operating 13 campuses across the country.[7] Beyond this is the effect of Suva hosting USP's largest campus—attracting students from across the region and acting as the principal incubator for academic pursuit in the region. Its staff have included illustrious indigenous and non-indigenous Pacific thinkers such as Epeli Hau`ofa, Teresia Teaiwa, Albert Wendt and Ron Crocombe. It has also proved to be a training ground for the region's elite, producing scores of parliamentarians, including prime ministers of Tonga, Tuvalu and Vanuatu.

Born of the regional independence movement of the 1960s and 1970s, USP's early years are celebrated as helping to shape notions and the practice of a 'Pacific Way', which combined cultural values, local histories and academic endeavour (Crocombe 1975). In recent decades, it has been criticised for becoming a site for training rather than learning—something that has been exacerbated by the emigration of many of the Pacific's brightest young minds to universities outside the region (Corcoran and Koshy 2010; Gibson and McKenzie 2009). Epeli Hau`ofa voiced this concern in 1992 when he referred to the Suva-based Laucala Campus as a 'beautiful cemetery' (cited in Lal 2015: 58; Teaiwa 1996: 216). Fijian civil society activist Kris Prasad repeated this concern in an interview:

> Student activism is dead. There are no radical groups happening. There is nothing happening around women's issues, as well. That sort of stuff used to happen quite a lot in the Sixties when USP started. There were more active movements around the nuclear-free movement and women's rights and there was lots of activism happening back then, but now it has become a beautiful cemetery, as poetically described by the late Epeli Hau`ofa during USP's silver jubilee celebrations in 1993.

This is not to say that there is absolutely no culture of critical inquiry among the youth in either country. To the contrary, I have been exposed to numerous young academics and activists—some of whom are represented

---

7   University of Fiji, two campuses; USP, three campuses; Fiji National University, eight campuses, some of which focus on specific disciplines.

in this book—whose intellect and insight are both inspiring and intimidating. These young people are prominent in Suva than in Honiara, which likely reflects the cause and effect of having a larger population of tertiary students and qualified research professionals and a more active critical civil society. The truth remains, however, that these youth are the exception rather than the norm.

The logical result of the limitation of young people's ability to speak freely and to question authority and accepted wisdom is that young people internalise the belief that their opinions are not valid. The risk of this is that youth self-censor not only their speech, but also their thoughts. First coined by democratic theorist and economist Anthony Downs (1957), 'rational ignorance' describes a situation where people disengage from critical thought when they believe their input is not valued. As international development researchers Lawrence MacDonald, Bobby Fishkin and David Witzel (2014: 8) remark, 'it's rational not to invest time and energy in understanding an issue on which their opinion will make no difference'. In the education system, this plays out daily as students understand that their role is to accept the information provided to them without question. The longer-term impacts of a lack of training in critical thinking become more apparent when students are expected to make informed decisions about their lives beyond secondary school, where a focus on attaining skills that connote social status as opposed to skills with more obvious livelihood benefits leads to a saturation of applications for a narrow scope of university degrees.

The lack of diversity in career ambition can be seen to impact on what is considered a worthy career, as well as to crowd the market for certain skill sets at the expense of others. Nilan et al. (2006: 902) report that, in Fiji, approximately 20 applications are made to the appropriate institutions for enrolment in tertiary nursing places for every place granted. This has further impacts on gender relations, as nursing remains primarily the domain of women, who are, correspondingly, reticent to apply for tertiary places in male-dominated workforces. The effect of this, according to Nilan, is that:

> Despite marked improvements in Fijian women's educational performance in the past 15 years, and greater labour force participation, the inferior status of Fijian women in the labour market has not changed much, not least because the position of women overall in the labour market of the country has not changed much. (2009: 30)

Educating girls

Any inquiry into the formal structures that are understood to most promote the potential of individuals and communities, such as formal education, must be cognisant of the social role of women and girls and how this impacts their engagement in these structures. Numerous academic works have noted that in many Pacific countries, women have significantly lower social status and less decision-making power than men (Bennett 1987: 13; Lee 2017; McLeod 2015; Morgan 2005: 11; Vakaoti 2012: 3; Vakaoti and Mishra 2010: 22; Woo and Corea 2009: 11).

One of my informants, Tura Lewai from Fiji, is a women's rights activist and a member of the UN Secretary-General's Network of Men Leaders as part of the campaign to end violence against women (UN Women 2008). He spoke to me of the socialised understandings that underscore the inferior social status of women and girls in Fiji:

> When I say young people, I really mean young men. When people refer to young people in Fiji, they often refer to young men and not young women, as well. There is something about the word 'people' that refers to men rather than men and women … You can see this in the way that a village or family eats, in the order they eat: the man will come first; then the children come and eat; then the young people; and then the women will eat the scraps and whatever is left on the table. Of course, they are doing all the hard work in the kitchen.

As stated previously, the marginalisation that Oceanic youth experience should not be read as a homogeneous representation of how youth in the region are regarded and engaged. Hierarchies are present across and even within disadvantaged and marginalised groups. Typically, at the apex of these hierarchies are able-bodied, cisgender, heterosexual young men from dominant ethnic groups. Joshko Wakaniyasi, a Fijian disability advocate, shared how this hierarchy can impact on the opportunities for young people considered to be of lower status. Discussing the education opportunities available to young people with disabilities, he told me:

> If there are other siblings and if the family parents have to invest in the child's education, it would take a very strong mother and father, if they have limited resource[s] themselves, to invest in the child [with a disability] to go to school. It's more costly to send a disabled-bodied child to school than [an] able-bodied child,

because somebody has to take them to school, they may need constant care whilst in school and because, in Fiji, we don't have accessible forms of transportation. It becomes a very costly exercise.

While the chiefly and big-man systems that dominated traditional Oceanic social structures indicate that men have disproportionately held positions of decision-making influence, there are strong suggestions that the status of women diminished because of interaction between Pacific cultures and European missionaries and colonisers (Lee 2017: 70–73; Vakaoti and Mishra 2010: 22). Rosie Catherine, a women's rights activist from Fiji, told me that a struggle with contemporary Fijian men, particularly iTaukei, is that 'Christians misinterpret the Bible based on "a wife should submit to her husband", but the next Bible verse says that a husband should respect his wife'.

I do not intend to imply that the role of women is not valued at all in Oceanic states. In Fiji, for example, women's roles may be separate from formal decision-making procedures, but they have traditionally been valued for their contributions to the livelihoods and social activities of their communities. Buell Quain (1948: 178) commented on this in his ethnographic study of a Fijian village from 1935 to 1936, while noting that a 'sexual division of labor in industrial activities' existed. Anthropologist Martha Macintyre (2017: 2) has also written about the fact that women did not have to struggle for suffrage or access to education and employment opportunities during the independence movements of the Pacific. Despite gender discrepancies that showed men were more likely to participate in formal education at higher levels, women's status was not universally low in the region. Similarly, Vakaoti and Mishra's (2010: 9) more recent analysis of youth leadership in Fiji noted that while 'ascribed forms of leadership in the formal sense are dominated by male adults … women have important support functions'.

Why women are seen to occupy a subordinate position to men matters for two main reasons. First, by understanding the causes of marginalisation, communities can debate the worth of the reproduction of such structures. Second, if women's status is understood to be natural and part of *kastom* when it is something that has been at least partially imposed or enforced through European intervention, then arguments for the maintenance of the status quo as a means of upholding tradition dissolve. This is one of the great tensions for the outsider academic or development practitioner who is attempting to maintain a sense of cultural relativity, and is summarised thus by legal anthropologist Jean Zorn:

> We who would like to do better are faced with a problem. We want to respect the integrity of the indigenous cultures of the Pacific, but we also want those cultures to act in ways that affirm the integrity and dignity of all persons. (2003b: 137)

It also presents a conflict for activists within communities which promote their 'traditional' livelihoods and belief systems in contrast to those of the West—most notably, as embodied in the feminist movement, which has sought methods to hybridise and indigenise concepts of women's and human rights in spaces where they may be rejected under the auspices of tradition (Domingo et al. 2014; Fletcher et al. 2016; Jolly 1996; Merry 2006; Moser 1993; Okin 1998).[8]

The studies into young Fijian women's lack of autonomy in education and career choices by Nilan (2009; Nilan et al. 2006) give evidence of the need to address how girls and women exit education into the employment sector, as well as the impacts this has on corresponding issues such as status and feminine stereotyping. This need is supported by Macintyre (2017: 7), who argues that men's superior social, political and economic status in contemporary Oceanic states reflects the greater number of men who achieved formal education in the years following independence. Anthropologists Stephanie Lusby (2017) and Jenny Munro (2017) further argue that the differences in educational attainment of men and women in the past 50 years have contributed to juxtaposing attitudes that educated men should navigate cultural interactions with modernisation while women should maintain 'tradition'.

Tura Lewai spoke of the prevailing cultural attitudes that place higher value on male upskilling:

> If you had $50 and school fees are $50 and you had two kids, they would often send the male because you will be the head of your household one day, so you need to be educated, so you can look after your family.

---

8   For a broader discussion of the contestation of the universal applicability of human rights and gender rights to non-Western belief systems and practices, see Mutua (2001) and Narayan (1998).

This is a problem that has existed in the Pacific for generations. Reflecting earlier comments about young women's status in relation to that of young men, Seah Chee Meow (1983: 13) referred to this in a study of education and employment challenges facing youth and women across Asia and the Pacific in 1983, saying: 'Females are thus a minority group, not in numbers but in status vis-à-vis their male counterparts.' Naidu summarises:

> With the relatively high population growth rates and the demand for education there is a severe shortage of both schools and teachers in Melanesia. The prospect for girls being educated in larger numbers continues to be limited in the Melanesian countries. (2003: 24)

This is not simply an issue of rights or equality. As mentioned earlier, educating girls also has widespread social and economic benefits. Klasen and Lamanna (2009) have found evidence from across the Middle East, North Africa, East Asia and South Asia that gaps in formal educational attainment and employment between girls and boys are correlated with significantly weaker economic growth, as well as poorer health and social indicators. As they write: 'The costs of discrimination toward women in education and employment not only harm the women concerned but also impose a cost for the entire society' (Klasen and Lamanna 2009: 117).

Comparing Fiji and Solomon Islands

It is important to note that while the formal education systems of both Fiji and Solomon Islands appear to not be providing an avenue for positive social and economic opportunities for most of their young people, the reasons for this and the way it is experienced by different youths vary significantly.

Youth with whom I spoke uniformly identified the discouragement of critical thinking as constraining the ability of young people in Fiji and Solomon Islands to achieve their potential. Rather than being encouraged to analyse social issues and use ingenuity to understand and address them, young people are expected to learn by rote. The cultural expectation that youth be deferent, combined with minimal social pressure to reform the curriculum in a manner that best represents the needs of Fijian and Solomon Islander societies, is resulting in recurrent generations learning similar material in a similar fashion with similar social and economic results.

Fiji's establishment institutions of education—most notably, the Queen Victoria School and Adi Cakobau School, which were established to educate elite boys and girls, respectively—demonstrate the gulf in the social presence of education institutions between Fiji and Solomon Islands. Though secondary education institutions are present throughout Solomon Islands, they carry less social cachet with citizens than do Fijian schools, which is evident by the prevalence of students and alumni from the latter tattooing the initials of their secondary school on their hands. The establishment schools are also symbolic of the difference in educational opportunities. In general, Fijian secondary schools are long-established and cater to children of all social backgrounds, while many schools in Solomon Islands are still recovering from the impacts of the Tensions (Commonwealth of Nations 2020) and service provision is uneven. Further, Suva's tertiary offerings, which are both a cause and a consequence of its status as a regional hub, are much more expansive than those found in any part of Solomon Islands.

Similarly, in both Fiji and Solomon Islands, those in rural locations appear to have a lower likelihood of access to quality formal education. In each location, it appears that difficulties in attracting qualified staff and providing regulatory oversight are contributing to rural young people not being provided with the same educational opportunities as their urban peers. With both countries displaying this difficulty in adequately training staff and enticing them to rural locations over a protracted period, this trend seems likely to continue, at least in the near future.

A greater focus on vocational training was offered by informants of all ages from both countries as one potential remedy for the disconnect between education and employment outcomes, as well as rural–urban migration. Achieving this would require a substantial overhaul not only of social attitudes to vocational education, but also of the structure and delivery of TVET throughout each country. This is not a quick or easy fix, but it is one that surely bears consideration.

Conclusion

It is clear that formal education systems across Fiji and Solomon Islands are inadequately designed and administered in relation to the skills and knowledge they provide young people to secure their individual livelihoods and contribute to the social and economic development of their communities. Central to these problems are formal education institutions not operating in accordance with local needs but more closely replicating foreign modes of teaching and learning, unequal standards of teacher training, and a mismatch between the outputs of secondary and tertiary education institutions and the demands of local employment sectors. The impact of these issues is that young people are receiving an education in name, but not necessarily being equipped to better engage with local, national and global societies.

The limitations of education on Fijian and Solomon Islander young people are not restricted to formal education. The social expectation of youth being passive observers rather than being supported to take control of their own learning pathways reinforces ideas about which forms of education are desirable and assist to stymie critical thinking. Rather than youth being provided with the skills to forge their own futures and be partners in driving national and regional initiatives through their education experiences, they are being further enculturated to be seen but not heard.

At an individual level, this has clear implications for the capabilities of young people to achieve self-actualisation. The systems that are theoretically designed to help them discover their individual abilities and desires instead approach them with formulaic standards to which they are expected to conform. For young people better suited to vocational training, social pressures dissuade them from engaging in this with little regard for its potential holistic livelihood benefits. A lack of adaptability in the system results in a lack of adaptability being inculcated into them. At a broader societal level, the lack of focus on critical thinking further limits the ability of young people to contribute to public discourse about the imagined self-determined developmental futures of their communities.

Those with whom I spoke discussed the limitations of the education system largely in response to issues of unemployment and a failure to prepare young people for their post-schooling livelihoods. The issues associated with formal education in these states go beyond a mismatch between formal training, qualifications and formal employment opportunities. The shortcomings of formal education in Fiji and Solomon Islands speak to larger issues of youth agency and opportunities for active, informed engagement in their societies. The civic engagement of youth is minimised in a manner that seems to simultaneously reflect cultural notions of young people being expected to learn through passive observation, as well as structures introduced and maintained through formal education that privilege the authority of the teacher over the critical inquiry of the student.

3

The recurrent issue of under/employment

Only a few percentage of young people manage to find further education or some form of employment, whether it is formal or informal.

— Andre Tipoki, Solomon Islands

As the Acting Director for Youth in the Solomon Islands Ministry of Women, Youth, Children and Family Affairs, Andre Tipoki is acutely aware of the challenges faced by young people across the country. Andre sees the lack of employment opportunities as the greatest community concern for youth, whether they are urban, rural or from the outer islands; male, female or non-binary; rich or poor; able-bodied or otherwise; university graduates or have not completed primary school. His was a sentiment I heard expressed over and over.

In every community in which I conducted focus groups in both Fiji and Solomon Islands, unemployment was raised as the most pressing issue facing youth. In the cities of Suva and Honiara, the problem is omnipresent. In rural areas, the problem does not present as obviously; village settings appear to offer sufficient subsistence provisions and daily activities to keep citizens of all ages busy. In reality, however, young people in both rural and urban areas feel the pressure of livelihood demands and social expectations even if they manifest in different ways (Tagicakiverata and Nilan 2018: 545).

Tura Lewai has worked in urban and rural settings in Fiji and across the Pacific region, which has exposed him to young people from multiple social, economic and geographical backgrounds:

> Urban youths are very concerned about employment; what do they do when they finish school? What is it that they can do so that they can earn money so they can get a nice car? So they can afford a flat or a nice place to live? Where they can buy nice phones and stuff? But young people in the rural areas are more concerned about how they put food on the table; what will enable them to put three meals a day on the table?

The number of young people walking the streets of Suva and engaged in the visible informal economy, such as shining shoes and pushing wheelbarrows, is a constant reminder of the lack of livelihood opportunities for many of the youths living in the Suva–Nausori corridor of villages and informal settlements, which is where the greatest concentration of people in Fiji lives (Phillips and Keen 2016). The sight of similar groups of youths in Honiara is one of the city's defining features, though here they are less likely to be engaged in regular work of any kind—formal or informal. These youths in both cities exist alongside young professionals, students and newly arrived rural migrants. They are drawn to urban areas largely by the prospect of securing work to support their own livelihood and that of their families through remittances. Their engagement in employment and employment-seeking practices also needs to be understood in terms of the representation of employment as a status indicator, bridging the divide between being a youth and being an adult.

This chapter looks at the issue of youth employment in Fiji and Solomon Islands. What emerges from this discussion is an understanding that the meaning and value of employment reach far beyond economic ends. While capitalist approaches to development see the value of employment primarily in promoting economic growth and consumption, employment also has significant social utility. Certainly, employment is a critical factor in ensuring livelihoods for youth and non-youth alike, but its impact on social status, self-actualisation and the creation of opportunities for individuals and those they support should not be overlooked. The hopes for employment of most Pacific youths and their communities begin with basic needs and livelihood provisions but are also shaped by formal structures of how employment opportunities are created and of what type, as well as informal structures of the social value placed on employment type and associated status.

Like the limitations evident in young people's determination of their own education pathways, employment options for Pacific youth are strongly influenced by community attitudes towards desirable and undesirable forms of employment. This results in skills shortages in certain sectors and an oversupply of skilled labour in others. Institutional responses to date have been inadequate in addressing the social and economic factors impacting on youth employment prospects and there is little sign of this changing soon. This chapter discusses how young people's livelihood options are constrained by social expectations and formal institutions, as well as noting examples that counter such obstacles. Both the normalised nature of youth unemployment and the examples of livelihood innovation demonstrate a lack of context-appropriate avenues to enhance youth livelihood capabilities.

Employment, unemployment and underemployment

Measuring unemployment in Pacific island countries and territories is difficult due to the high number of people engaged in subsistence and informal work. If a young woman provides for her family by selling produce from a makeshift roadside stall six days a week, making sufficient tax-free money to meet the family's needs, but expresses a desire to secure full-time formal employment, is she unemployed? Is she underemployed? Is she neither or some combination?

There are countless young people who are actively engaged in providing for their families who wish for full-time formal employment. It is difficult to state with any certainty that unemployment figures provide an accurate insight into the situation of young people who wish to be engaged in formal employment but are not (Duncan and Voigt-Graf 2008: 3). For example, while the World Bank determined that youth unemployment rates for Fiji and Solomon Islands in 2014 were 18.6 per cent (World Bank 2021a) and 9.5 per cent (World Bank 2021b), respectively, in 2016, the ILO (2016b) projected more broadly that youth unemployment in Fiji was between 13 per cent and 20 per cent and in Solomon Islands was more than 35 per cent. Human geographer John Connell (2011: 124) asserts that even in urban areas across Oceania, where employment prospects are typically better than in rural locations, unemployment is never realistically less than 10 per cent, and is 'usually much higher'.

While it is difficult to collect reliable unemployment figures, there is sufficient evidence to identify youth unemployment and underemployment as significant social and economic issues. In Fiji, for example, only approximately 2,000 new jobs were created in 2002 for the 'usual annual figure of 17,000 school leavers' (Mausio 2003: 445). Current figures are unavailable, but this trend appeared to improve marginally between 2002 and 2009, though estimates still suggested that at least half of secondary school graduates failed to secure employment (Woo and Corea 2009: 9).[1]

Regardless of the accuracy of employment figures, unemployment is a clear social concern in both Fiji and Solomon Islands. In the focus groups and interviews I conducted in both countries, unemployment was the most commonly raised issue that young people are facing and was identified by every focus group. Similarly, in 24 of the 37 interviews I conducted, unemployment was named as the most pressing social and economic concern for youth in the Pacific today. This sentiment was captured by Peni Tawake of Fiji, a development industry professional with experience working in regional programs, who stated: 'Youth unemployment: that's a Pacific-wide issue that young people talk about, that they're concerned about in rural and urban areas.'

One of the prominent reasons for the significant numbers of unemployed and underemployed youth, as discussed in the previous chapter, is a mismatch between the skills produced by formal education systems across Pacific states and the needs of their employment sectors. Numerous scholars have noted the outdated focus of the region's education systems on producing potential workers with skills for a service economy, which in reality is already oversaturated (Curtain and Vakaoti 2011; Duncan 2014; Kidd 2012; McMurray 2006; Nilan 2007; Nilan et al. 2006; SPC 2009a; Veramu 1992; Woo and Corea 2009)—compounding the problematic nature of perpetuating a system that has been identified as ineffective for many decades. Nilan et al. (2006: 897) found in their research into the career ambitions of final-year secondary students in Fiji that deficits in suitably skilled employees in certain sectors have resulted in offshore recruitment to fill employment vacancies in such diverse areas as 'skilled garment cutters, pattern-makers and embroiderers, building construction managers, qualified dive instructors, beauticians, chefs and air-conditioning technicians'. This has recently extended to other

---

1   Accurate, up-to-date figures are difficult to find as they are not reported by age demographic or time since completing formal education (see FBoS 2021b).

sectors. Fiji's sugar industry—the country's largest export producer—announced in 2018 that it intended to import foreign workers to make up for a recurrent shortfall in domestic labour (Boyle 2018).[2] And in 2019, Fiji's Attorney-General, Aiyaz Sayed-Khaiyum, announced plans to import tilers from 'Bangladesh, the Philippines and Indonesia because we have a shortage of people who know how to lay tiles professionally' (RNZ 2019).

Jai Narayan, Director of Secondary Education at Fiji's Ministry of Education, Heritage and Arts, explained to me that the mismatch between fields with employment opportunities and those in which young people are being trained was a persistent issue in Fiji:

> In October [2014,] … we had a stakeholders' meeting. We had [representatives] from the tourism sector, from the building and trade sector, the government … [All were expressing] that we have shortages and it is mainly expatriates working in these areas.

This has led to parallel problems in the employment sector, where young people are being trained in areas with limited job prospects, while certain skilled jobs—and now low-skilled rural jobs—remain difficult to fill. As mentioned in the previous chapter, this has created high unemployment for those seeking white-collar employment in contrast with skills shortages for blue-collar work. It should be noted, however, that the employment shortages go beyond simple issues of skills shortages or mismatches between education systems and the employment sector. The proposed importation of canecutters and tilers into Fiji provides an insight into the social determinants of worth attached to different jobs. As reflected in the previous chapter's discussion of the influence of elders and high-status community members in shaping the desired career paths of young Fijians, this is more an issue of community mindsets about what forms of employment are held in high esteem than a matter of youth making an autonomous choice to avoid undertaking such work when it is available.

Highlighting the issue of skills shortages in certain industries of which Jai spoke, Roshika Deo, a feminist activist and former political candidate from Fiji, spoke to me of the increasing prevalence of young people gaining qualifications in fields with little prospect of absorbing them:

---

2   Where these canecutters would be imported from was not specified.

> With unemployment, there is a lot more underemployment. You have a lot of young people who are employed part-time or casual or not employed in areas where they have qualifications. Last month, I was in MHCC [a shopping centre] and one of the girls in a women's retail store came to me and said, 'I actually have a teaching certificate but the Ministry of Education doesn't recognise it because I got it from University of the South Pacific and the ministry gives preference to Fiji National University [(FNU) graduates] first because the Ministry of Education runs FNU.

The young woman of whom Roshika speaks is an example of the tertiary system in Fiji absorbing students with little concern for the available employment opportunities or coordination between private industry, government and the education system. This example speaks to the multiple and complex social and economic factors that shape the importance with which employment is regarded. Though waged employment promises relief from the pressures of needing to provide basic needs, these are not the only—or, indeed, necessarily the primary—determinants of how, why and where young people seek employment in Fiji and Solomon Islands. Although the economic structures fail many Pacific youth in the mismatch between education outputs and employment opportunities, the social structures not only inhibit young people from engaging with the employment opportunities that do exist, but also shape their perception of why, and which forms of, employment should be pursued (Nilan 2009). Thus, issues of skills shortages and mismatches can be understood as reflecting not only the social values of Pacific communities, but also the minimisation of young people's autonomy.

The purpose of employment

With unemployment raised as the primary issue facing young Pacific people by a majority of focus group and interview informants, the importance of employment in Oceanic contexts requires interrogation. As Jack Maebuta, a peace and education academic from Solomon Islands, explained to me, when different people talk of unemployment as a problem, their reasons can differ significantly:

> From an academic perspective, when you say the real issue is unemployment and you write that unemployment is very high and whatever, you don't really know what people mean when they said 'unemployment' because it is something that ties into other

areas. When we all work together, you start to see the real cracks, that unemployment gives birth to other livelihood issues. From a qualitative perspective, when you talk to these people, you can get the real insight of their stories—their life stories of what that really means.

The mismatch between the qualifications and skills achieved through formal education and their practical utility beyond the classroom is a significant problem facing Pacific island countries and territories (UNICEF Pacific et al. 2005). Some of the ramifications of this mismatch are clear, such as an ever-increasing number of skilled unemployed, but what appears to be lacking is an understanding of the value of employment as a social and economic good in an Oceanic context. This is a particularly fraught question in the context of Fijian and Solomon Islander communities. While there are long histories of subsistence living in both countries (Barrau 1958), they also have complicated colonial legacies resulting from indentured/slave labour (Ali 1979; Connell 2010; Hunt 2007; Moynagh 1981; Munro 1993) and the division of ethnicities in plantation labour. The impacts these histories have had on different individuals and communities, in terms of their mental models of what employment represents, are difficult to establish.

Important distinctions exist in relation to livelihood provision between those living in rural and those in urban areas. Chief among these is the fact that urban lifestyles are more likely to revolve around income-generating activities to facilitate the purchasing of goods, including food, while in rural communities, subsistence farming not only continues to provide a social safety net, but also is critical in the provision of daily diets. Thus, the responses I received from interviewees and focus group respondents stating unemployment was the paramount issue facing young people across rural, peri-urban and urban locations need to be viewed for their social, as well as economic, implications.

Understanding employment desires as being purely related to the economic benefits afforded the individual through work overlooks other motivations, both intrinsic to the individual and reflective of social norms. The combination of status, livelihoods and self-actualisation resulting from employment is not limited to the Pacific. As international development researchers Jaideep Gupte, Dolf te Lintelo and Inka Barnett (2014: 10) write of the social and economic issues facing urban youth in sub-Saharan Africa:

> Being in employment is not just instrumental in fostering young people's ability to gain access to food, but the right kind of work may also have intrinsic value and bestow a sense of self-worth to foster wellbeing.

Vince Nomae, an economist from Solomon Islands, spoke to me of the dual social and economic benefits of youths being engaged in formal or informal employment. Despite the issue of mismatches between the products of the education system and the opportunities available in the employment sector, he identified value in both the livelihoods provision that employment provides and the way employment promotes positive civic engagement among young Solomon Islanders. He told me:

> There are people who come back [from school] with qualifications and instead of joining the formal sector they join the informal sector. There are people who come back and work in the offices and there are others you will find in the street—for example, selling betel nut. Either way it is good. At least he is employed and making money.

While it is important to accept that employment provides both social and economic benefits to the individual, from an international development perspective, it is vital to probe deeper to attempt to understand the purpose of employment in countries and local communities. There are multiple ways to view this purpose through different development approaches.

If the purpose of development is simply to provide greater opportunities for individual and collective economic improvement, employment can be argued as a moral good. This perspective most closely aligns with the Rostovian modernisation approach to development, which promoted the partnership of employment and mass consumption as leading to improvements to industrial societies and the individual lives of their citizens (Rostow 1959: 9–10).

A basic-needs perspective on the worth of employment would value wage labour as both an end point (as a result of investment in poor people's health and education) and a means to meet the individual's physiological and security needs, as initially applied by the World Bank (Ul Haq 1981: vii–viii). A more comprehensive reading of Maslow, though, illuminates the confluence of social, economic and livelihood requirements, as well as intrinsic and extrinsic motivators of an individual. Maslow (1943: 383) viewed self-actualisation as occurring through the interconnectedness of basic, psychological and self-fulfilment needs.

From a capabilities perspective, the benefits of employment are realised when it results in increased levels of individual agency and the promotion of equality of opportunity, not simply in the potential for increased wealth. From this viewpoint, employment needs to lead to the creation of a more equitable society (Nussbaum 2003: 33) and act as a vehicle for individual and community freedoms for self-determination (Sen 1999). As Sen (2003: 4) writes, 'economic prosperity is no more than one of the means to enriching lives of people. It is a foundational conclusion to give it the status of an end.'

The holistic livelihoods approach I advocate concerns basic-needs provision and critical agency for the individual, which allows for their self-actualisation, as well as for communities to determine their own desired path of development. This can be through formal structures such as those related to education and employment or through informal structures by which self-actualisation is socially understood, as in iTaukei culture when an individual is recognised as *yalomatua*.[3] Thus, the purpose of employment from this perspective cannot be tied to specific or singular outcomes. The value of this approach has been repeatedly reinforced through my own practice, as well as engagement with informants and focus group participants throughout my research. As an example, Andre Tipoki presented the difficulty of summarising a singular purpose for employment by relaying a previous conversation on the topic:

> Very interestingly, when we talk about unemployment in Honiara, I talk to a lot of young persons in workshops and training, they are referring to the formal employment sector. One day, I went home in the deep rural area, back in the village, and caught up with a friend and asked, 'What are your problems?' And he said, 'Unemployment.' 'What do you mean when you say unemployment? Because that is what I have heard in Honiara, where they are closer to industry. So, what do you mean when you say unemployment?' 'It's about the resources,' is what he said: 'It is a disempowering situation in that we are not able to enter into formal or informal employment for our benefit.' So, you have youth in the urban areas and youth in the deep rural areas and they have a shared problem in how they look at this issue.

---

3   Fijian, meaning 'mature', 'reasonable', 'respectable'.

Andre elaborated about how material goods and sometimes agricultural products were effectively the possessions of chiefs and big-men in many Solomon Islands communities. Anthropologist Keir Martin (2007: 292–93) writes of this situation as being a neotraditional cooptation of traditional big-man customs, where greater levels of financial wealth have resulted in less accountability for big-men, instead making them 'Big Shots'. For the villager of whom Andre spoke, the desire for resources was a desire for money, material goods and a secure livelihood. Just as importantly, however, it was a desire for empowerment through agency.

Hearing this village perspective highlights not only the fact that concerns about employment are prominent in both rural and urban areas, but also the multiple meanings behind descriptions of unemployment as an issue. In some instances, it relates most closely to material gain; in others, food security; and in others, it highlights a tension between what is represented as maintaining 'traditional' lifestyles and exercising autonomy. Significantly, it also relates to cultural values and social expectations. One example of this is the improved status of young people who are employed, allowing them to be seen as adults. Another example lies in their increased capacity to provide for themselves and support their own family. As is discussed in the case studies in this chapter, starting and supporting a family are paramount ambitions for youths and adults alike, particularly men.

Case study: Pesa, Fiji

Pesa[4] is a 17-year-old male from a village in the Naitasiri Highlands of Fiji where I conducted focus groups. During my visits to his village, Pesa became one of my main contacts and generously showed me around his community. This extended beyond a tour of the village to a trip deeper into the interior of Fiji, where Pesa was able to show me harvested bananas being transported down the Wainimala River on *bilibili* (bamboo rafts) and motorised banana boats. At one point, Pesa pointed into the distance to where his family's land lay, where they farmed a mixture of subsistence items and cash crops to sell at the weekly markets in Nausori and Suva.

The extended periods I was able to spend with Pesa provided the opportunity for me to ask him about his ambitions and the issues facing Fijian youth in more detail than the focus groups allowed. Unsurprisingly,

---

4   Due to his age, a pseudonym is used in this case study.

when I asked him what the biggest issue facing youth in his village was, he replied, 'Unemployment.' I asked him what he meant by this and he informed me that for young people in the village to achieve their potential, they would need to move to Suva to find full-time work, most likely in an unskilled role such as a labourer. He then offered that this was also his plan.

When I probed about what he hoped to gain from moving to the city and becoming employed, Pesa responded that he wanted to earn enough money to be able to return to the village after a period of years. He did not say how many, but I understood this to be five to 10 years, with the prospect of it being significantly longer as he told me that on his return he hoped to settle down with his own family, build a house and farm a plot of land for subsistence living as well as extra money through cash-crop sales. Such a practice would mirror that of numerous Suva-based Fijians I have known who have returned to, or expressed a desire to return to, their village communities on retirement.

Employment as a status marker

It struck me that what Pesa was suggesting he wanted to gain from employment was much of the stability and lifestyle that, on the surface, he seemed to be currently enjoying, with two important accompaniments: the prestige of economic success that would graduate him from youthhood to adulthood, and the capability to figuratively and literally begin his adult life with a family and home of his own. This indicated that the allure of employment for him is connected to issues of agency, identity and status, on one hand, and the realisation of culturally valued social goals on the other. The nature of this type of migration and return migration has been noted in Solomon Islands by indigenous anthropologist David Gegeo, who notes in an article on the strength of indigenous beliefs and practices against a backdrop of globalisation that this is a common practice in the country:

> [I]n the Solomons, people have not tended to permanently migrate to a metropolitan area, locally or internationally. Even when they leave their home islands to work or attend school, they ultimately return to their villages after a few months or years away, and certainly on retirement. (Gegeo 2001: 496)

The extent to which this assertion will hold true as greater numbers of people live away from their home island or rural community for significant periods—during which they will develop identities and lifestyles tied to urban locations such as Honiara through employment, raising families and developing social networks—will be an interesting site for future research.

The appeal of employment is a result of economic and social factors. The economic factors are primarily financial security and the ability to purchase material goods. The dominant social factors appear to be related to improved social status and the ability to start and support a family. With youths' opinions and participation undervalued until they reach milestones of adulthood, it is easy to see how employment becomes a desirable goal for its social as well as economic impacts. Employment provides young people with an opportunity to progress from the marginalised social concept of youth to functioning adult. Further, by relocating to the city, Pesa could assert his independence from those in his village who did not see him as an adult. As Fenton Lutunatabua, of Fiji, told me: 'As long as you're [living] under the roof of your parents … you're not the adult yet.' In these ways, migration, employment and beginning a family act to accelerate the self-actualisation process for young people, providing both social and livelihood gains.

The basic supposition of this assessment can be read as an indicator of the desire of young people to have greater agency over their individual livelihood trajectories. To what extent this proves a shift in Oceanic cultural norms away from the sociocentric towards the individualistic is a site of wider debate (for example, Besnier 2011; Brison 2007; Gegeo 2001; Sahlins 2005; Strathern 1988). There do seem to be clear links, however, with the lack of agency afforded youth in traditional settings and the desire for employment to break these barriers. Links can also then be made with the propensity of rural youth to express a desire to seek work in urban locations.

Further, allowing youth the opportunity to expand their individual livelihood possibilities speaks to both the basic-needs and the capabilities approaches to development. From a basic-needs perspective, it can be theorised that gainful employment that secures young people against threats to their livelihood provides the basis for continued personal growth (Maslow 1943: 383). From a capabilities perspective, employment can be viewed as providing opportunities for the individual that can be reinvested into the community to provide similar opportunities to an ever-expanding pool of young people, offering 'an adulthood that is beneficial to themselves, their families, and their societies' (Saraswathi and Larson 2002: 346).

The reality of employment opportunities

Regardless of the purpose employment serves to the individuals and communities of the Great Ocean States of the Pacific, the mismatch between the available formal employment positions, the skills required by the formal employment sector and the skills obtained through formal education persists. Repeatedly, studies have determined that a significant proportion of Pacific youth overwhelmingly desire white-collar careers that are in critically short supply (McMurray 2006; Nilan 2007; Nilan et al. 2006; SPC 2009a; UNICEF Pacific et al. 2005; Woo and Corea 2009). The reasons for this include what Nilan et al. (2006: 897) document as 'little present alignment of the education system with manpower needs' and social perceptions of what types of work are desirable (Nilan 2009).

To illustrate the impact of mindsets on limiting critical thought about career opportunities, a 2006 study by Nilan et al. looked at yearly tertiary nursing applications. They write that,

> according to the Lautoka Teachers College 2003 prospectus, each year approximately 6,000 applications are made for less than 300 actual places. Similar numbers apply to the Fiji College of Nursing for a strictly limited quota of places (around 210). (Nilan et al. 2006: 902)

In a follow-up study, Nilan (2007: 5) found that 'all Fijian females who wanted to be nurses identified a relative as their role model, and the same was true for all Fijian males who wanted to be lawyers'. This phenomenon is not unique to Fiji, with Mary Good (2019: 41–42) reporting similar findings for young women in Tonga. Through these examples, we can see that the social constructs of what it means to be successful and what are acceptable roles for one to play in their community hold greater influence over the actions of youth in making career choices than objective information about opportunities and the likelihood of success measured in terms of full-time employment or financial gain.

This sentiment was reflected multiple times by those I interviewed. Former chair of the Fiji National Youth Council Usaia Moli said:

> We are brought up … you grow up, you are going to be a policeman, you are going to be an army officer, you are going to be an engineer and you are being told all this throughout your life and anything that you try to do apart from that is discouraged.

Regional development worker Peni Tawake added: 'A lot of it is also the mindsets of parents. If your child wants to do liberal arts, it's like, "Get a real job".'

A colleague of Peni's, Emily Hazelman, noted that youths' decisions regarding desired livelihood pathways are strongly influenced by ethnicity:

> There is also a racial mindset. [Fijian] Indians will do accounting and science and, for them to do arts it's like there is something wrong with their child—they're not smart enough. There is that racial divide in Fiji.

Despite the assumption that may be drawn from the considerable literature outlining the mismatch between skills gained and skills required, the mindset that white-collar work must be pursued is not all-pervasive; Nilan et al. (2006) found in two of the nine schools they surveyed that roughly half of the students stated ambitions to work in areas other than the government or corporate arenas. They mentioned of these schools that '[i]nnovative approaches to careers education are taken in those two schools and both have well-supported and extensive Technical and Vocational Education and Training programs' (Nilan et al. 2006: 900). These findings suggest that investment of energy and finances in demonstrating alternative livelihood paths can alter societal perceptions of what is desirable and how it may be achieved. This aligns with alternative development, capabilities development and adaptive development approaches, which promote the primacy of agency and informed decision-making in communities in developing countries (Berner and Phillips 2003).

Further to these problems are the very real logistical difficulties of expanding employment opportunities in Pacific states. Due to their geographical isolation and small population sizes, the Great Ocean States of the Pacific are at a significant disadvantage in terms of their ability to scale up their economies through increased or preferential terms of trade. Regional development economist and governance expert Yongzheng

Yang (2014), for example, suggests that the remoteness and population sizes of Pacific states may have negatively impacted their GDP growth by around two-thirds since the mid-1990s. Providing a sense of the difficulty of scaling up Pacific economies to promote significant employment growth, economists Neelesh Gounder and Biman Prasad's (2013: 16) evaluation of the risks and opportunities for the Fijian economy suggests that achieving mass employment would require 'sustained and inclusive growth' in 'a supportive macroeconomic environment', as well as '[p]rivate sector expansion and structural transformation', requiring 'quality investment', particularly foreign direct investment. According to Prasad (2012a, 2012b), these challenges have been compounded in recent times due to political instability harming the confidence of foreign investors.

On paper, these concerns display the macroeconomic impacts of domestic political troubles and unavoidable attributes that limit market engagement such as population size and spread (Connell 2016; Dornan and Pryke 2017).[5] For youth in rural and island communities, these are ever-present factors dictating their livelihood opportunities. Kinivuwai Naba, representative for the rural Nadroga-Navosa Province on Fiji's National Youth Council, told me how the lack of access to opportunities in rural areas was increasing a sense of marginalisation. When he told me that unemployment was the greatest issue facing youth in his district, I asked him to elaborate. He said: 'Unemployment in terms of finance. We have [this issue] from the upper area in the interior because of accessibility to town. Town is where employment opportunity is.'

Similarly, Sarah Tafo`ou, the youth council's representative for the island Lomaiviti Province, discussed how a lack of access to markets and services negatively impacted on some island communities:

> The two main islands that currently have more accessibility to markets are Koro and Ovalau, because the shipping companies normally take that route once or twice a week. Compared to the other little islands, [where] they have to get their own fare there [to Viti Levu], which costs around $600–$700 [approximately US$285–335] one way.

---

5   Though Allen (2012: 165) notes regarding Solomon Islands that economic development problems are also representative of issues of who has access to the benefits of development as well as debates about what positive development looks like to local communities.

These insights concisely capture the marginalisation experienced by young people in rural and remote communities in the Pacific. While sustainable agriculture and kinship support systems still exist to some extent, previously established perceptions that village communities have little or no poverty have since been disproven (Connell 2011: 126). Further, rural and island locations do not provide the same level of opportunity as urban centres for securing and furthering livelihoods. Marginalisation and poverty, to these communities, are best understood as poverty of opportunity. As development economists Michael Clemens and Timothy Ogden (2014: 2) write: 'Location, too, is a form of human capital.'

Examples of how location is used as a form of human capital play out daily on the streets of Suva, where individuals and groups take advantage of the large population and access to economic activity. One enterprising group of unskilled labourers is even working as a collective to improve their earning capacities in the 'undesirable' informal employment area of wheelbarrow porterage.

Case study: The Suva Crime-Free Wheelbarrow Association

Since at least the late 1990s, male, predominantly youth,[6] street-frequenters in the urban centres of Fiji have engaged in the informal economy by pushing wheelbarrows for clients (Vakaoti 2009). These 'bara boys' push their wheelbarrows to cart goods such as produce and luggage for individual customers at markets and bus stands, as well as to shift loads of goods for retailers.

Despite the economic initiative shown by bara boys, throughout the first decade of the twenty-first century, these men were renowned for their antisocial behaviour. Fighting, drunkenness and theft were common traits ascribed to them by the public—and not without cause. Further, their operations were illegal and police crackdowns on individuals were common. With the stigma associated with them damaging their esteem and hurting their business interests, in 2007, the Suva-based bara boys started a collective, the Suva Crime-Free Wheelbarrow Association.

---

6   Bara boys are not exclusively youths, with some long-term members being well into middle age. However, most practising members are young, as are almost all new members.

When I met with representatives of the association, they explained that it is now a joint initiative of the practising bara boys, the local police and the Suva City Council. The practice has been legalised, with licences limited to 100 and all members have to be owner-operators, removing the previous exploitation whereby a handful of owners rented out wheelbarrows to between 300 and 400 operators.

While some operators have criminal records, the association welcomes them provided they can commit to abstain from criminal activities. New offending incurs immediate revocation of their licence by the council.

A public stigma around the work of the bara boys remains—a hangover from the period before the practice was well-regulated, according to youth leader and volunteer officer for the association, Usaia Moli. This is even though they provide a useful service with minimal risk thanks to internal and police oversight. They report earning anywhere between 25 per cent and 70 per cent more in an average week than they would earn as a security guard. Beyond this, they each donate a small amount to a central fund each week to act as insurance in case one of them experiences an injury or bereavement; the fund has also been used to assist elderly homeless people since 2015.

Though stigma around the group still exists, the successes of the association are notable: a reduction in petty theft, increased incomes and active participation in civic life. Previously defined by the seemingly antisocial elements of their existence—namely, crime, homelessness and alcohol abuse—as street-frequenters, the bara boys are a subset of what Vakaoti (2012: 9) argues is 'the longest surviving group of young people engaging in "active citizenship"' in Fiji.

Given the association comprises almost entirely unskilled workers and continues to be held in low regard by the public, it is remarkable that these men have positioned themselves as entrepreneurs of sorts. While several of them informed me that they hold out hope of engaging in seasonal migration for greater income, the ability to provide for their families motivates them to continue as engaged members of their society through the association. As one bara boy told me—to nods of approval from others in attendance: 'Family's the number one thing. Once our family's okay, everything's okay.'

Usaia Moli, who introduced me to the bara boys, discussed the practicalities of the livelihood opportunities available to them. The quotation below highlights not only their pragmatism, but also their resilience. The example of the bara boys acts as a hybrid practice of adaptive development (ODI 2014) within capitalist structures. As Usaia observed:

> The common thing with all of the jobs these boys can do and want to do—wheelbarrow, security, fruit picking ... is that they don't need [specialised] skills for these jobs. They will look for the best kind of work they can with the skills they have. A little child, you can ask them what they want to do when they grow up and they can still dream because they have all of their options open to them, but these boys have to rely on the skills they have.

Youth unemployment and civic engagement

Beyond the obvious impacts of increased idleness and fewer opportunities to provide a livelihood through formal employment, there are wider social ramifications of entrenched youth unemployment. Communities become more prone to repeated acts of antisocial behaviour (White and Wyn 2013: 121), young people are less prone to engage with their communities as 'active citizens' (Bessant 2004; Vakaoti 2016), increased internal migration creates pockets of disenfranchised people and functioning social norms are disrupted. Perhaps most crucially, significant numbers of young people are prevented from realising their potential as engaged citizens, 'thought leaders',[7] economic consumers and job creators.

As has already been stated and will be explored in more depth in Chapters Four and Five, current social structures limit the ability of youth in the Pacific to participate meaningfully in community discussion and decision-making processes. Employment offers one avenue to bridge the divide between being considered a youth and being an adult, providing greater influence as a senior member of a community, particularly for men. If employment opportunities are few and poorly linked with the skills with which young people are equipped, it is conceivable that they will view themselves as being caught in a position where their social status

---

7   That is: as critical and engaged thinkers who can test, debate and influence concepts related to the public good, whether social, economic, political or other.

has the potential to stagnate. As young people themselves stated in the Suva Declaration from the second Pacific Youth Festival: 'Opportunities for formal employment are few. Unemployment breeds discontent, loss of identity and low morale, causing many young people to practice risky behaviour or engage in exploitative work' (SPC 2009b: 3).

While this lack of security will most likely occur in localised situations, inherent risks can be understood as credible both at greater social levels and to individual youths. As previously noted, in the relatively short period since the turn of the century, there have been multiple instances of civil conflict with significant youth participation in Fiji, Kanaky/New Caledonia, Papua New Guinea, Samoa, Solomon Islands, Tonga and Vanuatu. Peace studies scholar Helen Ware (2004: 1) sees this as squarely an issue of unemployment, arguing that 'violent unrest in the Pacific Island countries and Papua New Guinea is increasingly common because of the lack of employment for large cohorts of young people'. There are numerous examples globally of unemployed young people feeling a lack of social engagement and civic responsibility (OECD 2016: 52; Urdal 2006), from youth in India passing time through substance abuse (Jeffrey 2010) to the role of young people as agitators of the Arab Spring (Moghadam 2013: 398; White and Wyn 2013: 13). Curtain and Vakaoti echoed this claim in 2011, highlighting the potential for negative individual and societal consequences because of limited livelihood opportunities:

> Denial of economic and social opportunities leads to frustrated young people. The result can be a high incidence of self-harm and anti-social behaviour, including a greater risk of social conflict and violence. (Curtain and Vakaoti 2011: 9)

The decreased community security resulting from the high youth unemployment rates in the Pacific reflects both the sense of purpose that is attached to employment and the hopelessness caused by protracted denial of livelihood opportunities. The political and economic uncertainties in Oceanic states present a disconcerting picture for young people that opportunities are not only few, but also tenuous. This is perhaps one explanation for employment in the civil sector being positively regarded in Fiji (ECREA 2002; Nilan et al. 2006: 902). Despite the dearth of opportunities, government positions are at least theoretically more stable than those in the private sector, which is more prone to bankruptcy or capital flight.

Employment is a significant indicator of prosocial civic engagement. Indeed, Judith Bessant (2004) argues in her writing on youth participation and democratic practice that it is through employment that full citizenry is realised. She offers that

> citizenship is gained through employment, a living wage and an adequate standard of living while it also demonstrates the value of being moral, independent and able to meet one's civic obligations. (Bessant 2004: 390)

Arguments can be made against the applicability of such a view in rural communities throughout the Pacific based on the propensity for subsistence living. However, there is merit in this thinking if employment desirability is considered for its social status equally or more so than for its livelihood benefits. With young people's opportunities to participate in decision-making processes limited, in both rural and urban communities, it is reasonable to expect that they will seek to create their own pathways to participation. As previously argued, employment provides one socially acceptable method of promoting oneself as an engaged citizen worthy of trust and responsibility.

The earlier example of Pesa illustrates several possible insights into the desire for employment expressed by youth across the Pacific. His wish to move to Suva exhibits the practice of migration as a strategy of economic investment (Clemens and Ogden 2014), with Pesa hoping to earn enough money to return to his village and engage in socially valued practices of beginning and supporting a family, and simultaneously being recognised as an adult in his community. Through migration and employment, Pesa can chart his own path, be free of daily village impositions associated with his age and return as a full and active member of his community. Employment, in this reading, provides an avenue to self-actualisation— although, importantly, this is marked not by the attainment of employment but by the process of his personal growth.

This perspective challenges the perception of young people as apathetic towards politics and decision-making processes and deficient in civic engagement. Rather, it suggests that young people will engage actively with their society when they feel they are being denied opportunities for participation in decision-making processes. In such circumstances, they are likely to create their own opportunities for engagement, whether prosocial or antisocial. Nevertheless, for Pacific youth, their civic engagement is inhibited by established expectations of young people's subservience to elders (Morton 1996; Vakaoti and Mishra 2010). Another factor is the increasing precarity of livelihoods created by global market forces and the diminishing social safety nets provided by local communities in the Pacific (Mohanty 2011).

With the considerable constraints on growing the economies of the Great Ocean States of the Pacific—their small populations and geographic isolation—it is difficult to imagine that youth unemployment will not continue to be a social and economic challenge for the foreseeable future. For this reason, it seems vital that these states engage in deliberative discussions about the developmental futures they desire. If employment and/or economic growth are key to this, they will need to find ways to grow their markets, supplement their economies or create windfall opportunities that will allow for significant economic redistribution through measures such as a universal basic income. Alternatively, they may wish to envision different forms of locally relevant development that are self-determined and not contingent on economic growth. Whether such visions can be realised is difficult to predict; however, it is clear that current models are not working sufficiently and the economic limitations are having profound social impacts.

Migration and the disruption of social hierarchies

The lure of independence, both social and economic, is seen as a chief motivator encouraging many Pacific youth to leave rural village communities and migrate to urban centres. Despite the subsistence affluence of many Oceanic communities, particularly in Melanesia, large numbers of young people continue to relocate from rural villages to urban and peri-urban settings. UN-Habitat reported in 2015 that the Pacific is urbanising faster than any region in the world, with an average annual urbanisation rate of 4.3 per cent, compared with a global average of 1.7 per cent—a figure that balloons to 16 per cent in peri-urban areas (UN-Habitat 2015: 14).

Census data for Fiji showed an increase in the urban population of around 18 per cent between 1996 and 2007, while the rural population shrank by approximately 1 per cent in the first recorded period when the urban population was larger than that in rural areas (FBoS 2021a).[8] This trend

---

8   The discrepancy in these figures represents population growth in this period.

continued between 2007 and 2017, when the urban population increased by more than 16 per cent while the rural population decreased by approximately 5 per cent (FBoS 2018), which reflects Sarah Mecartney and John Connell's (2017) assertion that Pacific urbanisation is becoming more permanent. The rapidly increasing establishment of homes and informal communities in the Suva–Nausori corridor is testament to the continued internal migration of Fijians to urban areas, with the United Nations estimating in 2015 that 53.7 per cent of the total population was living in urban areas (UN DESA n.d.[a]). A similar situation is apparent in Solomon Islands, with Honiara expanding at a rate of approximately 5.8 per cent per annum between 2009 and 2019—above the national average of 2.7 per cent (SINSO 2020). The proportion of the total population living in urban areas has increased from 20 per cent to 26 per cent during this time (SINSO 2020). Such urban population growth is faster than previous forecasts that were already predicting a doubling of the 2015 urban population by 2032 or earlier (Keen and Barbara 2015: 1). While this is a slight decrease from government statistics that found the urban population to have grown by an average of 4.7 per cent annually between 1999 and 2009 (Government of Solomon Islands 2011: 21; see also Allen and Dinnen 2015: 391), together, these figures suggest an established pattern of increasing rural–urban migration. With 2015 UN estimates that only 22.3 per cent of Solomon Islanders were then living in urban areas (UN DESA n.d.[b]), this represents a significant shift in the demographic composition of the country if the trend continues.

The reasons for rural–urban migration are many and varied across the region, though one dominant motive pervades: economic opportunity (Connell 2006; Kiddle 2010: 88; Maron and Connell 2008). Fijian youth activist Elisha Bano believes this is increasing partly due to the forces of modernisation making urban lifestyles and associated employment attractive to rural Fijians. Linking migration with the desire of Fijian young people to gain white-collar employment, she told me:

> With migration … there is a lot of rural to urban drift. That's our migration issue. Especially with young people, because more jobs are in urban areas. [In r]ural [areas], you might have more agriculture jobs, but parents are not encouraging their children to take up agriculture. They want their children to have white-collar jobs. That's the problem.

A catch-22 for the development community exists in attempting to address the issues associated with rural–urban migration without providing further incentives for young people to relocate to major cities and other urban hubs. As disengaged youth are most concentrated and visible in urban areas, they appear to be the perfect locations in which to run social assistance programs. The problem with this, however, is that similar opportunities are not available in rural settings. This is particularly pertinent in Solomon Islands, where the population remains much more concentrated in rural areas than in Fiji. As Honiara Youth Council President Harry Olikwailafa told me, a certain program may be good, but it attracts 'young people from rural communities to come to Honiara'.

Jack Maebuta agreed that the focus on urban youth results in youth livelihood issues being responded to where they are most visible, but not necessarily where they are most needed:

> We need to see the reality that the majority of persons are living in the rural areas. There has not been tangible rural development going on in the rural areas that will capture the livelihood of people in the rural areas, so it all comes back to the willpower of the government of the day. If they are serious in responding to the needs of the mass of the people of Solomon Islands, then they need to do something in the rural areas.

Andre Tipoki reflected similarly:

> We are having this shift from rural areas to the urban centres and the question is, 'If they are not able to find an opportunity here then why are they staying?' There are a lot of factors … In Honiara, young people can stay as long as five to seven years with their relatives with the hope that one day opportunities might arise. This [Honiara] is where opportunity arises. Some of the family members encourage extended family to stay with them. This is where opportunity comes.

One of the most visible representations of Solomon Islander youth engaging in rural–urban migration in the academic literature refers to the *masta liu* in Honiara. *Masta liu*, meaning people who walk around aimlessly (Allen 2013; Evans 2019), are groups of people, mainly men, who have travelled to the capital to find work and/or increase their livelihood skills. Due to the lack of livelihood opportunities, however, the *masta liu* are instead conspicuous for their lack of engagement in formal employment or education. As Jourdan wrote in her study of the *masta liu*:

> Their main characteristic is being unemployed: some have lost their jobs, some have dropped out of school, others are simply waiting for the departure of the ship that will take them back to their home village. (1995: 202)

They rose to public prominence in the 1970s when the Masta Liu Project was created to engage the large number of 'young people who come to Honiara and cannot find work' (The Solomon News Drum 1976). Their lack of engagement in 'productive' tasks, such as employment or education, does not appear to be a burden for the *masta liu*, however. Rather, Jourdan (1995: 211) claims it is indicative that while the allure of urban migration may be the possibility of increased wealth and livelihood opportunities, it is the freedom from hard subsistence labour and constraining social roles that encourages young people to stay in cities, even when their financial prospects are poor. Free to navigate their daily activities with autonomy, the *masta liu* travel for economic opportunities and stay for the social freedoms.

Remarkably, none of the youth advocates and activists with whom I spoke in Honiara raised the *masta liu*. When I broached their social role with youth development worker Sandra Bartlett, she recognised that *masta liu* are a somewhat prominent subculture within Honiara that skew towards being from younger generations, but she said there is a social distinction between those identified as *masta liu* and the broader general youth population. This is a particularly interesting social development given the continued visible street presence of young people in Honiara with no obvious engagement in employment.

It is interesting to note the differences between the street-frequenting populations of Suva and Honiara. Young people in Honiara are noticeable for their large numbers, seeming idleness and age range, from late teens to early twenties. In contrast, street-frequenters in Suva are less conspicuous and are more often young men—typically but not exclusively in their twenties and early thirties—engaging in informal employment as individual traders such as the bara boys and also as shoe-shiners or roaming street vendors (Vakaoti 2012). Where large groups of youth are apparent, they are likely to be in transit to or from school or social activities.

One explanation for this difference is the greater density of Honiara, where not only do migratory youth have less space to meet each other and seek out livelihood opportunities, but also these youth are more likely to have moved from other islands to settlements and villages close to the city centre, while Suva-destined migrants are more likely to settle in the expansive peri-urban fringe between Suva and Nausori. Though further exploration of the motivations and activities of street-frequenters in each space would shed more light on their daily practices, the stark differences in how they engage with public spaces are evidence that rural–urban migration is experienced differently in different parts of Oceania. Interestingly, considering the above comments of Harry, Jack and Andre regarding how youth projects unintentionally attract further streams of migrants, Vakaoti (2013: 87) found in his research on forms of youth participation in Fiji that municipal administrators in Suva are reluctant to promote youth gathering spaces 'because of the fear that they will attract more young people to the city'.

As formal employment becomes an accepted mechanism for advancing one's status and urban migration provides an escape valve from the cultural constraints of *kastom*, traditional Oceanic lifestyles and social norms are evolving at a rapid rate. Although culture is not static, the pace of such changes threatens to significantly break down established and understood cultural practices. Previous practices of hierarchy and the transition of authority over protracted periods are being undermined by the changing composition of village communities and the means of ensuring basic needs for individuals and families. Employment and the increasing association of status with individual educational attainment and financial success lend greater authority to those employed, while increasing rural–urban migration is diluting the support networks for village-based youth and elders alike.

This changing dynamic holds great promise and great danger. Increased youth exposure to, and participation in, decision-making processes acts as a form of futureproofing for Pacific societies. However, when young people leave the family unit in search of livelihood opportunities, or when their parents leave them for the same reasons, the strength of the family unit is weakened, 'leaving young people without adequate support mechanisms', as Noble et al. (2011: 112) write in their UNDP investigation into the social and economic risks facing Pacific youth. This results in both familial care and discipline being left wanting (Woo and Corea 2009: 12). Further social risks beyond those to youth demographics have also been noted by Connell (2011) and development studies scholar Pamela Thomas (2001) in relation to the social disruption caused by associated issues of employment seeking and rural–urban migration. Connell writes:

> Social consequences of poverty and other difficult urban conditions include the growth of domestic violence, though not an exclusively urban phenomenon, and the increase in the number of female-headed households following family breakdown and social disorganisation. (2011: 127)

Allen (2012) even attributes the discrepancies in perceived wealth and access to opportunity as a significant causal factor of the civil unrest experienced in Solomon Islands at the turn of the century. When traditional lifestyles and contemporary livelihood pressures meet, the balance between progress and destabilisation appears to be very delicate.

It must be remembered, however, that culture and what is understood as tradition are constantly changing. The tension of change is the uncertainty about how it will affect people and the prospect that some will be worse off. The promise of adaptive and alternative approaches to development is not only that local peoples have the capacity to determine their own development path, but also that in their doing so any chosen developmental direction will be more reflective of the values they hold rather than externally driven indicators (Andrews et al. 2015; Nederveen Pieterse 1998; TWP Community 2016).

Institutional responses to unemployment

With recognition that the current education–employment paradigm is failing many young Pacific people, greater diversity in pathways to employment is now being tested in both Fiji and Solomon Islands. Both government and nongovernmental organisations have been placing a greater focus on equipping youth with skills that formal education has not provided them. This takes the form of one or a combination of life-skills training, work-ready training, industry engagement, vocational training and entrepreneurship.

Life-skills training—a program in which I was involved through previous employment in Fiji—is targeted primarily at youth who have not undertaken tertiary education and are not engaged in formal employment and attempts to instil in them critical skills for sourcing or creating employment, as well as dealing with the stresses associated with unemployment. Originally created as a socially based method to mitigate youth experimentation with drugs and alcohol in New York (Botvin 1985; Botvin et al. 1980), the approach has been adapted for a more general application in Fiji and Solomon Islands, primarily through NGOs. Maintaining the dual focus of improving the social and personal self-management skills of youth (Botvin and Griffin 2004: 216–17) that will assist them to navigate real-world complexities, life-skills training aims to provide a platform from which youth can launch themselves towards possibilities while also boosting their capacity to withstand failure.

The step beyond providing life-skills training typically results in work-ready training and industry engagement. Industry engagement has largely taken the form of volunteering and interning with government and private-sector organisations, occasionally with a small stipend earned by the youth participants. Two of the larger programs in Solomon Islands are the previously mentioned REP, facilitated by the World Bank, and Youth@Work,[9] which is funded primarily through the Australian Government and administered by the Secretariat of the Pacific Community (SPC). Each of these programs progresses young people through life-skills and work-ready training, including topics such as professional presentation, communication and financial literacy, before connecting them with a work placement; Youth@Work focuses on private-sector and civil service positions, while REP participants are mainly engaged in road-building and similar civil works (World Bank 2015). A 2015 evaluation of Youth@Work found that between 31 and 43 per cent of participants found ongoing formal employment (McDonald and Kyloh 2015: 33–35) but cautioned that the reliability of these figures was uncertain. Regardless of the success rate, the evaluation noted sustainability issues in the industry engagement approach—notably, that a risk of employment substitution saturation exists where interns may be rolled over from one cohort to the next without being hired post internship and that the REP is yet to prove that its focus on engaging participants in civil works projects provides career pathways (McDonald and Kyloh 2015: 56).

In Fiji, the focus on industry training is even greater. In fact, volunteering is one of the four official employment streams promoted by the government's National Employment Centre (NEC 2021), alongside formal employment, self-employment and foreign employment. NEC Director Viliame Cagilaba informed me that with the twin aims of engendering community spirit (NEC 2021) and building capacity for improved employment prospects, the NEC is promoting volunteerism as

---

9   Websites for each program are listed in the Bibliography.

a pathway to formalised employment in its official approach to tackling unemployment. To date, I have been unable to locate data testifying to the success of this approach, including from the NEC directly.

An alternative approach to job-seeker training has emerged in recent years, with significant investment made through government and NGOs in Fiji and Solomon Islands in providing youth with entrepreneurial skills.[10] This is a trend seen throughout the region, as noted by Good (2019) in Tonga. The justification for this focus is summarised by Mia Rimon, Solomon Islands Country Director for the SPC, with reference to the self-employment stream of Youth@Work:

> The Young Entrepreneur Program [YEP] is the key, however. There are not enough formal employment positions in Honiara so the Youth Market and YEP are there because there are not enough jobs in Honiara, so we have to create self-employment opportunities, which is great for the economy as well.

As mentioned above, self-employment is also one of the official approaches of Fiji's NEC. In fact, entrepreneurship has arguably become the cornerstone of the national government's approach to addressing youth unemployment since the launch of the Young Entrepreneurship Scheme in 2018, which provides seed funding to small and microenterprise endeavours (The Fijian Government n.d.). Such investment seems to be predicated on the understanding that young people are both 'the most at risk of unemployment, and also the best placed to respond to new opportunities in the private sector economies' (Roberts 2003: 486). My previous employment in Fiji incorporated microenterprise training and assistance into its project design to improve youth livelihoods and development. Like other projects focused on inculcating entrepreneurial skills, the project provided basic training in financial literacy, identifying market viability for the intended business and creating a business plan. Once signed off by an independent third-party expert, participants were provided funding to assist the establishment of these microenterprises.

---

10   Although arguments could be made that this approach recycles previous attempts at developing the human capacity of youth, as demonstrated by Evans's (2019: 83–84) reflections on the Honiara-based Masta Liu Project, which commenced in 1976 and included a 'focus on soft skills (personal development such as punctuality and reliability) and technical skills (carpentry, agriculture and electrical work)'.

Joining this project during its participant recruitment phase, I was struck by the assumption that entrepreneurial skills could be transferred to participants in a matter of weeks. In communities where the *kerekere*[11] practice of sharing goods communally informs both social and economic customs, I wondered how the individualist nature of entrepreneurship would be absorbed. After all, to be an entrepreneur requires more than capital and an identified gap in the market; as Andreas Rauch and Michael Frese's (2012) examination of the psychology behind entrepreneurial people and their behaviour identifies, it also requires personal traits related to a desire for high achievement, risk-taking, innovation, autonomy, locus of control and self-efficacy. Although these traits are not necessarily unobtainable for Pacific youth, some— particularly autonomy and locus of control—run counter to established cultural norms of reciprocity and communalism.

Project manager Sina Suliano informed me that of the twin arms of the livelihoods project, job-seeking and entrepreneurship, the success rate for those who completed the job-seeking stream far exceeded that of the youth entrepreneurs. As to why, she postulated:

> I don't know if it's a cultural thing or a Pacific islander thing, but when it comes to small businesses, especially in the villages, they [are] set up to fail. It really takes a strong, hard-willed person to run a successful business … One of the main issues we picked up from our monitoring, especially with the businesses that have failed, [is] they have all failed because of … always giving things out on credit and not being able to collect that back.

Patrick Mesia, who worked on a project almost identical in ambition, hosted by a Honiara-based NGO, offered a similar analysis:

> We tried doing some small income-generating activities, but very few have entrepreneurial thinking. There are others that, even if you provide them with the best skills training, if they are not in the mindset to do that, [they won't succeed].

This is not to say that entrepreneurialism is nonexistent among youth in Oceania, as there are a few examples that speak to the positive impacts of emerging entrepreneurialism in the region. For example, Aaron John Robarts Ferguson (2019) offers case-study analyses of young entrepreneurs

---

11 Fijian: literally 'please', *kerekere* is a custom by which family members and others with close ties may request assistance of some kind with no expectation on the behalf of the provider that the debt will be directly repaid.

in American Samoa, focusing on three individuals. Meanwhile, in Honiara, cheaper and more reliable internet access has been identified as a sufficient enabler of entrepreneurial behaviour for a group of young women who use social media to sell second-hand clothes directly to consumers (Aumanu-Leong 2021). Notable among these and other examples (Youth Co:Lab 2021), however, is that none of these entrepreneurs appears to have had their initiative emerge from involvement in microenterprise training delivered by development organisations.

Despite a lack of evidence of the success of programs and policies focused on youth self-employment, entrepreneurialism was raised as one possible response to youth unemployment in 15 of the interviews I conducted.[12] This included four informants who had direct involvement with an employment program that utilised microenterprise training and support as at least one of its streams. All four of these informants agreed that focusing on improving the self-employment capacities of Pacific peoples was folly without greater societal change. As Jack Maebuta, who was involved in the design of aspects of the REP in Solomon Islands, said: 'Entrepreneurial skill training on its own, without being based in a real need, is a waste of time.'

Interestingly, however, of the other 11 interviews in which entrepreneurship as a focus for addressing youth unemployment was raised, none had a directly negative view. Nine could be classified as neutral, with two favourable. Four of the neutral respondents were civil service bureaucrats, one of whom was involved in a program that had only recently established a microenterprise stream for youth, and the remaining four were civil society and/or development organisation representatives. Of the two positive respondents, one was also involved in the program that had recently established a microenterprise stream and the other reported on his knowledge of the Tutu Training Farm on the rural Fijian island of Taveuni—long recognised for its success in training and providing livelihood opportunities for the young people it engages through cash-crop growth and sales (Hill 2001: 20).[13]

---

12   Seven in Solomon Islands; eight in Fiji.
13   When discussing entrepreneurship as a framework for promoting youth livelihood opportunities in Fiji, the example of the Tutu Training Farm on the island of Taveuni is regularly raised as an example of success. Tutu trains students as cash-crop farmers and is widely acknowledged as providing positive livelihood outcomes to its graduates. It is worth noting, however, that it is not a program focused on entrepreneurship. As Mishra-Vakaoti (2013: 108) notes: 'The programme ... includes education in farming, financial independence and leadership. The programme works on a holistic approach to personal development.'

What is apparent from these responses is that the concept of utilising entrepreneurialism to address youth unemployment holds cachet with those involved in youth development policies and projects in Fiji and Solomon Islands. This is despite the experiences of those with whom I spoke who viewed this style of intervention as ineffective. The fact it continues to be utilised in development projects suggests it is a mode of intervention favoured by donors. The irony of development organisations promoting youth entrepreneurialism through interventions that have repeatedly failed to produce positive outcomes has been remarked on elsewhere (see Evans 2019) and was noted specifically by Georgina Cope, an Australian based in Fiji working on developmental reform–focused projects throughout the region. She noted: 'The culture of the development community and civil service is geared towards finding flaws and [is] not very entrepreneurial and trying to address things in a creative way.'

Life-skills and entrepreneurship programs offer an example of the propensity for development organisations to promote programs of mimicry rather than engage in testing adaptive approaches based on local contextual realities. The insufficient regard for social and cultural contexts is an example of the limitations of 'intentional' development interventions (Cowen and Shenton 1996). This is not to say that greater levels of entrepreneurialism, coupled with a more supportive social and legislative environment for such activities, are not possible. The stories of the Suva Crime-Free Wheelbarrow Association and the significant numbers of people engaged in roadside trading in both Fiji and Solomon Islands and, more particularly, betel nut vendors in Solomon Islands are testament to the abilities of Pacific peoples to engage in self-employment practices. It needs to be noted, however, that all these initiatives are undertaken by large populations through informal practices and thus, while clearly commercial ventures, are not truly entrepreneurial.

Seasonal migration

Another avenue for addressing unemployment in Oceania is seasonal or permanent migration. Temporary economic migration to Australia and Aotearoa/New Zealand has increased in size and scope since the New Zealand Recognised Seasonal Employer scheme began in 2007 (Gibson and McKenzie 2014) and the Australian Seasonal Worker Programme[14] commenced in 2008 (Reed et al. 2011). It is worth noting, however, that such migration was significant in parts of the region before these schemes, particularly from Polynesian countries that have long histories of circulatory migration, mainly to Aotearoa/New Zealand, but also to Australia (Connell and Corbett 2016: 587; Good 2013; Woo and Corea 2009: 6).

Viewed as a 'safety valve' for unemployment pressures and the potential antisocial conflicts they can drive (Woo and Corea 2009: 6), seasonal migration is theorised to not only provide relief from unemployment, but also act as a key driver of local Pacific economies through remittances (Connell and Corbett 2016: 595). Research undertaken for the World Bank has found that seasonal migration opportunities have strong potential to provide significant direct and indirect benefits to the economies of both origin and destination countries and, importantly, to create possibilities for developmental growth for Pacific peoples. Referring to the concept of a 'triple win', Curtain et al. write:

> For Pacific Islanders, migration generates significant employment opportunities. For labour-sending countries, remittance flows contribute to increased income and consumption at the household level, reducing poverty, loosening credit constraints and providing insurance against negative shocks … Labour-receiving countries in the Pacific Rim benefit from the filling of labour shortages and by using migration access as a major policy lever to lift the prosperity, security and stability of their low-growth neighbours. (2016: 1)

The effects of labour mobility on human capital are difficult to predict. One perspective views the increased economic opportunities as having clear links to human capital gains as remittances are invested in improvements in health and education resources in origin countries (Curtain et al. 2016). This line of thinking is not founded in blind faith, but is supported by Clemens and Ogden's (2014: 3) study of migration as a financial strategy that suggests that people with limited access to opportunity are savvy investors in their own potential and that of future generations and that labour migration, in particular, is 'the most profitable investment, by far, available to many of the world's poor'. Such findings support alternative, adaptive and capabilities understandings of the

---

14   Known as the Pacific Seasonal Worker Pilot Scheme from 2008 to 2012.

expertise of local communities concerning their own livelihood stressors and opportunities (Esteva and Prakash 1998; Leftwich 1994; Nussbaum 2003, respectively).

On the surface, employment migration schemes appear to be a perfect remedy for the youth developmental challenges perspective that sees 'investments in youth as critical to economic development' (Fussell and Greene 2002: 26). In exploring such schemes, it is important, though, to be cognisant of the social and economic benefits and disadvantages that are represented. These cross individual, family and societal boundaries. Benefits include financial gain, increased access to further training and exposure to new cultures and environments (Gibson and McKenzie 2009; Gibson et al. 2008; Maron and Connell 2008). This is not to mention the impact of remittances in providing financial assistance to families, communities and even national economies in the origin country (Curtain et al. 2016: 7). Indeed, research on migratory employment practices both outside[15] and within the Pacific highlights this as the primary motivation for much migratory work (Brown 1997; Gibson et al. 2008; Maron and Connell 2008). The disadvantages of seasonal migration noted in both Pacific and non-Pacific contexts include breadwinners being absent from the family for months at a time, disruption to social hierarchies causing social friction (Guendelman and Perez-Itriago 1987; Maron and Connell 2008; Rogaly 1998) and the risk of worker exploitation in countries where their knowledge of legal protections may be limited (Ball et al. 2011; Curtain et al. 2016; McKillop 2017). Further, the periodic nature of seasonal work—with long times of idleness and a limited number of years when one can reasonably expect to be physically able to engage in such work—may disrupt household dynamics and fail to provide ongoing livelihood security for participants.

Comparing Fiji and Solomon Islands

Unemployment is the topic on everyone's minds in both Fiji and Solomon Islands. Any conversation about opportunity and capabilities invariably is directed to problems with securing work. As discussed, the meanings that individuals and groups attach to unemployment as an issue vary widely and underscore deeper social, cultural and economic concerns.

---

15   On Mexico, see Guendelman and Perez-Itriago (1987); on Europe, see MacKenzie and Forde (2009); and on India, see Rogaly (1998).

Perhaps the greatest similarity the countries hold in this space is in the allure of their capital city. Both Fiji and Solomon Islands are experiencing significant rates of rural–urban migration by young people in search of livelihood opportunities. The combination of population mass, industry concentration and tertiary education bases provides the appearance of opportunity abundance in both locations. The reality, though, is that young people in Suva and Honiara are experiencing entrenched unemployment and underemployment, with education levels playing a minimal role in improving employment outcomes.

How urban unemployment is experienced by the young people in these locations is vastly divergent, however. As mentioned, the visible presence of idle youth is drastically greater in Honiara, where the *masta liu* loiter in groups large and small. With many unemployed youth having travelled from islands beyond Guadalcanal, they are less connected to social and cultural mores and expectations than those living with family in the Suva–Nausori corridor, for whom the imposition of social obligations remains more present. Both the betel nut vendors of Honiara and the bara boys and shoe-shiners of Suva demonstrate that informal income-generation opportunities exist for young people, but even the statements of the members of the Suva Crime-Free Wheelbarrow Association that they would seek alternative forms of employment if possible demonstrate that these are not highly desirable forms of livelihood generation.

In rural locations, unemployment is experienced in a different manner again. Subsistence agriculture and sociocentric lifestyles continue to offer something of a safety net for rural Fijian and Solomon Islander youth. While my engagement with youth beyond Honiara was limited, conversations with young people who had travelled to the capital for livelihood opportunities demonstrated an important similarity with their rural Fijian counterparts regarding the allure of migration. Rather than the move to the city being purely emblematic of economic migration, it provided an opportunity to display greater individual levels of agency and autonomy.

Conclusion

Unemployment was highlighted as the most recurrent and urgent issue facing young people in Fiji and Solomon Islands by those I interviewed and the community members with which I ran focus groups. At face value, this may appear to reflect concerns about livelihoods provision or even fears about the potential social problems of idle youth. In reality, the pre-eminence of unemployment as an issue of concern unearths deeper and wider social and economic attitudes in Oceanic societies.

Youth development and employment issues are reflective of wider debates about what development should look like and how it should be achieved in any one location. This is where a holistic livelihoods approach is useful. At its base level, employment acts to complement subsistence lifestyles in livelihood provision, securing the basic needs of individuals and their loved ones. Beyond this, however, lie important formal and informal structures that shape ideals of self-actualisation and community development and, further, act to promote or inhibit the achievement of such.

The formal structures of employment generation—namely, the private sector as an employment provider and government as policymaker, mass employer and education provider—must be understood in terms of how they create employment opportunities. The history of entrenched youth unemployment in Fiji and Solomon Islands demonstrates both a lack of jobs available for willing workers and a failure to marry skills development to such vacancies. Both problems are represented by the high numbers of skilled unemployed looking for white-collar employment and the difficulties of locating employees for skilled blue-collar roles. Whether or not it is even possible for the Great Ocean States of the Pacific to generate enough employment opportunities to meet the skills of their peoples, with consideration to geographic isolation and small population sizes among other issues (Connell 2011; Duncan 2014), is an area for further exploration. Ideally, this is a question that must be asked in any comprehensive evaluation of the scope for expansion of the employment sector in these countries.

What must also be understood is the impact of informal structures on employment and its purpose. Employment is not merely an economic issue, but also has social implications. For young people, these factor into their desire to seek white-collar skills and employment, as discussed in the previous chapter. Further, employment is one means by which young people can socially transition from youthhood to adulthood. Employment acts as a medium for the realisation of an individual's identity and agency, and for community engagement, status and respect.

This is not to say that this is the best way for employment to be understood and pursued. Indeed, the way Pacific societies conceive of employment, the importance with which they consider it and the impacts it has on creating new understandings of tradition are in a state of flux. This is partly due to the tensions between modern and neotraditional modes of living, and partly because cultural norms are constantly shifting. For an increasingly large cohort of Pacific youth populations, social influences and formal institutions are not moving at a similar rate— acting as a compounding factor in their entrenched unemployment, including for those with strong formal education qualifications. The examples of Pesa and the bara boys highlight that employment functions both as a livelihood provider and as an indicator of status. The differences in the way that employment is perceived and experienced in these two case studies suggest that where opportunities may not exist—such as in bridging the gap to adulthood in a village setting for Pesa and in securing a stable income for the bara boys—alternative and innovative pathways will be sought.

Rather than focusing on the ways in which unemployment acts as a signifier of the social and economic challenges facing countries like Fiji and Solomon Islands, perhaps a more pertinent line of inquiry is to consider the role of economic growth as an enabler of positive developmental futures for Pacific peoples. The current models for improving individual employment opportunities and growing national economies are not fit for purpose through most of Fiji and Solomon Islands. With the spectre of COVID-19 set to loom over Pacific states for some years, these challenges are likely to become even greater—with diminished international travel impacting on the number of people who can remit earnings from seasonal migration and likely ongoing negative effects on local tourism. Reconsideration of the benefits of employment and how these might otherwise be realised may be a more appropriate path for Fiji and Solomon Islands to follow, rather than reproducing more of the same.

4

Civic engagement and leadership

You cannot have young people questioning what is happening when the church and tradition are interlocked and where they have no voice at all. You need to be able to get them to think critically: 'Why is this?' 'You say for me to do this. Why?'

People say that's annoying: 'Don't ask why. Just do it.'

No. Ask why. Ask your leaders why they are doing that; why you have to do this. That is important. Only then can young people be well-informed, well-equipped and have access to resources. It is often there but they don't know how to access it and who to ask for it.

— Tura Lewai, Fiji

For Tura Lewai, the suppression of critical thinking is a vital issue for youth in Fiji. Well-known in the country for his social justice and prodemocracy advocacy, Tura remarked on how formal and informal structures discourage young people from being curious about how their societies work, let alone holding authority to account. His sentiments were echoed by Mereia Carling, regional youth advisor for the SPC, who told me that Fijians 'avoid confrontation and just follow suit, generally'.

The image of civil society in Oceania is one of juxtapositions. Though village settings are often represented as supportive, cohesive, family-like units, critical civil society is still seen as uneven, even weak, throughout the region (Corbett 2015; Haley 2008: 10). Conventional theories of civil society posit the legitimacy of the state through an active populace holding its government to account (Post and Rosenblum 2002: 1) by engaging in civic action outside formal state or parliamentary structures (Woods 1992: 77). These concepts reflect Western norms and are indelibly linked to notions of liberal democracy, and their applicability to Pacific contexts varies between communities and countries.

Superficial readings of civil society across the Pacific suggest that citizens play a passive role in the functioning of the state. Social roles are culturally prescribed and hierarchies well established. This is not to say that civil society within the Great Ocean States of the Pacific is weak. If we take an alternative starting point—that the core premise of civil society is that 'individual well-being is tied to, and understood to be tied to, the well-being and independence of groups' (Post and Rosenblum 2002: 6)—it can be strongly argued that the sociocentric norms of Pacific societies have created robust endogenous versions of civil society.

In this chapter, I argue that understandings of civic activity in the Pacific appear to represent a limited band that lionises civic engagement with overtly political ideals. Everyday civic engagement is just as, if not more, significant in its impacts on social norms and mores through the subtle challenging or reinforcing of social roles. For young people, the roles that are socially acceptable for them to occupy are quite restrictive, relegating them as observers to decision-making with an eye to being future leaders in an undetermined time frame.

Civil society in the Pacific context

The strength of civil society across Oceanic communities varies. The hierarchical nature of traditional communities can act as a limiting factor on citizens' active participation in civil society, with Oceanic societies generally prescribing the roles that each member of the community is allowed and entitled to perform. Thus, despite the long history of group decision-making processes for most Pacific societies, power is primarily wielded by adult men (McLeod 2015; Prasad 2017: 331; Sahlins 1963), though senior women have greater influence in some matrilineal societies, particularly outside Melanesia (McLeod 2007: 10–12; 2015).[1]

---

1   This is further structured hierarchically according to factors such as chiefly lineage, religious roles such as being a pastor, and big-man attributes such as wealth and influence.

Despite this, change has been present in recent years, resulting in an expanded and emboldened civil society sector in certain spaces. The combination of enhanced information flow through telecommunications technologies, growing levels of educated citizens and the influences of globalisation such as the expansion of the international development industry—including through regional multilateral bodies—has resulted in civil society groups and development organisations critically engaging with and, at times, challenging authority in the region (Brimacombe 2017; Slatter 2006; Titifanue et al. 2017). Moving from 'sporadic' responses to issues of immediate concern, such as Fiji's 1987 military coups (Slatter 2006: 29), these groups, both formal and informal, are now engaging in sustained campaigns that are both sociocentric and issues based. Fijian LGBTIQ+ activist Kris Prasad even theorised that events that risk repressing civil society can act to fortify critical civil society. He told me: 'Every time we have a coup, social movements start, civil society groups start, human rights groups start. There is always a people's response to tyranny and dictatorship.'

Notably, the increasingly politicised civil society activities of the recent past have largely been driven by, or made inclusive of, youth. This is despite the continued structural minimisation of the roles they play and have the potential to play in their communities. Particularly in fields related to social justice, such as gender rights, sexuality rights and climate change, young people are at the vanguard of change and forcing their way into the public consciousness and conversation. This does not overcome the fact that the reach of civil society and civil society organisations remains limited. To begin with, these spaces are mainly apparent in urban hubs, particularly those with significant cosmopolitan populations, such as Suva.

Rationalising power imbalances

A number of those with whom I spoke talked of the frustration they felt within Pacific youth communities regarding the lack of opportunities for their active engagement in civil society. In some youth populations, their minimisation was being met not with passivity but with resistance. Not content to be seen as citizens-in-waiting, they were agitating to be viewed and included by their societies as active citizens.

Child protection specialist Salote Kaimacuata informed me that this is a problem throughout Oceania. Having lived and worked throughout the Pacific region, including in Aotearoa/New Zealand, she has witnessed youth struggling to be included in decision-making processes. She reflected on her experiences working with young i-Kiribati women for UNICEF Pacific, telling me:

> i-Kiribati youth have been asking for a long time: 'Can we sit there?' 'Can we participate?' 'Can we input? Because our time will come sooner than we want and we need to learn now from you and be mentored by you.'

Usaia Moli, who has a long history of youth leadership in Fiji, conveyed the same experience of engaging with and resisting adult leaders:

> No longer can they point to us and say, 'You'll be the leaders of tomorrow', because we are making changes right now. We look at every issue that comes up around the country and we have become champions on these issues in our own way. We represent the country in international meetings and presentations and everywhere we go, but yet they keep telling us, 'You are the leaders of tomorrow. Your time will come.' Our time is now. I don't have to wait a few more years.

Interestingly, this is an issue that also arises in critical civil society spaces in Oceania. Mamta Chand, a women's rights activist from Fiji, described her dismay at the women's movement's rigid leadership structures and lack of acknowledgement of the successes of its young members:

> When we are in the intergenerational spaces, young women are told: 'You're not leaders. You're the leaders of tomorrow.' It was really frustrating. We would say, 'We are leaders of today. We are doing things. We are mobilising young women. We've mobilised young women to go and vote. We did that ourselves.' They refused to see us as leaders of now, of today. They say, 'No, when we die you become leaders.' We are leaders. We are leading. They refuse to accept that.

Resistance to youth engagement and participation has significant precedence on a global scale. Power is classically held by adults and elders, for whom weakening this hold on power would have little clear benefit. Whether consciously or not, their status and significance are tied to their social role and to share power with those who do not hold it would serve not only to undermine their own authority, but also to risk the development of their communities in ways that run counter to their interests. As youth worker and scholar Andy West (2007: 126) finds, 'adults resist and control the development of children's participation often because it disrupts adults' established working patterns and challenges existing norms'.

Issues related to the difficulties of engaging Pacific youth in prosocial civic behaviours, including decision-making processes, are not limited to the region. As international development youth worker Claire O'Kane (2003: 1) asserts: 'Children and young people have traditionally been excluded from decision-making processes in all parts of the world.' To challenge such power imbalances would require going beyond improving access to decision-making processes for youth and other marginalised groups, to facilitating their prosocial participation in civil society and, further, to promoting cultures of deep critical thought. Public planning scholar Sue Brownhill (2009: 360) writes of the 'inevitable rationality of power' as undermining true modes of participation. Only by disrupting accepted ideas of whose voice counts, when, where and why, can such power be countenanced.

Across the Pacific, the power imbalances divided along age and status lines are prevalent across all aspects of society. From the expectations of young people to undertake most menial labour in household and village settings to the limited representation of youth interests in formal governance systems, including parliaments (Noble et al. 2011: 19),[2] the opportunities for invited, engaged participation in civil society are few. Further, when youth attempt to create space for themselves to represent their views, they are derided for disrespecting how their cultures operate and the wisdom of vesting authority in their elders, as discussed in Chapter Two with quotations from Mereia Carling, Tura Lewai and John Firibo.

Beyond maintaining the status quo of power relations, inhibiting youth participation has direct negative impacts on the self-actualisation processes of young people. When ignored and left unnurtured, the skills and creativity of young people may fail to develop. As they internalise the idea that their abilities are not valued, they are less likely to invest their own energy in engaging critically with their surroundings. Engaging

2   It should be noted that this is not a phenomenon limited to the Pacific region. For example, the 2015 national election in Australia and the 2017 national election in Aotearoa/New Zealand resulted in the election of people aged under 35 years at levels of 3.1 per cent (Evershed et al. 2016) and 10 per cent (Farrar 2017), respectively.

in practices of rational ignorance may then lead to the perpetuation of power structures that are overtly or opaquely oppressive and embed such communal mental models into understandings of young people's place within their societies (Saraswathi and Larson 2002: 346).

Structural minimisation

The influence of hierarchy in Oceanic societies can scarcely be overstated. Social roles are generally well established and align with an individual's lineage, gender and age[3] (Brimacombe 2017: 144; Cox 2017: 77; Jolly 1994; Morton 1996: 22–24). Other factors with greater variability— such as ability, sexuality, education, occupation and marital status—also play a part. For youth, such hierarchy underscores the roles and influence they can have in their communities. This is commonly marked by an expectation of deference and a lack of deliberative participation. As Tura Lewai eloquently phrases it: 'Young people are taught to be seen but not heard.'

This extends to youth representatives often not being young themselves. While in Fiji, I met with Kaajal Kumar, who established the Aspire Foundation as an organisation to promote youth civic engagement and action. Of note, the Aspire Network hosted the 2014 Fijian Youth Parliament—the first time the event had been held in more than a decade. Kaajal spoke to me of the propensity of such representatives to be disconnected from current trends and issues affecting youth but holding on to the position of influence they have obtained. She told me:

> What you see in the Pacific—you come across young people who are 30 or 40 who are in the youth movement. If you look at [name of organisation], the person holding the youth desk, how old is that person? Because it took them time to get there, they have an ideology. And the youth movement, the way it functions, is that our ideas keep changing.

Discouraging youth participation enculturates young people to occupy a subordinated position in society. In a report on increasing youth participation in the Pacific, commissioned by the World Bank, youth development advocates Shasheen Jayaweera and Kate Morioka (2008: 11)

---

3   Though forms of hierarchy differ significantly throughout the region (for example, Besnier 2004; Jolly 1994).

explain: 'Young people are expected to accept authority without question, to the extent that they are discouraged from sharing their ideas and suggestions with elders.' Despite this, examples exist of young Pacific people expressing a desire to be more actively involved in the planning and decision-making processes of their communities, countries and cultures. At the second Pacific Youth Festival in 2009, more than 300 young people from across the region declared:

> [A]s young people, we are important human resources to development, and have an important role to play in building families, communities, institutions and nations; and in all sectors, both formal and informal. (SPC 2009b: 2)

This sentiment is mirrored in the responses to which Jayaweera and Morioka (2008) were exposed from young Pacific people discussing their wishes to be engaged citizens. They point out:

> Whilst some cultures actually discourage young people from expressing their views, it was the heartfelt desire of youth to become active citizens who could make a worthwhile contribution to their nation. (Jayaweera and Morioka 2008: 10)

Moreover, it is evident in growing examples of young people inserting themselves into spaces of active civic participation, as highlighted in case studies presented in the following chapter.

The minimisation of youth engagement in home and village settings is replicated in formal decision-making policies and processes. Such minimisation even flows through to academia. Vakaoti (2012: 8) notes that the 'literature on Fiji's political history has failed to offer any detailed analysis about young people's involvement in politics'. Regionally, this minimisation is most notable in the repeated lack of mentions of youth in progress reports on the Pacific Plan (Noble et al. 2011: 16) and similar documents outlining the focuses and ambitions of the 18 member states of the Pacific Islands Forum. Such examples act as evidence not only of the assumed lack of influence of youth within Pacific societies, but also of the recurrent failures to acknowledge, understand and address their realities.

Whether by design or simply reflecting *kastom*, the result of the youth voice being ignored amounts to a structural minimisation of the worth and potentiality of youth. To borrow a term from citizenship scholar David Owen (1996), youth are considered not as active citizens, but as 'apprentice citizens' who need to be managed, rather than consulted; taught, rather than learned from (see also Bessant 2004; Harris 2006). As Jayaweera and Morioka (2008: 11) note: 'Even if adults understand youth concerns, they are perceived as unlikely to prioritize them or take action to address them.'

A disjuncture is evident here between the ambitions of young people to be active participants in their communities—to be involved in decision-making processes, to share their knowledge and to learn—and their systematic marginalisation. This not only results in a vicious cycle in which many young people internalise their own subordination, but also leads to ineffective policy responses to youth issues, such as those discussed in earlier chapters in relation to education and employment. This inability to enact effective youth policy outside occasional ad hoc successes can be attributed to any or all of three factors. First, the simple notion that youth voices are not valued makes it less likely that poor policy will be challenged openly, nor will it represent risk at the ballot box. Second, when youth are consulted on issues they face and asked how these may be addressed, their internalised belief that their opinions matter little may result in them struggling to identify and enunciate their positions. Third, even when they are consulted and can articulate their thoughts and values, their participation is often tokenistic, with elders and those in authority determining the appropriate responses regardless of youth input. This sentiment was articulated in interviews I held in Fiji and Solomon Islands. Jope Tarai's role as an educator at USP's Laucala Bay campus in Suva exposes him to a great number of youths from across the region as well as Fijians active in critical civil society who attend events at the university's campus. He told me:

> I am sad to say that when youth interests come up, it's tokenistic branding, rather than anything that is really genuine. When we are needed for publicity, we will have to stand with the minister and shake his hand. [Former UN Secretary-General] Ban Ki-Moon or whoever—these top-brass delegates come over for these ticking-the-box consultations and then they leave and we go back to the same crap. We go back to the fact that our young people are facing the same struggling issues as they did before.

Jope's frustration regarding what he considered to be the token engagement of young people was shared by informants in Solomon Islands. Of the tokenistic and formulaic responses to issues youth are facing, youth development worker Sandra Bartlett told me: 'The older generation just don't get it. I find it so annoying. Even the leaders say, "Let's do something for youth: we'll do training."' Another informant from Solomon Islands said:

> The youth issues are there. We know about the youth issues. In terms of people in decision-making positions, of course they know the youth issues. But in terms of the strategies to address them, they always fall back to: 'Let's throw them some balls and nets and let them have fun with sports.'

This sentiment mirrors the observations of Pacific youth and development scholar Daniel Evans (2019: 87) that policy and program interventions aimed at developing youth potential in Solomon Islands are routinely 'low-cost, narrow and discrete'.

The lack of meaningful consultation with, and participation by, Pacific youth reflects cultural understandings of the social roles that subsections of Pacific societies are expected to play. Primary to this is the paramount authority of male elders, which is evident as much in the formal roles they play as village chiefs and big-men as it is in the parliaments of the region, where women account for only 8.6 per cent of parliamentarians (PacWIP 2012–21).[4] Two of these women are aged under 35 (PacWIP 2012–21)— a significant change from the longstanding norm through the region of female youth having no representation at all (Noble et al. 2011: 19).[5] The lack of social and political leaders outside the parameters of male and middle-aged or older permeates through the formal and informal institutions of Pacific societies and is reflected in the lack of political will expended on issues related to youth, women, people with disabilities and other marginalised groups, and remarked on throughout this book. Further, as discussed in the case study below, the deficit of role models for these groups plays out in the understandings of youth, and others, of who can and cannot be a valuable participant in decision-making processes— that is, who can and cannot be a leader.

This minimisation begins in the home and extends to the village, the schools, the provinces, right through to the policies of governments and the programs of their ministries. Though young people worldwide wield less authority than their elders, the extent to which this is true in

---

4   As of May 2021.
5   Also based on research of existing databases identifying Pacific parliamentarians by gender and age, as of July 2021.

Oceania exceeds countries such as Australia and Aotearoa/New Zealand. As was touched on in Chapters Two and Three, the influence of parents and communities in the decision-making processes impacting on young people's lives and livelihood opportunities in the Pacific is difficult to overstate, including shaping their decisions to pursue careers held in high esteem, yet with few opportunities for practice (Nilan 2007: 5). Vakaoti's (2014) commissioned study on youth participation behaviours in Fiji confirms the influence of elders, even to the point of stymieing the self-actualisation of young people. He illustrates this when discussing focus groups he ran with Suva-based youth who identified parental expectation as a limiting factor on participatory decision-making processes, with one respondent stating that 'an individual who is under 23 years of age cannot voice an opinion or make a decision on something like moving out of the family home' (Vakaoti 2014: 18). Solomon Islands youth development worker Patrick Mesia sees this structural minimisation as being rooted in cultural practices of hierarchy:

> Because of some of the cultural context here in Solomons, like the big-man system, the elders in some places dictate what should happen sometimes for a young age group like that. They don't give them space and when they hear them raising issues, they ignore it as being from a *pikinini* [child] point of view.

Even in the most acceptable mode of democratic participation for youth aged over 18, voting, the influence of elders is strong. Jayaweera and Morioka (2008: 19) note that 'most young people [in Fiji] vote for the same political party as do their parents, or, if they have a relative running for Parliament, are compelled to vote for them'. This reflects the strictly hierarchical social norms of Pacific communities, but also signifies the practice of rational ignorance (Downs 1957), as even at the most basic levels of participation, youth are expected to act in socially determined ways. Not only does this support Vakaoti's (2014: 5) suggestion that 'voting does not mean that young people are meaningfully participating in democratic processes or that they are equal partners in decision making', it also is further evidence of how youth are practically discouraged from expressing critical thought or being active participants in civil society. Young people are expected to be passive (McMurray 2006: 5), but such customs so marginalise their value as to render them largely submissive and truly subordinate—a risk identified by youth studies academic Anita Harris (2006: 224) as prevalent among young people cross-culturally in contexts where they feel their participation is not valued, with specific reference to Australia and Aotearoa/New Zealand. The impact this has on their capabilities, agency and critical thought is crucial to understanding how youth are preparing for their future as active citizens and leaders of their communities.

The marginalisation of youth participation appears to traverse ethnic boundaries. The indigenous cultures of Fiji and Solomon Islands have both been long understood to operate their societies hierarchically, where youth 'occupy a subordinate position and play a passive role' (Vakaoti 2012: 3). I was also informed of the strict deference youth must pay to their elders within Indo-Fijian communities. One notable difference between the indigenous Melanesian cultures and the Indo-Fijian culture, though, is that the social boundaries to participation within Indo-Fijian communities apply much more strictly to females than to males (Carling 2009: 107),[6] as they are expected to occupy a subordinate position, first, to their parents and, later, to their husband. As Mamta Chand expressed to me:

> The Indo-Fijian community, where I come from, it is very difficult for an Indo-Fijian young woman to be out—just to speak up, to get opportunities in these kinds of organisations and these kinds of spaces. As soon as we are born, we are groomed to get married. Education level is just probably up to high school. Education is not a priority. Getting married is a priority.

Thus, we can see across a range of ethnicities in Fiji and Solomon Islands that youth agency and decision-making capacities are minimised. One obvious impact of this minimisation is apparent in the lack of young people occupying visible and influential leadership positions.

Qualities of a leader

Across five of the six communities in which I worked during my fieldwork periods in Fiji and Solomon Islands, I asked several questions designed to gain a basic insight into the daily activities of youth in these communities. One question sought insight into role models with whom young people

---

6   Though young women in Melanesian communities are further marginalised than their male counterparts (Vakaoti 2012: 3), this is less restrictive than in Indo-Fijian communities according to multiple informants.

may identify who would also be classified as youth.[7] The intent was, first, to gain insight into the types of role models young people looked up to and, second, to gently test the critical thinking abilities of youth in response to an unanticipated question. This was inspired by a conversation with Mereia Carling, who told me:

> When I first came to Fiji and worked in television, I would go to schools and see children who couldn't answer a question where they had to use their own thoughts or their own dreams. They had to be told what to say about what they wanted to be when they grew up and what their favourite food was and then all the other children in the class would follow suit—the first one having asked the teacher what to say.

The responses from the five groups are detailed in the case study below.

Case study: Identifying youth leaders

To have the youth focus group participants thinking about leaders and leadership, I posed a lead-in question asking them to identify the characteristics of a good leader. None of the five groups across urban, peri-urban and rural Fijian and Solomon Islands communities struggled to respond to this question, providing lists of five or more traits in short succession. Some examples included: 'Honest', 'Compassionate', 'Neutral in decision-making', 'God-fearer' and 'Inherit from ancestors'.

Once asked to identify a leader who could also be considered a youth, however, the participants in all groups struggled. When they were broken into groups of between five and 12 people, silence was common where only minutes previously there had been a steady hum of discussion. No individual group was successfully able to identify a youth leader within five minutes of being asked the question, with multiple subgroups asking for clarification that the answer was to be someone who was both a leader *and* a youth.

With some prodding from within the group and some clarification from me and my research assistants, all groups eventually named their youth leaders. Their answers provide significant insight into the limited mental

---

7   This question followed earlier discussion of how 'youth' was defined in these communities. The example that groups were asked to identify could be from the local community, from their country or from anywhere else in the world.

space such people occupy in their communities. Among the answers were then US President Barack Obama and Fijian Youth Minister Viliame Naupoto, neither of whom was within even a decade of the upper age limit of 35 that the focus groups had previously identified as the cut-off point of youthhood. Closer to the mark was one response from a subgroup in Solomon Islands identifying the young King David, who was reported in the Bible to be 30 years old when anointed King of Israel in 1025 BCE (2 Samuel 5:4).

Two responses unquestionably met the two criteria—one for a person and the other for a group. Notably, both took time to be reached and only after considerable consultation. One Fijian subgroup identified then 30-year-old Iliesa Delana, who won Fiji's first Paralympic gold medal and was at the time the Assistant Minister for Youth and Sports. However, his name was only reached after that group agreed with the prompting suggestion of a research assistant. Another group identified the Fijian advocacy group Youth Champs 4 Mental Health. This answer was reached after extensive clarification of potential parameters for a youth leader between me and the subgroup and was suggested by a group member who had volunteered in a campaign run by Youth Champs 4 Mental Health.

Youth leadership as an oxymoron

The inability to identify youth leaders can be attributed to several forces. First, the number and visibility of youth leaders are most notable for their insignificance: Pacific youth occupy few positions of ceremonial or official power and their public stage is mostly limited to the sporting arena. Second, cultural concepts of youth and leadership make it almost impossible to conceive of someone being identified as both a leader and a youth. Once a young person achieves a position of recognised leadership, whether formal or informal, they are no longer socially associated with youthhood regardless of age. Third, the lack of opportunities for engaged participation in civil society provides the perfect mental environment for rational ignorance to develop, making it difficult for young people to challenge established mental models, such as that youth and leadership are antithetical traits, to identify individuals who challenge such notions.

This case study supports a recurrent theme throughout my interviews related to the socialised concept that young people cannot be leaders. For Georgina Cope, a regional development worker based in Fiji, the responses from these focus group informants reflect a simple truism of Oceanic conceptions of leadership legitimacy: 'People are conditioned to think of a leader as someone who is not young. You are not credible if you are young.'

Salote Kaimacuata, of Fiji, further suggests that elders' lack of willingness to share or relinquish leadership positions limits opportunities for new leaders to be nurtured and developed. This mirrors the assertions of West (2007), discussed earlier, that leadership in cultures throughout the world is marked by practices of maintaining and consolidating authority rather than developing it in others. Salote told me:

> When you get older, your priorities change. When you get older, you hold on to things that maintain your power base, whatever that is. When do we know to give over to young people? I'm happy to mentor now and I'm happy to nurture a leader. I really believe a good leader breeds other leaders and, as difficult as it may be, knows and discerns when they need to start moving back and putting that young person forward. They will not be forgotten. They will be remembered for putting forward that other person that continues good leadership for sustainability.

Perhaps this problem is cyclical in nature. There are few young leaders because limited opportunities exist for them, but also because there are few role models. Further, political models that are not liberally democratic and that privilege those already in positions of power limit the avenues through which young people can assert their leadership qualities. They provide little space for political discussion among youth and limited opportunities for genuine representation. Perhaps this is why Mereia Carling reported witnessing a huge shift in young people putting themselves forward for leadership positions in the time between writing her master's dissertation on youth citizenship in Fiji in 2009—during the period of unrepresentative governance following the 2006 coup—and the 2014 elections. This is further evidenced by young candidates standing for parliament, like Roshika Deo (as discussed in the case study below) and Usaia Moli. As Mereia told me:

> I remember writing a paper on youth participation 10 years ago and I was scratching around. I could think of one or two youth leaders then but there is quite a movement now which has emerged in the last 10 years and it is growing. The fact that we had Usaia [Moli] and other young people standing at the last election was great.

Given the boon in youth leadership examples in Fiji in such a short period, it will be interesting to see whether this trend continues. It also suggests that such an increase may be possible in other Pacific locations with fewer such examples, including Solomon Islands.

Cultures of silence

The restricted nature of youth participation and the flow-on effects this has on civic engagement and critical thinking processes hint at greater suppression of full participation in Oceanic societies. The strictly hierarchical nature of these societies makes the overt questioning of authority figures taboo. Woo and Corea (2009: 14) refer to this culturally encoded restraint of criticism as a 'culture of silence' that is evident throughout the region. Benjamin Afuga is a Solomon Islands civil society activist who helped to create and moderate a Facebook page, 'Forum Solomon Islands International' (FSII),[8] which provided a space for Solomon Islander citizens domestically and in the diaspora to engage in civics discussions. Benjamin contextualised the concept of a 'culture of silence' to me when explaining the role of FSII in opening spaces for citizen engagement in the political realms of civil society:

> Solomon Islanders have a culture of silence: even though things don't seem right, people won't talk, people won't protest, people won't use their democratic and constitutional rights to ask and to question. That is the biggest problem we have in this country and I think it is one of the stumbling blocks to development in this country. We think if leaders say something, you don't question it. If you want to question it, we go and sit under the mango tree or under the coconut tree and question, 'Why is John doing this?' We cannot face people and ask them. We cannot go to the media and ask them to tell them [the government] they are wrong. So, when FSII started doing that, people started thinking: this is a new thing, this is wrong, this is not respectable, this is not respecting the leaders.

This silence is held at individual and community levels and its impact is seen in the difficulties youth have in voicing the issues with which they are struggling. Through the cultured understanding that their opinions and voices are unimportant, they embody not only rational ignorance but also a stoic muteness. Rosie Catherine, of Fiji, explained to me:

---

8   FSII is discussed in a case study in Chapter Six.

> Because of the way we were brought up, if you are not given the
> opportunities to speak, that continues and when it comes to talking
> about things that really matter ... you don't feel like you can.

Compounding this problem in Fiji in recent decades has been the political
climate of coups, media censorship and restrictions on citizen political
engagement. Discussion of political issues was severely suppressed
between the most recent coup d'état, in 2006, and the 2014 election.
I experienced this first hand before the 2014 election when friends and
colleagues would actively disengage from conversations if issues of politics
were raised. This occurred to such an extent that I distinctly remember
the two people who would discuss political matters with me: one was an
activist known for outspoken criticism of the then regime and the other
only after becoming a good friend and developing a trusting relationship
with me.[9] Further enforcing the culture of silence during the 2006–14
period of military administration, the mainstream media was subjected
to significant measures of formal censorship, as well as self-censorship
(Perrottet and Robie 2011). The imposition of government censors in
newsrooms famously led to the *Fiji Times* redacting whole sections of the
daily newspaper where a censored story was to run and replacing them
with the text, 'The stories on this page could not be published due to
Government restrictions' (cited in Hayward-Jones 2012).

This censorship was extended to the public sphere through the Public
Emergency Regulations decree that was in place between April 2009
and January 2012. The decree limited the ability of citizens to meet in
groups, allowing police and local district officers to 'prohibit absolutely
or place conditions on "any procession, meeting or assembly in any place,
or building whether public or private" unless a permit has been granted'
(Bhim 2011: 9; see also Vakaoti 2017: 701). The justification for such
restrictions was, in the words of Bhim (2011: 4), the assumption by the
government of the time that 'a state of emergency exists in the country
because elements planning activities to destabilise the government
may exist'.

As with other forms of marginalisation, the stifling of criticism creates
perfect conditions for the internalised repression of critical thinking
development in the individual. Mereia Carling views the lack of revolt

---

9   Leading up to and following the 2014 election, I have noticed a marked shift in people's
willingness to discuss political matters, including commentary published alongside identifying details
in online spaces, such as social media.

against the coup regime, particularly after coup leader Frank Bainimarama was democratically elected as prime minister in 2014, as reflecting the feebleness of opposition to power, which is socialised into most Fijians, not only young people:

> It is amazing that we have had a dictatorship in Fiji that has told people what to do and pretty much the whole nation is happy with that. I think that is a symptom of this way we are brought up. People say, 'He's a man that knows what to do', 'He's a leader'. Whether it's right or wrong, it's a leader telling us what to do and we'll go and do it. I once spoke to my housekeeper about, 'Why do church ministers have to scream and shout at their congregation?', because to me that's abusive and it makes me want to run away and she said, 'We need it. Fijians need it. We need to be told what to do.' Maybe that is a cultural thing that I just don't understand. That's how I think it affects people and nations, that we can then be happy with dictatorships.

This criticism indicates that the cultures of silence evident in Oceania are more widespread than simply youth communities. As has already been mentioned, the role of hierarchy in Pacific societies and how it shapes roles and relationships for and between citizens are ever-present. Though young people are among the most marginalised in terms of participation and voicing opinions, there is evidence that these silences can be employed in other circumstances over larger groups of people, as argued by Mereia.

Deep and deliberative democracy

Despite the structural minimisation of youth and other groups being normalised in contemporary times, Pacific societies are reported to have had a long and rich history of democratic practices before colonisation. Differing from modern forms of liberal democracy based on citizen consultation, formulation of policy platforms and legitimisation through voting, these practices more closely resembled systems of deliberative democracy. As defined by political philosopher Joshua Cohen:

> The notion of a deliberative democracy is rooted in the intuitive ideal of a democratic association in which the justification of the terms and conditions of association proceeds through public argument and reasoning among equal citizens. (1997: 72)

In short, deliberative democracy encompasses methods that seek the constructive feedback of the cohort of people affected by a decision, not power vested purely in a concentrated individual or group of decision-makers.

Traditional village practices in both Fiji and Solomon Islands appear to have upheld the concept of deliberative democracy for decades. Ravuvu wrote of this in relation to the need for Fijian leaders to justify their position in terms of the continued communal benefit to the village, stating that

> a person who is *veidokai*[10] does not impose without consultation any idea or action beyond his traditionally defined boundary of social expectation. He must concur with others who are going to be affected before he makes any public proposition. (Ravuvu 1983: 104; see also Quain 1948: 205)

Writing of Solomon Islands, missionary and amateur anthropologist Charles Elliott Fox contrasted the methods of customary decision-making, which combined aspects of centralised decision-making and deliberative democracy more explicitly with Western concepts of liberal democracy. He wrote:

> In each village, separated from the next, perhaps by language or dialect and perhaps at war with it, when some matter of importance to the village had to be decided all the people of the village met together and discussed it. All would say what they thought about it and all were listened to. The chief might give his opinion, but anyhow it was he at the end who gave the decision, and not a majority of the people in the British way. (Fox 1967: 74)

Both Ravuvu and Fox write of deliberative democratic processes that were inclusive of all those affected by the decisions. Whether the deliberative democratic methods employed in villages included women, youth and others or whether only men were considered to be affected and thus consulted is unclear. What is clear, however, is that such processes were much more consultative than the oppositional nature that marks the equivalent processes of liberal democracies (Ravuvu 1991: 87), even if final decisions were ultimately made by chiefs, as stated by Fox.

---

10   Literally 'respectful'—one of four qualities of *vakaturaga* (befitting a chief; also, behaviour befitting the presence of a chief). The others are *vakarokoroko* (deference), *vakarorogo* (attentive and complying) and *yalo malua* (humility) (Ravuvu 1983: 103).

Salote Kaimacuata spoke to me of how she has seen these approaches used less and less over time. She explained to me her fear that these customs and the skills to follow them may be lost:

> The old Pacific way was consensus-reaching. There was a lot of dialogue and politicking outside and inside and during side meetings. We don't know how that was done anymore because it wasn't passed on or trained.

The importance of an active civil society in fostering democracy is well documented in international development and public policy literature emanating from Europe and North America (for example, Diamond 2015; Fukuyama 2001; McLaverty 2002; Scholte 2002). Mirroring the traditional Pacific models of deliberative, participatory democracy, many social scientists see fault in the functioning of Western liberal democracies in recent decades and their turn away from consultative engagement with their constituencies (Armingeon and Guthmann 2013; Pharr et al. 2000; Putnam 1995). Genuinely participatory modes of governance are seen to create a truer sense of democracy, emboldened by the general populace's ownership and their continued engagement in decision-making processes (Gallagher 2008: 404; Putnam 1995; Regan 2003; ECOSOC 2007). As Western democracies move away from these models and citizens become more disconnected from the systems and structures of governance, however, they may feel a sense of 'democratic disarray', leading to a 'broad continuing erosion of civic engagement', as explained by social theorist Robert Putnam (1995: 77).

This critique of contemporary Western liberal democracies provides interesting fodder for analysis when transposed over the emerging establishment of democratic models across the Pacific and compared with traditional participatory democratic practices. As Mellor and Jabes note:

> In nearly all developing countries … Western/liberal democracy is a relatively new concept and practice; in the Pacific region, especially, the system is laid onto the base of a longstanding traditional culture whose values and institutions often seem at odds with it. (2004: 13)

Ravuvu writes of this phenomenon and its alien characteristics in the Fijian context when discussing how villagers were introduced to the workings of contested democratic representation, noting:

> Villagers could not understand the necessity for an opposition, it made no sense to them to actually pay people to work against the government and against their chosen leaders in parliament. (Ravuvu 1991: 87)

Similarly, Connell (2011: 131) notes of Pacific governance institutions: 'Democracy requires time, experimentation, new habits of tolerance, mutual commitment to giving and taking, everyday respect for difference, strange ideas of a "loyal opposition", etc.' Here an interesting paradox emerges where the introduction and propagation of democracy from outside forces may, in fact, have acted to weaken established democratic norms. Where once everyone affected by a decision had, at least theoretically, an opportunity to engage in the decision-making process, now citizens are constrained to expressing their views through discreet acts of civic engagement and parliamentary voting—itself limited to those of a certain age.

Comparing Fiji and Solomon Islands

Cultural conceptions of the extent to which young people are expected and allowed to participate as critical and active members of civil society are similar in both Fiji and Solomon Islands. Perhaps more so than in any other space, this is where the notion that young people are to be seen but not heard is most uniform. Youth in both countries are unlikely to be provided access to decision-making processes and, in turn, be recognised for their leadership capabilities.

It was notable that across urban, peri-urban and rural communities in both countries, examples of youth leadership could not be identified without significant assistance. It appears that the settings are few and far between in each country where young people's leadership potential is viewed as a possibility for the present rather than a promise for the future.

Conclusion

Cultures that exclude young people from decision-making and holding authority to account are not unique to Oceania. Indeed, the consolidation of power by adults has been identified as common across the globe. Two notable differences in how this impacts Fijian and Solomon Islander societies and those beyond the Pacific bear remarking on, though. First, the permeation of youth minimisation through formal structures, such as education, and informal structures, such as village-level everyday civil society, renders deeper and more perpetuating the minimising effects on youth engagement. A strong argument can be made that this minimisation is furthered due to more widespread repression of criticism of authority, whether because of limits on democracy or through cultural norms that discourage open condemnation. Second, the representation of this minimisation as reflecting long-held traditional power systems, marked by chiefly and big-man systems, overlooks histories of deliberative democratic practices.

It should be no surprise that identifying examples of youth leaders proved such a difficult task across all the engaged communities. After all, youth is seen as a disqualifying factor for someone to be considered a leader and even if individuals overcome this barrier, once they become a leader, they are no longer culturally considered a youth.

Young people in Fiji and Solomon Islands should not be painted merely as passive observers to either their communities or their own lives. To begin with, recognition must be given to the myriad ways they positively contribute to their communities, cultures and countries through their engagements in everyday civil society. In no region of the world are all citizens expected to be activists, advocates or agitators and this should be no different for Pacific youth. Further, the rich histories of deliberative democracy that exist in Fiji and Solomon Islands, while apparently diminished, still offer a guide to engaging youth participation more deeply. The biggest threat to the ongoing engagement of Fijian and Solomon Islander youth in critical civil society appears to be twofold: the assumption that youth will learn how to become leaders through passive observation, and the denial of their engagement in decision-making spaces where such observations of leadership can be made.

5

Emerging youth activists

The older generation are so disconnected from young people … They are the ones who are responsible for training them and teaching the values that they need to actually succeed in life and they are not doing that. They treat them as less.

— Sandra Bartlett, Solomon Islands

The structures restricting Pacific youth from engaging with their communities critically as full and active citizens are multiple and complex. Contemporary social expectations of deference to leadership—hybridised from the traditional forms of reverence previously discussed—create a foundation for the marginalisation of young people's engagement across much of civil society. As youth development worker Sandra Bartlett notes, this is compounded by adults' attitudes that problematise youth without reflecting on their own responsibilities to be mentors.

These, of course, are not the only structural barriers to young people's full engagement as active citizens. Additionally, young people face societal notions that their role is to be passive observers, doing the bidding of family and community, and there is a lack of role models exhibiting active and positive youth leadership. At an institutional level, their minimisation is reinforced through the propagation of systems and structures that should be designed to assist their active citizenship, critical thinking and self-actualisation—namely, formal education and employment—and a lack of recourse to decision-makers regarding the ineffectiveness of these social and economic pillars. The forms and means of marginalisation of youth engagement and personal development vary in relation to demographic factors and are compounded by other factors such as gender, ethnicity, sexual orientation, and physical and intellectual ability.

Despite recent iterations of *kastom* that have normalised youth marginalisation, there is a small but growing recognition that providing opportunities for young people to develop their skills is required not only as a safeguard against antisocial behaviours and civil unrest—as per conventional readings of the youth bulge theory (Sukarieh and Tannock 2017; Urdal 2006)—but also to create and sustain positive developmental futures for the Great Ocean States of the Pacific. This is particularly true in institutional settings that address youth development issues directly or indirectly.

This chapter analyses examples of how young people in Fiji and Solomon Islands are engaging in emerging spaces of civic discourse despite the formal and informal structures that act to exclude them, including social understandings that it is the position of youth to be passive citizens as they exist as leaders-in-waiting. The chapter concludes by reflecting on the current state of youth engagement in civil society in Oceania. I note areas where young people are staking their claim as active citizens and how they may be better engaged by governments, development organisations and others. Looking at overtly political civil society activity as well as more everyday subtleties, I note the nature of Pacific civil society is that, while an increasing number of youths are engaging as active agents of change, the majority remains somewhat marginalised by cultural norms.

Young people and critical civic engagement

Several of my informants discussed with me not just how young people are discouraged from engaging critically in civil society, but also their capacity to positively engage if allowed opportunities. Luisa Senibulu, who has run anticorruption workshops with young people from across the region, said:

> Youth have a lot to contribute. It is often said that they are the leaders of tomorrow. They have a lot of capacity. They have a lot of knowledge that we don't really utilise.

Similarly, former chair of Fiji's National Youth Council, Usaia Moli, stated: 'If you're going to plan for the future, then it is only right that you include those that are going to be there, and that is the young people.' These sentiments were shared by Mereia Carling, who has researched youth citizenship in Fiji and is the primary author of the current *Pacific Youth Development Framework*—the guiding document for youth policymaking and benchmarking for Pacific governments. She said:

> We are never going to solve the problems that we want to solve by ignoring what young people think and not involving them. We are creating problems when we don't involve young people.

Beyond this, some young people continue to demonstrate their willingness to be leaders of their communities. This is particularly evident in responses to issues that have social as well as economic consequences. On issues of climate change and civil rights, youths are the ones making themselves experts and demanding that their voices be heard. No two examples better display this than the work of 350 Pacific in relation to climate change and Roshika Deo's 'Be the Change' political campaign of 2014, which are discussed in this chapter as case studies. These examples support political scientist Patrick Kaiku's (2017: 7) criticism of the application of the youth bulge theory in Melanesian societies: '[W]here the youth bulge discourse generally depicts young people as impulsively violent and conflict-prone, it disregards youth-led initiatives that are worth knowing and supporting.' Notably, in each of these cases, the youth involved created the space for their engagement in areas where deficits existed that traditional ideas of leadership had not filled and reinforced: climate change and social justice–led politics.

The active and open participation of increasing numbers of Pacific youth in civil society reflect a growing sense of both optimism for change and despair at the status quo. Though their numbers remain small, their influence is growing. This shift cannot be attributed to a singular cause. A combination of access to information, a growing network of youth engaged in critical civil society, political disenfranchisement and a renewed focus on democracy throughout the region also appear to be playing a part.

Access to information has long been recognised as important to shaping individual and collective thought patterns. From Alexis de Tocqueville's (1947) assertion in 1835 that the strength of democracy in the United States was largely a result of a free and informative media, through to the impact of television on the civil rights movements globally in the mid-twentieth century (Klarman 1994: 11; Winter and Eyal 1981), the flow of information has shaped politics and political engagement. As critical race and gender activist and author Bell Hooks writes: 'Watching television in the fifties and sixties, and listening to adult conversation, was one of the primary ways young black folks learned about race politics' (cited in Torres 2003: 2). It also appears that the increasing reach of internet communications and particularly social media is expanding the scope of youth knowledge and engagement in civic discourse (Tarai 2015). Sionlelei Mario is a civil society activist from Fiji who has worked on civics education programs. She explained to me how social media is opening channels of dialogue across the citizen spectrum of Fiji:

> Social media has a lot of groups that are discussing stuff. Policy people are having discussions, youth are having discussions and then there are others who have gone past their time and they're still talking.

Facilitator of Forum Solomon Islands International (FSII), Benjamin Afuga, sees the power of social media to communicate public sentiment to leaders and agitate for social change: 'We believe that people's views on Facebook can be a useful tool to bring issues across to our leaders and others who might have an answer to these things.'

Political disenfranchisement appears to be increasing youth civic engagement. Multiple interviewees spoke of political processes that discriminate against marginalised communities and push the concerns of youth to the side as motivating their own engagement. Jope Tarai expressed his frustration that '[t]he current power structures that we have in Fiji are pro-elite, anti-youth, anti-poor. Not them personally, but the way the parliament is structured.' Such an assertion is echoed by Honiara Youth Council President Harry Olikwailafa, who told me: 'We have a lot of good policies but the political will behind those policies [is lacking]. Sometimes you can see the political interference at [the] administrative level.'

This reflects Daniel Evans's (2019: 85) assertion of the lack of political will behind youth policies in Solomon Islands: 'Despite the steady stream of [youth] policies ... youth-related objectives have more often than not been left unrealised.' Similarly, findings from a study of seven youth communities across Central, North and South America by sociologists Jessica Taft and Hava Gordon (2011, 2013) identified frustration with political systems as a driver of youth civic engagement. Taft and Gordon (2013: 98) even suggest that youth engagement in activist civil society demonstrates that 'these youth are deeply committed to meaningful democracy and participation'. Rather than embodying identities focused on individual ambition and achievement—and shaped by forces of modernisation including international development discourses of capabilities and empowerment (Cornwall and Brock 2005; Kleine 2010; Makuwira 2018)—a number of Pacific youths are finding ways to engage in their societies to benefit what they perceive to be the common good.

This commitment to democratic engagement with civil society was a recurrent theme in interviews I held with young civic activists. Young people engaged in critical civil society in Solomon Islands saw it as their duty to promote the interests of youth and to hold government to account for transgressions and corruption. John Firibo, of Solomon Islands, stated:

> In the schools, especially when it comes to history, we talk a lot about the politicians and there is a growing tension between us and the politicians. Many of us are trying to stamp out corruption in a way that they will see us, they will hear us and maybe make change.

In Fiji, this sense of frustration among youth interviewees with their marginalisation from civic and political practices was even more palpable— due at least partially to the fact that 2014 had seen those aged under 30 voting for the first time in the eight years since the beginning of military rule. The 'coup babies', as they are known (Vakaoti 2014: 5), appeared to revel in the opportunity to finally exercise their democratic rights and openly discuss their concerns with friends, family and the public more generally. Sionlelei Mario explained this enthusiasm:

> I'm in my twenties and most of my friends are around that age group and, for most of us, it was our first time to vote. We thought we had some obligation since we were sensitised in that area of national development and youth roles [as civically engaged young people]. We needed to get involved with other young people who are just coming out of their late teens to discuss what we think your role is, what your level of interest is in the general elections and what does it mean as a young person to actually tick that box [on the ballot paper].

This should not be taken as a generalisation of youth approaches to engaging with governance structures. Indeed, the youth activists I interviewed were notable precisely for the depth of critical engagement they have with political agents and structures in comparison with their peers.

Case study: Be the Change

Before the 2014 elections in Fiji, Roshika Deo decided to run for parliament. With a professional background in law and international development, as well as a long history of social justice activism, Roshika sought to use the campaign process to highlight inequities she saw in her home country, providing a voice for youth and women.

Roshika built a small support team and consulted with established parties about standing for them, before choosing to run as an independent. As she explained:

> In the beginning, we went to two political parties. We sat in meetings, spoke to people and we realised that they were very much conformist and there were rigid hierarchies. I realised that if I went in that party, I would only be perpetuating the same systems that are there by being part of it. I wouldn't be doing anything new. Nothing would change.

When determining to run as an independent, however, Roshika decided to acknowledge the significant support network she was building and labelled her campaign 'Be the Change'.

Running on a social activist platform, Roshika and Be the Change challenged social and political orthodoxy not only by openly discussing issues such as abortion, domestic violence and same-sex marriage, but also by taking progressive positions on each of these issues, which contrasted with the conservative stances of the major parties. Her campaign shaped much of the public narrative of the election by pushing these boundaries. She told me:

> Fiji Sun [newspaper] was running an opinion article, so the candidates could write opinions and submit. Parties could write, so I said, 'Be the Change is like a party. It's functioning like a party, so let's write.' Then I started getting other young people to write together with me. When we wrote about mental health issues, the next two or three days after, we noticed the media had started asking all the candidates about mental health. Once, when we wrote about LGBTIQ rights, on [television station] Fiji One, they asked all the candidates about same-sex marriage.

Of the campaign's influence, Roshika said:

> We are very proud of our achievements. We raised a lot of issues that
> no-one else was talking about: things around LGBTIQ rights—
> no-one used to talk about it, so as soon as we started talking about,
> the media started talking about it. Violence against women: no-
> one talked about violence against women as comprehensively as
> we did. Also demilitarisation—people did talk about militarisation
> but we talked about it in terms of the impact on young people and
> women, moving away from generic discussions on militarisation.
> It was a bit more abstract, so we started contextualising it.

The campaign not only influenced media reporting and forced other
candidates to discuss uncomfortable topics, it also opened Roshika up to
significant criticism across the community, which regularly went beyond
analysis of her political positions. She was criticised because of her gender,
religion and culture, among other things (Chattier 2016; Palet 2014).
She told me: 'They had a [picture of a] full-born dead baby that they
circulated all over Facebook, saying "Roshika Deo supports abortion."
Very aggressively and loudly, I got attacked in that space.'

The impact of such criticism did not silence Roshika, however. She
continued her campaign, narrowly falling short of being elected. Her
influence can be seen in her ability to attract more than 1,000 votes in
the general election and more than 14,000 likes on the Be the Change
Facebook page (Chattier 2016), and the ability of her campaign to
dictate much of the election's narrative. Demonstrating the capacity
for organised youth to influence civic discourse, Roshika highlighted to
me the motivation she took from some of the more distasteful forms of
criticism she received when she realised why it was occurring, stating:
'We're challenging the status quo.'

Developmental benefits of civic engagement and participation

As has already been discussed, many see a robust civil society having
significant benefits to ideals of democratic deepening. Political sociologist
Larry Diamond (1994: 8–9) suggests that full citizen participation
in decision-making processes goes beyond the promotion of deep
democracy, however, and results in holistic capacity strengthening. As the
most disadvantaged and marginalised, including young people, develop

a greater sense of social inclusion and participate more actively in their communities, the rest of the community is exposed to their knowledge, skills and experiences (Gaye and Diallo 1997: 10). Multiple respondents expressed this sentiment and discussed what they saw as a clear necessity for young people to be engaged in decision-making processes from both rights and sustainability perspectives. Mereia Carling stated:

> I love people's first experience of working with young people because they're always like, 'Gosh, the young people really have a lot to say and they really know about sustainable development', and they are shocked that they have a lot to contribute. There is this perception that they have nothing to say of value, and that exists everywhere [in the Pacific].

Confirming this theme, former member of Fiji's National Youth Council Elisha Bano urged:

> We just need to be believed in. We need to be given the spaces. We need the support. If we were given the mix of those three things, people would be surprised at how much we can achieve.

Harry Olikwailafa agreed and went further to state that youth representatives—from village youth groups through to national youth councils across the Pacific—need to be stronger in advocating their own legitimacy as leaders who should be included in decision-making processes regarding youth issues:

> If we stay outside of the decision-making table, outside the decision-making process, if we don't speak to our leaders, sometimes they will forget us. We need to come into the circle, involve provincial youth structures, so that when elected youth leaders talk to elected national leaders they will listen and they will understand that there are thousands of young people's voices behind them. When we talk to leaders, we can say to them, 'I'm a leader as well. I represent the young people and I know my facts and I am prepared to give recommendations.' And when you present yourself as a leader, they're less likely to overlook you because of the Melanesian big-man system.

Communal ownership of the direction of development and the building of civic capacity provide for the sustainability of development ideals. Reverting to more traditional modes of deliberative decision-making across Oceania provides the potential for historically marginalised groups, including youth and women, to not only contribute, but also feel a sense of ownership over future plans. A considerable strength of this ownership is that it can be seen as a safeguard against corruption (Pinkney 2003: 13). The social capital benefits of enabling participation promote further participation (Bryer 2010: 271) and expand the network of those whose critical opinions and knowledge can help shape visions of locally relevant and sustainable development.

Case study: 350 Pacific

350.org is a global grassroots social movement focused on combating human-induced climate change (350.org n.d.). The organisation has a diversified structure, with the main office in New York and satellite bodies throughout the globe, representing cities, countries and regions. Most of its members are volunteers who engage in advocacy campaigns that can be locally led or coordinated through a regional office.

350 Pacific is the arm of the organisation representing the region incorporating Australia, Aotearoa/New Zealand and the Pacific islands,[1] and has a permanent staff member based in each of Australia, Aotearoa/New Zealand and Fiji.[2] There are active 350 Pacific groups across 15 Pacific states. Though membership across the 350 global network is not restricted by age, the Pacific groups comprise almost exclusively people aged under 35 years. Their membership reflects their belief that as young people will most feel the effects of human-induced climate change, they should lead efforts to combat it.

The Pacific-based group, who identify as the 'Pacific Climate Warriors', have not let their age negatively impact on their engagement in advocacy and reform programs across and beyond the region. Rather than relying on recognised government, private-sector or civil society leaders to guide climate change advocacy and reform efforts, the members of 350 Pacific have insisted on having their voices heard by domestic, regional and international leaders and change-makers.

---

1   350 Pacific was created by a group of volunteers whose values aligned with the global 350.org movement, which developed into a formal partnership. Its volunteers are recruited through member networks.

2   At the time of fieldwork in 2015. The structure of the organisation has evolved multiple times since and is likely to continue to do so.

The traditional methods of advocacy in which they have engaged include direct lobbying of decision-makers and facilitating protests (350 Pacific n.d.). Overcoming some of the barriers related to geography and timeliness, 350 Pacific has engaged in electronic campaigns to contact local representatives, as well as sharing images and videos of their daily climate-affected realities with the global community (Carter 2015: 216).

To register an impact that is both current and sustainable, 350 Pacific has recognised that the ideas of leadership held by their communities are vital to influencing change, but instead of ceding authority to those seen as leaders purely because of their age, they have instead questioned what leadership looks like. Fenton Lutunatabua, 350 Pacific's Fiji-based communications coordinator, explains that the organisation seeks to embed a sense of ownership and leadership in the communities with which it works by responding to their needs 'in ways that make sense to them so they can take full ownership of and encourage leadership from the ground up'.

Beyond this, 350 Pacific actively targets young Pacific people whom it sees as agents of change to become members and lead their home-country initiatives. Regional representatives include members of the Pacific Youth Council and Commonwealth Youth Council and senior staff from Pacific-based development organisation offices. Fenton claims of their worth to the movement:

> These people are well connected. They're leaders in their own right. Really, they're doing the climate movement favours. Do we take claim to developing them? No. They have built their own reputations, they have networked so well, they have empowered so many people. It is us just connecting with them and trying to look at ways in which we can take their experience with the justice movements that they're in and apply that to the climate justice movement.

These youth leaders have been influential in securing positions in regional decision-making processes, such as the drafting of the current *Pacific Youth Development Framework*.

The most disruptive 350 Pacific campaign took place outside the Pacific islands and focused on the damage being done to the planet by the region's neighbour Australia. In 2014, 30 young Pacific people blockaded Newcastle Harbour—home to the largest coal port in the world—

on traditional canoes, with scores of non-Pacific people joining in support, stopping all 10 ships scheduled to pass through that day (Packard 2014). The success of this action led to a second 350.org blockade in 2016 (Connell et al. 2016). Explaining the action, Fenton states the purpose was

> to send a very clear message to the fossil fuel industry saying that, as Pacific islanders, we will do what it takes to stand up for our Pacific and show the world that, if they continue to expand the fossil fuel industry, that's literally exporting destruction to the Pacific.

Facilitating youth participation

The campaigns and structures of 350 Pacific and Be the Change illustrate how some Pacific youth are identifying gaps in how their leaders are addressing issues of social justice. Where such deficits exist, young people are acting decisively to fill these gaps as advocates and activists. Further, they are proving they have the talent to do so in ways that are meaningful and have impact. Providing opportunities for young people to be positively engaged in civil society opens the prospect for a far greater number of youths to affect the futures of their communities, countries and regions for positive developmental change. The case studies also document the ability of a cohort of young people to create their own opportunities for civic engagement when none is provided to them. These case studies only highlight the positive, prosocial civic engagement Pacific youth create in a vacuum of opportunities, but potential also exists for more antisocial responses, as touched on in Chapter Three.

As has been discussed, social hierarchies inhibit youth participation through both perceived and actual diminishment of the involvement of those towards the bottom of the hierarchies. To circumvent this issue, one mooted technique is to allow Pacific youth to engage in decision-making processes in small groups rather than individually, which lessens the weight of perceived expectations of their behaviour and reflects their preferred method of problem-solving. When researching the democratic participation practices of youth in Fiji, Vakaoti (2014) supplied a questionnaire to participants across four rural and urban locations to understand their knowledge, attitudes and practices. He found:

> When asked who they would turn to [to] address an issue they felt strongly about, the majority (64%) of young questionnaire respondents preferred addressing issues as part of a group compared to 18% who prefer to address issues individually. (Vakaoti 2014: 20)

Too often, appropriate modes of participation are determined through an adult-centric lens. Parents and elders minimise youth participation daily and yet expect young people to be able to engage in systems designed for and by adults when the adults believe that engagement is necessary or beneficial. Again, Vakaoti's study provides valuable insight into how freely youth feel they can engage as valued contributors:

> Nuclear families, schools and social media were identified as popular spaces where young people could express their opinion. Adult spaces like community and church meetings were the least comfortable spaces for young people. (Vakaoti 2014: 24)

The mention of online platforms as spaces for youth civic engagement supports my own observations and data drawn from informants. Thus, it appears appropriate that when desiring youth engagement and participation, thought is put into where, when and how young people will feel most comfortable and valued to share their knowledge and opinions.

Mereia Carling suggests that where youth input is required in more structured ways, guided participation is favoured. Rather than recruiting young people to be involved in non-specific tasks or tasks for which the parameters are unfamiliar, they should be guided in areas where the facilitators are looking for their perspective and informed of how it will be beneficial. Mereia recounted a recent experience regarding a consultation with female youths to highlight the failings of engagement when participation is invited but not guided:

> The leader of [name of organisation] sent out our strategy to the women and said, 'Please comment', and I feel like that is really pointless. We might get one or two comments from the ones that always comment. Really what we need to say is to extract out of that strategic plan: 'This is the thing that I want you to comment on. This question and what do you think about that?' We need to do that sort of translation because just sending a 30-page document out is not consultation. You need that facilitation process to happen.

Guiding youth participation and attempting to engage young people in spaces in which they are comfortable contributing also lessen the likelihood of their participation feeling tokenistic. This was a significant issue raised by many of my interviewees and was attributed to a combination of dismissive attitudes towards young people's views, maintenance of status quo processes and an inability to convert well-intentioned consultation to a meaningful response. Such remarks were made by youths, youth advocates and bureaucrats alike. Jai Narayan, Director of Secondary Education in Fiji, admitted to the difficulties of overcoming the established mental models of practice for policymakers: 'We, as teachers and educators, have our own mindset because we have been brought up in a different age and setup.'

This problem was also noted by Kris Prasad, LGBTIQ+ activist from Fiji, who expressed frustration at the lack of commitment to ideals of youth participation. Kris described how spaces are created for youth engagement but rarely result in youth voices being valued and used to inform decision-making processes:

> In terms of having a national space, they'll bring youths together and make them come with their issues or speak about their issues and they'll listen, but it doesn't trickle down. 'Okay, you've listened to us, you have this report but what are you actually doing?' Because, at the end of the day, it just comes down to a senior person at the Ministry of Youth who signs off on the report and that's it. They're good at listening, but they're not good at implementing or finding strategies on how we can work around the issues that these youths have raised.

Similarly, Sionlelei Mario expressed frustration with current attempts at participatory practice in Fiji. Viewing many such practices as tokenistic, she explained that often what is considered participatory by adults in positions of authority instead reinforces power imbalances. One way this is done is by limiting participation to observation, which is anathema to true participatory ideals (Hart 1992). Sionlelei stated: 'That's something I think young people should be doing: observe and action, not just observe and have someone come and tell you what to do.'

My own experiences working with and researching youth, prior to and during this study, confirm the truth in these claims and approaches. The most valuable tool I have found in sourcing information from youth is to create an environment of trust. In the absence of time to create a stable dynamic of trust with individual young people, allowing them to interact with peers with whom they have already created trust networks allows the freedom to express ideas, debate approaches and feel equally comfortable agreeing or disagreeing with each other. Further, I have found it vital when conducting this research not only to be upfront about the limitations of what the study can materially offer my research participants, but also to conclude each interview by asking what the interviewee would like to see occur as a result of the research and their individual engagement. It was reflected to me on multiple occasions throughout my fieldwork that this was a unique experience for many interviewees and they appreciated the attempt to ensure each party was aware of the motivations for the other's involvement and what reasonable outcomes could be expected.

The engagement of youth through mediums who value their full participation and with whom they are comfortable would require a rebalancing of typical understandings of the social roles of youth that complement *kastom* but also reflect contemporary social and economic realities. As Vakaoti (2012: 11) writes: 'This is the enduring challenge for young people's participation in Fiji: how to successfully negotiate the past and the present?' Against the sociocentric backdrop of traditional communities and the increasing global influence of materialism and individualism, their challenge is to negotiate change in the roles they play in society and in the roles their societies play in the global environment. McMurray summarises this difficulty:

> Especially difficult for young people is that many of the values and practices of a modern society are in direct conflict with those of their traditional societies. Traditional societies tend to resist change and questioning of their identity, whereas modern society promotes freedom and democracy, new ideas, discussion and debate. (2006: 5)

Overcoming hierarchical hindrances to youth participation requires more than soliciting information from young people regarding issues important to adults or organisations they represent. For long-term, meaningful participation of young people, youth need to be empowered to appreciate that their contributions are valuable and people in decision-making positions need to truly recognise that value. A key tenet of international development approaches since the 1980s—such as alternative development, capabilities and adaptive approaches—has been an understanding that individuals are the experts on their own situation. In the words of Berner and Phillips (2003: 19), this is 'documented by their very survival'.

This understanding evolved through post-development scholars and practitioners in the Global South who sought to displace the belief that Western knowledge was superior to all others (for example, Escobar 1992, 2000; Esteva and Prakash 1998). Ideas about who is 'expert' enough to have their opinions considered have provided insight into the power with which knowledge is seen to be held, both by governing powers (Brownhill 2009: 360) and from Western centres of thought, such as academia and bilateral aid agencies (Mahiri 1998). Reversing this trend is not simple. It requires commitment by experts, policymakers and young people alike to be open to the possibilities of youth engagement leading to positive outcomes. Examples such as those from Be the Change and 350 Pacific demonstrate that such outcomes are possible.

Comparing Fiji and Solomon Islands

The differences in critical civil society spaces within and between Fiji and Solomon Islands are considerable. First, it must be noted that if one is seeking activists and agitators in either country, their respective capitals should be the first port of call. Of course, this is not necessarily significantly different to how critical civil society is exhibited throughout most of the world.

Between the two countries, the visibility and scope of critical civil society are appreciably larger in Suva than in Honiara. Whether as a result of Suva being a regional hub, exhibiting greater cultural diversity or some other factor, it is hard not to be struck by how active and present activism and activists are in Fiji's capital. With minimal effort, one can find themselves at a social justice demonstration or a performing arts event free of the ominous badging of a local diplomatic mission or multilateral agency. In Honiara, these spaces are harder to find. Building relationships and a reputation opens doors, but they are less numerous outside displays of 'traditional' culture or through 'development' sponsorship. Bearing this in mind, it is not surprising that the two most obvious examples of youth-led organisations creating space to demonstrate their civic engagement and leadership, Be the Change and 350 Pacific, both had their base in Suva.

Even within Suva, though, the numbers of engaged civil society activists and allies remain small. A core cohort can be found at the same events, supporting women's rights one evening and spoken-word poetry the next, while the majority of the city's inhabitants go about their daily lives unaware and/or without care. I have come to know many of the people of Suva's critical civil society space as much through repeated exposure as through intentional efforts to cultivate personal and professional relationships. In fact, several of my interviews strayed at times into recalling shared experiences at previous events, generally before personal connection had been made between me and my informant.

This space is expanding, though. New waves of university students from across the region and the globe are sharing their experiences of what the future could and should look like. The impact of the short-term migrant[3] diplomatic and development communities has a clear influence, too, in influencing 'progressive' debates in Fiji's capital. Undoubtedly, this is a contributing factor in the greater and more visible number of active citizens in Fiji forcing their way into decision-making spaces on causes of social justice. Similarly, social media is having a significant impact in opening spaces for civic discourse in Fiji, but also in Solomon Islands, as demonstrated by FSII. The long-term impacts of such spaces opening will provide fodder for fascinating research into the future.

Conclusion

Despite cultural conventions discouraging their active participation in critical civil society, many young Pacific peoples are regularly finding new ways to engage in civic discourse. In particular, they are locating ways and means of engagement with critical discourse in relation to issues where they are yet to have their involvement and perspective minimised. Each of the organisational case studies presented in this chapter has found one or more ways to forge a path into public discourse. For Be the Change, it was in raising social issues in public discussions during the 2014 Fijian election campaign that had been considered taboo for the major parties to broach. For 350 Pacific, it has been in the ownership and representation

---

3   They are often referred to as 'expatriates'; I avoid this term as it connotes a dichotomous worthiness attached to the professional classes of typically Anglophone countries in comparison with less-worthy economic migrants moving from less to more developed states.

of Oceanic indigeneity to a global audience. The influence of information and communication technology (ICT) cannot be overlooked in each of these examples and is discussed further in the next chapter.

It must also be noted that the youths engaging in public discourse are the exception rather than the norm. The structural minimisation of young Pacific peoples discourages their active citizenship beyond prescribed roles that do not extend to participation in decision-making processes. As I have argued, this risks creating a form of rational ignorance, where their dismissal from civic engagement results in a disinclination to future deep engagement.

With numerous young people currently making their voices heard in various ways—such as those discussed in the case studies—it will be interesting to see how young leaders are framed, understood and acknowledged moving forward. It remains to be seen whether these examples will turn out to be outliers or whether their actions are emblematic of a trend of increasing civic engagement by Pacific youth. Viewing how the people in each of these examples have navigated their way into public discourse by identifying gaps where their participation has not already been denied suggests that even if these groups are to close themselves off to newcomers, future generations of young people will continue to find new means by which to insert themselves into civic discourse and public consciousness.

6

Navigating tradition and modernity

> You are divided into two. One half of you is modern Fijian, but
> the other half is still very much the traditional, laidback person.
>
> — Luisa Senibulu, Fiji

Within Pacific societies, a tension remains between perceptions of what
is 'traditional', what is 'modern' and how each influences the formal
and informal structures of society, politics and culture. Being iTaukei,
living in Fiji and working in a multilateral development agency, Luisa
Senibulu reported to me being acutely aware of how concepts of tradition
and modernity impact on her and influence her differently in the
multiple social roles she inhabits. Expanding beyond the individual to
the societal, Mecartney and Connell (2017: 57) write: 'Modernisation
and globalisation have brought fundamental changes to Pacific societies,
affecting values, goals and social norms.' While friction in response to
processes of cultural adaptation to foreign influences is not new, the pace
of change experienced in the Pacific in relation to factors such as ICT,
trade and travel makes the current challenge to cultural identity appear
more urgent. Writing of strategies to manage the benefits and pitfalls of
globalisation on an outer island of Vanuatu, Katherine Wilson identifies
the impact of modernisation on the Great Ocean States of the Pacific,
noting that

> the combined forces of national independence, globalisation and
> the penetration of the free market economy have all contributed
> to changes in aspirations in the Pacific, even on the outer islands.
> (2013: 246)

Meanwhile, Jayaweera and Morioka (2008: 10), in a World Bank report on youth participation, see the quickening pace of change as a challenge for Pacific communities, writing that 'most Pacific societies are experiencing conflict between traditional and modern ways of living and thinking. They struggle to find ways to accommodate the pressures of globalization.' For Mellor and Jabes (2004: 13, 16), in a report on Pacific governance for the Asian Development Bank, the conflict between tradition and modernity is identifiable in the ways modern states extol the virtues of individual merit, equal access to opportunity and participation in contrast to traditional Pacific sociocentric structures and big-man and chief–led hierarchies.

Such social flux is not new and need not be seen as a threat to cultural identity and practice. After all, all cultures are in a state of constant hybridity. As Zorn (2003a: 97) writes: 'Every society is changing all the time. The societies of the Pacific were always changing.' Good (2012: 293) notes for Tonga that even the popular usage of terms such as 'youth' to categorise groups of people 'has become a powerful index of global modernity', and the same can be said of other Pacific countries.

This chapter explores some of the ways in which 'traditional' identity is represented and challenged in Oceanic contexts and how young people negotiate pressures to maintain their cultural identity without forgoing the opportunities offered by globalisation and modernisation. The chapter first considers social attitudes towards youth, as well as youth attitudes to customary roles and rules. This is followed by a discussion of the real and perceived conflict between sociocentric and individualistic values. Investigating the opportunities created by exposure to global capital and ideas, a case study of how Solomon Islanders have used ICT to enhance civic engagement is introduced. This opens discussion about the potential for young people's further inclusion and participation as active citizens representing broad and multiple subsections of their societies. This chapter presents the argument that Pacific youth, through their navigation of indigenous and foreign influences on their livelihoods and beliefs, will largely be responsible for what future generations come to recognise as 'tradition'.

Attitudes to youth and tradition

Discussions of tradition versus modernity are considered somewhat outdated in most contemporary literature. The discourse has largely moved on to embrace ideas of hybridity (Garcia Canclini 1995; Rosaldo 1995), indigenisation (Jolly 1996; Sahlins 1999) and vernacularisation (Levitt and Merry 2009), which reflect on the ways indigenous peoples in Oceania and elsewhere adapt foreign influences to suit local needs and customs. It is important to note, though, that concepts of tradition continue to have great social and cultural currency in the Pacific. People in Fiji and Solomon Islands talk about tradition as being relevant to everyday functioning and decision-making processes. And, for many of those to whom I spoke, navigating 'traditional' and 'modern' spaces is an everyday consideration. Just as it is important to note how concepts and practices of culture and tradition change and evolve, so, too, must we not overlook the ways that such changes are conceptualised and practised by those who are navigating these spaces (see Teaiwa 2006: 75).

The perceived tension between concepts of tradition and concepts of modernity in relation to Pacific youth populations is most prominent in social attitudes about appropriate levels of youth agency and participation with elders in decision-making processes. While tensions between generations are common across cultures, the ability to resist elders and concepts of tradition is a site of particular tension in Oceanic communities. As discussed in previous chapters, the role of youth in their communities is understood to be passive and deferential. To question authority is to be insubordinate and disrespectful.

Mereia Carling provided me with insight into how these mindsets play out in the Fijian setting. Partially raised and educated in Europe and having worked on Pacific youth issues for bilateral and multilateral development organisations, Mereia's cultural understandings straddle Western and Fijian contexts. She told me her parenting style reflects this, as she is attempting to instil in her children respect for tradition as well as nurturing individual curiosity. The benefits of this approach to parenting are not self-evident to some members of her Fijian family:

> My relatives look at me and think that I let my child just talk and ask questions. They might call them *siosio*—which means 'cheeky'—because they are always asking questions and they're confident. All my kids are confident and they always ask questions

and that's what we've always encouraged and given them space to ask questions. It is not about them being cheeky. Rather, these are the difficulties of nurturing a child that has the freedom to speak and has the confidence, knowing that they will never get hurt for speaking.

The conflicting ideals of traditional social protocols emphasising deference to elders and contemporary global values that promote individual endeavour and achievement are further complicated by formal institutions that endorse economic growth as the primary aim of development. This is no doubt strongly influenced not only by the resources bestowed on Pacific societies by international development organisations, but also by the use of seemingly neutral terms such as 'empowerment', 'rights' and 'participation', which in fact carry very Eurocentric connotations (Cornwall 2007; Cornwall and Brock 2005; Good 2012; Makuwira 2018). Development discourse perpetuates narratives that equate development with economic growth and the replication of Western-style structures of governance and civil society (Cornwall and Brock 2005: 1055, 1057; Kleine 2010: 675).[1] For Pacific youth, this begins with formal education systems that, despite persistent problems of quality and resourcing, increasingly attempt to encourage individual identity and awareness of global movements and cultures. McMurray spoke of this tension in a seminar hosted by UNICEF Pacific regarding how to facilitate the active participation of Pacific children and young people:

> The Pacific way of learning is by passive observation, whereas modern education systems promote active engagement and research. Passivity and unquestioning respect for leadership bring acceptance in a traditional Pacific society, whereas evaluation and initiative are the keys to success in a modern environment. (McMurray 2006: 5)

This creates a sense of cultural and identity confusion for some people. While young people may be taught to question and critique in school,[2] they are admonished for doing the same in the home environment. As Carling stated in her master's thesis on youth citizenship in Fiji:

---

1   Others, such as Jolly (1996: 184), counter that human rights are not simply the 'pious projections of wealthy western nations', and that even in Western states, their influence and pre-eminence have primarily been driven by women and other marginalised groups.

2   Though this is not uniform across educational settings, as discussed in Chapter Three.

For children and young people brought up in Fijian traditional settings, negotiating the conflicting values between tradition and those espoused by educational institutions presents [a] great challenge for them, affecting the development of a clear identity that can rationalise both traditional and educational settings. (2009: 107)

The tensions between 'traditional' and 'modern' modes of living are ever present as the lure of financial reward and freedom in urban centres provides an incentive for Pacific peoples to remove themselves from their lower-status positions within their home communities (McGarry 2014). This is evident in the examples of the *masta liu* in Honiara and the case study of Pesa presented in Chapter Three, as well as the continuous streams of youth engaging in rural–urban migration (Carling 2009: 80; Keen and Barbara 2015: 1). These examples speak directly to the challenge of forming an individual identity that receives the benefits of development and yet maintains a strong sense of self through culture. This is the pressing paradox between Sen's (1999) concept of 'development as freedom', which holds that access to the material and institutional markers of development provides the freedom for individuals to achieve their potential, and Kleine's (2013) 'technologies of choice' hypothesis, which argues that exposure to technological and developmental advances may limit our ability to consciously reject or resist change.

Though the pace of social change is undoubtedly quickening— influenced by factors such as increased global trade and transnational communication—the challenges arising from this should not be seen as new. The societal and cultural pressures of maintaining identity through 'tradition' in light of ever-encroaching modernisation are well acknowledged in anthropological case studies from around the world.[3] What remains less remarked on, however, are the social attitudes towards youth and their roles in actively navigating these changes. Some interviewees spoke of their frustration at being expected to uphold traditional values and practices but without an appreciation from adults of the livelihood pressures they face. They argued that young people are not simply seen as a subservient subclass needing to bide their time before becoming the gatekeepers to tradition and culture, but they are also

---

3   See, for example, Haley and Wilcoxon (1997) on Chumash Native Americans; Jakimow (2012) on the impacts of international development in India; Sahlins (2005) and van Meijl (2001) on Oceania; and Wee (1996) on South-East Asian populations.

viewed as problematic and disrespectful if they do not conform to social expectations. Daniel Evans (2019: 82) notes that this framing has been applied to youth in Solomon Islands since their emergence in the national conversation in the 1960s. Development workers Mereani Rokotuibau from Fiji and Patrick Mesia from Solomon Islands told me that village youth need to earn the respect of adults through acts of community service. Without engaging in culturally approved forms of civic engagement, they will struggle to be respected and have their opinions considered.

Left unchallenged, these social attitudes to youth and the roles they play in their communities allow for their continued marginalisation. Echoing the sentiments of Mereani and Patrick, Sandra Bartlett, who manages the Youth@Work program in Solomon Islands, believes the best way to reverse these perceptions is for young people to be seen to contribute positively to their society. With reference to Youth@Work, she discussed the positive social effects the program has had in Honiara:

> The big success, the social change success, is that we've put youth development on people's minds. In Solomons, it was always, 'Youth are a problem', 'Youth are a time bomb', 'It's an issue, it's an issue …', but now they see that youth are doing things. They think about putting money into youth development and that's the great social change success we've had.

The role that *kastom*[4] plays in this understanding of youth as problematic is difficult to unpack. History is awash with declarations that each generation of young people is marked by decreasing moral worth—a sentiment that continues to this day (Protzko and Schooler 2019). Plato is credited with pronouncing in the fourth century BCE:

> What is happening to our young people? They disrespect their elders, they disobey their parents. They ignore the law. They riot in the streets, inflamed with wild notions. Their morals are decaying. What is to become of them? (Cited in Merchant 2013: 91)

It appears to be an informal role of youth populations globally to be criticised as representative of perpetual social decay, despite a lack of empirical evidence.

---

4   As noted in Chapter Two, while *kastom* as a term may not be applied universally across Oceania, it is taken here to reflect the socially understood constructs of everyday Pacific life, imposed not only by elders but by ancestors (see Goddard 2010).

These common negative perceptions of youth are related to the perceived potential for loss of status and identity in older age groups, as discussed in Chapter Four. West (2007: 129) describes how some adults are reluctant to allow young people to critically engage with them, as this is seen as undermining cultural norms and respect for elders. Andre Tipoki, of Solomon Islands, explained this fear with reference to local context: 'What concerns elders is having development and this influencing our culture. This is more based on culture being lost at the expense of these influences.'

Immediately following this statement, Andre discussed the need for Solomon Islanders to acknowledge the realities of social change and globalisation as drivers of this. Echoing concepts such as hybridity and indigenisation, Andre spoke of the need to balance traditional knowledge and beliefs when planning for the developmental futures of Solomon Islanders at local and national levels:

> In terms of addressing some of the issues that we are facing, if we want to adapt some of the strategies to use and improve our livelihood and standard of living and those things, I think we should look [at] how best we can work with that in a very local context.

Even when Pacific youth view some aspects of traditional ways of living and the institutions attached to them as repressive and outdated, this does not necessarily imply that young people do not respect or value tradition and *kastom* more generally. Instead, this is where the tension between the contemporary and what is perceived as traditional is perhaps most pronounced. Many Pacific youth hold a strong sense of cultural identity and are proud of many of the traditions of their peoples, but they still hope to engage in the economic and social freedoms that modernity offers (Fletcher et al. 2009: 25).

Culture as fixed

One of the more prevalent challenges to modern Pacific societies is the friction between the conservative ideals of traditional societies and the social and economic changes demanded by global markets and democratic processes. When societies resist social change as defying tradition, as asserted by McMurray (2006: 5), the connotation is that what is traditional—and, by extension, what is *kastom*—acts as a safeguard against change. This implies that tradition is and has always been fixed. Coordinator of the Pacific Youth Council Tarusila Bradburgh spoke to me of this challenge in relation to how young people from across the Pacific can fully engage with their communities as active citizens when established structures minimise their opportunities:

> How do we use what we see as barriers that are structures within our families and communities to help us be able to grow, develop and be part of decision-making? Otherwise, we get the same: culture is a barrier, the church is a barrier; our families, our parents, our elders [are barriers].

The perception that social change is a fundamental threat to cultural purity or that the values and practices that underpin tradition are antithetical to social change is intriguing. Notions of culture and tradition are constantly in flux, evolving and adapting to different social, political, economic and environmental realities—as Kanaka Maoli[5] scholar Emalani Case notes: 'Everything ancient was once new' (2021: 66). Rather than viewing culture and tradition as static, they are better understood as representing the most widely accepted narrative of how a community sees itself at a particular point in time, whether this is according to a shared creation of ideals or reflecting the will of those with power in that community. From an international development perspective, this underlies concepts of capabilities, as well as thinking and working politically, where the exercise of power, whether overt or covert, is most clearly demonstrated. In the words of development philosopher Martha Nussbaum (2003: 42): '[A]ny society's account of its most fundamental entitlements is always subject to supplementation (or deletion).'

The people of the Great Ocean States of the Pacific face a delicate balancing act trying to accommodate the positives of increased global interconnectedness, such as improved health care and livelihood opportunities, while maintaining cultural traditions and activities that contrast with such interconnectedness. For locals and foreigners alike, it can feel like the states of Oceania are straddling a divide, with one foot in the future and the other in the past. This is acutely experienced in the differences between modern city living and the influences of *kastom* that can dominate village life only a short bus or car trip outside urban

---

5   Indigenous Hawaiian.

centres. As Luisa Senibulu's comment on being 'divided into two' alluded to, young Pacific peoples are forging identities that accommodate both traditional cultural norms and contemporary global pressures.

The notion of creating a hybridised form of identity and tradition is one that has been noted before, with particular reference to the notion of 'neotradition' offered by Marshall Sahlins (2005). Fijian development scholar Vijay Naidu, when discussing the modernisation of Pacific states, agrees with the notion that what is considered cultural and what is considered traditional alters over time:

> Sahlins maintains that the dichotomy between modernity and tradition is undermined by the fact that non-western peoples have sought to create their own versions of modernity. In any case what is regarded as traditional has usually been neo-tradition, already a hybrid of the old and the new. (Naidu 2003: 26)

The most obvious examples of this in the Pacific are the contemporary claims that Christianity is a cornerstone of culture, despite its introduction in only the past two centuries. Ravuvu's (1983) depiction of the Fijian way of life and Brison's (2001) writing on sociocentrism in Fiji highlight the fact that the success of Christianity's spread was partly attributable to the ways missionaries aligned Christian precepts with their understandings of traditional values. More recently, peace studies scholar Louise Vella (2014: 6) has written of how Christianity and *kastom* in Solomon Islands can be hybridised for the peaceful governing of conflict. These examples echo discussions of 'indigenisation' from Pacific studies scholars such as Margaret Jolly (1996) and Sahlins (1999), referencing the way that seemingly foreign concepts are shaped to be applicable to local circumstances. Similarly, beyond the Pacific, sociologist Peggy Levitt and anthropologist Sally Merry (2009) use the term 'vernacularisation' to discuss their findings in activist spaces throughout parts of Asia and the Americas of foreign concepts regularly being assumed and adapted for local contexts. They discuss this through the example of gender and human rights advocacy in developing countries:

> As women's human rights ideas connect with a locality, they take on some of the ideological and social attributes of the place, but also retain some of their original formulation. (Levitt and Merry 2009: 446)

Fijian civil society activist Tura Lewai explained to me how the introduction of Christianity by European missionaries brought with it the concept of divine right, which was extended to chiefly titles. This provides a hallmark example of how cultural institutions and people's understandings of what is and is not traditional can be supplanted relatively quickly. It also elaborates on writings by social scientists Morgan Tuimaleali`ifano (2007) and Stephanie Lawson and Elizabeth Hagan Lawson (2015: 3) that describe the interconnectedness of contemporary Fijian conceptions of land, politics and Christianity, including the 'embodied *mana* (divine power)' of chiefs. Tura stated:

> Because Christianity came in, suddenly your leaders are anointed … so you cannot question them. Before, our chiefs were not born into that. That status was not ascribed … You had to prove yourself; you had to be a good warrior; you had to be a good speaker; you had to be able to be influential. The people would sit down and talk about who they would nominate to be the leader of the clan, or chief, and they would vote for who would become the chief. So, we had something that resembled democracy. Then, when the church came in, they were like, 'Your leaders are anointed by God.' As soon as that happened—you know how the royal system worked, where you were born into royalty— that is how we took it on and said, 'Our chiefs are God-sent', and so we shouldn't question them, because questioning them is questioning God.

Governance and participation

While pronounced differences between rural and urban locations are apparent, the impacts of globalisation are increasingly felt in rural and island village communities where everyday livelihood activities remain more connected to subsistence farming and traditional social roles and protocols. These impacts are experienced as Pacific states seek to engage in economic and governance practices that support increased health and economic indicators, but with corollary processes and outcomes that run counter to traditional practices—notably, in the differing forms of citizen engagement and participation. Where modernised developed states extol the virtues of individual identities impacting on collective norms, in Pacific cultures, people are viewed as more sociocentric, with their identities more tightly linked with the consciousness of the collective (Brison 2001). Interestingly, in an analysis of weekly feature articles in the *Fiji Times* newspaper celebrating ordinary citizens, focusing on how they 'constructed emerging notions of what citizenship and nationhood might entail', Connell (2007: 85, 103) found they lionised traits that one would associate with modernisation, such as 'social mobility', 'economic success' and 'individual endeavour'. Michael Morgan (2005), writing about the sometimes awkward fit of liberal democratic institutions with traditional Pacific modes of governance, theorises that the tension between 'traditional' and 'modern' arises due to the separation of state, market and civil society. This gives rise to a tension between a Western emphasis on the rights of the individual and the 'indigenous socialities of kinship and community' found in Pacific communities (Morgan 2005: 4). It must be noted, however, that this tension is not absolute. As anthropologists argue, modern and traditional identities are not fixed polarities, but rather representative of relative positioning on a spectrum between purely individualistic and purely sociocentric (Englund and Leach 2000; Hess 2006; Robbins 2007; Smith 2012).

While there is certainly merit to the argument that there are greater levels of communalism in Pacific communities than in their Western counterparts, and that the differences between the individual and community focuses of Western and Oceanic states are stark at times, this assertion overlooks the substance of what community and civil society mean. Participation may be viewed as an individual right in Western states, but this does not need to be in contrast with Pacific communal values. Indeed, a strong argument can be made that increased participation in prosocial activities, such as decision-making processes, may have strong community benefits in traditional societies (Checkoway et al. 1995: 136; Frank 2006: 352). Increased active participation of young people in their communities may not only allow for individual self-actualisation, but also expand the capabilities of communities at village, provincial and state levels.

The challenge that such participation would make not only to notions of *kastom*, but also to power relations across these societies must be acknowledged. Such issues need to balance ideals of participation leading to good governance with the political realities of who holds power and why they would willingly share it. The UN Economic and Social Council (ECOSOC 2007: 4) advocates that 'participation can help to deepen democracy, strengthen social capital, facilitate efficiency and sustained growth, and promote pro-poor initiatives, equity and justice'. However, as Brownhill (2009: 360) writes, other accounts of participation 'are more pessimistic and argue that the rhetoric of increased participation is undermined by the inevitable rationality of power'. The risk identified here is that increased participation may only be tokenistic—utilised to protect the status quo rather than progress it. National Youth Council of Fiji representative Kinivuwai Naba expressed to me how this occurs in community meetings in his predominantly rural home province of Nadroga-Navosa, noting that 'youth participation in the village and district—it's well structured. But all the people who sit here, they tend to disregard youth.'

In the context of the Pacific, these challenges to socially constructed models of rank and authority need not be regarded as an attack by youth on traditional ways of living. Rather, the Pacific youth I have encountered express a strong connection to *kastom* and a strong sense of identity through a connection to their cultures. This is true both at home, as Carling (2009: 70) notes of the connection of youth identity to culture in Fiji, as well as in diaspora communities, with Fletcher et al. (2009: 25) finding through research into the education needs of Pacific migrants in Aotearoa/New Zealand that 'Pasifika parents and their children demonstrated a strong desire not only to engage with and succeed in the mainstream culture but also to maintain their own cultural identity'.[6] Even the critically engaged youth I have quoted as informants and in case studies clearly demonstrate the willingness of at least some Pacific youth to engage in their societies through advocacy and actions supporting what they view as the common good. These examples lend weight to the idea that while there is a tension between emerging and established knowledge, attitudes and practices, this should be seen not as a clash of distinct forces but rather as navigation of the synthesis of different social influences.

Former Fijian youth magistrate Salote Kaimacuata even suggests that youth who wish to participate in decision-making processes should try to use cultural procedures to their advantage. By thinking and working politically, she suggests, young people can demonstrate their deference to culture and authority, while positioning themselves to be influencers. Just as it is important that elders make time and space to understand youth, so must youth attempt to understand their elders. Salote says:

---

6   Although connections to cultural identity can be more difficult to maintain in subsequent generations born outside the islands (Lee 2011).

> One thing I've always advised young people is to be very respectful. Follow the traditional protocols, listen to their 'Blah, blah, blah' and say, 'Yes, yes, yes', and then: 'With all due respect, this is how we see it.' Let the old people do their 'Rah, rah, rah' and judgement and then listen very patiently. Once you have their ears and they see that you're listening and that you respect them, they will make time to hear you. That must always be the approach in the Pacific way. If we do it in the way that is going out and making a public comment against this person, you are shutting the doors. You need to be patient; you need to strategise on which leader has a youth your age; you need to look at it from all angles.

Furthering Salote's comments regarding the need for young people to consider the lived experiences and emotions of those in positions of authority, Usaia Moli noted the challenge in presenting to elders changes to culture and increased youth prominence in areas of decision-making:

> It's hard for Fijians to accept changes and things that have been introduced because we still try, very much, to hold on to things that have gone in the past. It is not hard to accept new ideas. It's about abandoning the old ones—that is the hard thing for them. We need to reassure them that they are not [at] risk. You can still hold on to that. We can [take] those learnings and move forward with that.

Several of my young Fijian informants have involved themselves in social debates in which they exhibit an acceptance of tradition as they push for social and political changes. Tura Lewai explained to me how he discusses with rural communities the applicability of human rights to cultural beliefs through a simple practice where he draws a circle and asks for the community to fill the circle with all the characteristics required to be a fully functioning human being. When the circle is complete, Tura explains that those attributes based on the needs identified by the community are the basis of human rights.

For 350 Pacific and their communications coordinator Fenton Lutunatabua (discussed in a case study in the previous chapter), working on the global issue of climate change requires communicating differently with different communities. While the Pacific Climate Warriors embrace Pacific dress and culture in their presentations to communities outside the Pacific, within the Pacific, they have recognised that they will receive more local support by having a less assertive presence. Embracing the cultural significance that religion holds in contemporary Oceanic societies, 350 Pacific created the 'Pray for Our Pacific' campaign for domestic audiences (350 Pacific 2016).

This example speaks not only to the use of perceived traditional values, but also to the way in which Christianity has become part of the hybridised tradition of Pacific societies. Further, Fenton updated me in 2018 on how the organisational structure of 350 Pacific, in which youth occupy most of the leadership positions, reimagines traditional indigenous structures, identities and processes of decision-making that exist throughout the region. This is represented in the titles given to 350 Pacific representatives and representative bodies, such as the Council of Elders, which provides strategic guidance and planning to the organisation; the Fellowship of the Fonua ('the Land'), comprising the executive committee; and the Custodians of Solwata ('the Ocean'), which is the subcommittee charged with overseeing 350 Pacific projects and fundraising.

Taking a more dramatic tone, academic, civil rights activist and social commentator Jope Tarai posted a blog on his website in 2017 titled 'God is Dead!'. In this post, Tarai questioned whether the traditions and hierarchy of Fijian churches had distanced them from their congregations and led to the gradual decay of the very morals they espoused. He suggested that religions were more concerned with their 'brand' than acting to uphold and advocate notions of the common good (Tarai 2017). Tarai's argument was not that religion was not or should not be important to Fijians, but that if people were to live in the image of their god, they needed to engage with their faith on a deeper level. In this way, he was appealing to the righteousness of Fijians to embrace the causes of equality and social justice.

These examples speak not only to how young people are utilising 'tradition' to engage with modernity, but also to the practice of thinking and working politically for individuals and groups whose civic participation may be limited in some forums. Like the ways the youth activists above engage the resources at their disposal, Spark et al. (2019) report on how women political leaders in Marshall Islands, Papua New Guinea and Samoa utilise their networks, knowledge and cultural ties to navigate historically male-dominated institutions of power. And, like Tura's methods of connecting culture and human rights, more than two decades ago, Jolly discussed how gender activists in Vanuatu were

> insisting that human rights are not necessarily inconsistent with *kastom*, by appropriating and indigenizing notions of the 'human' to suit their local context and by insisting … that tradition is not a static burden of the past but something created for the present. (1996: 183)

The necessity to navigate traditional and emerging forms of civic engagement is apparent through the burgeoning of ICT throughout the region. Political scientist Danielle Cave (2012), writing on how the rise in ICT use was influencing social norms in the Pacific islands, noted that the increasing youth populations throughout the region and improvements in access to internet network coverage and mobile phone technologies were resulting in a surge of active users even in countries where ICT usage had been below 10 per cent less than a decade earlier. It is reasonable to assume ICT reach and usage have continued to grow in the region since this time, in line with international trends (Internet World Stats 2021).

One space where increased ICT usage is having a clear impact in the Pacific is in social media–based civic engagement. The increasing opportunities for citizen interaction in online spaces have led to transformations in how some Pacific youth are engaging with social, political and economic issues. In Solomon Islands, this is best represented by the Facebook page of Forum Solomon Islands International.

Case Study: Forum Solomon Islands International

A curated Facebook group for Solomon Islanders and those interested in political and civic activities in Solomon Islands, FSII promoted dialogue between citizens, activists and politicians on a range of social and economic issues between 2011 and 2018. Created by four Solomon Islanders, including interviewee Benjamin Afuga, the page sought to act as a space where Solomon Islanders could freely express their opinions on matters that were important to them and use this information to advocate to government. FSII later moved to engaging in ad hoc acts of philanthropy such as renovating hospital wards and facilitating material responses to natural disasters. With more than 23,000 members at its peak,[7] the page developed a reputation throughout the region for its strong anticorruption advocacy and impact on domestic politics. I first learned of the page in 2015 from Jope Tarai of Fiji, who explained to me the depth of impact the page was having:

---

7   As of November 2017. Members self-nominated to join from their Facebook account pending an approval process from one of approximately a dozen page administrators.

> Their [Solomon Islanders'] prime minister literally checks up on
> that forum: what the people discuss; how are they discussing; how
> are they engaging. That shows that they are literally taking a sense
> of accountability demanded from an online group.

When discussing the impact of the page with me, Benjamin was keen to
point out that the forum had provided a new avenue for youth not only
to express their sentiments on matters political, social and economic, but
also to open conversations and seek counsel from others. In a culture in
which young people are expected to accept the word and decisions of
their elders without question, this was a particularly valuable outcome.
As Benjamin informed me:

> There are a lot of youth that have learnt so many things from
> the page. It gives them the opportunity to ask [questions of] our
> academics [and] other respectable people in the community who
> are members of FSII. Some of the youth go under aliases, some
> [adults] choose not to use their real names, but these are very
> respectable people in the community. These youths are given the
> opportunity to talk to these people, to question them, to tell them
> that you are wrong. This is a very, very new experience for these
> people and it's teaching our young people a lot of new things and
> that's the good thing about FSII.

The greatest evidence of the impact FSII had on creating a culture of civic
engagement and political accountability were the government's attempts
to neutralise the group's impact. Speaking to the *Solomon Star* newspaper
in August 2015, Special Secretary to the Prime Minister, Rence Sore,
claimed: 'Their continuous involvement in political decisions from the
Cabinet forces us to seek [the] option to de-register them' (cited in John
2015). Benjamin countered that the page represented the voice of the
citizenry—the 'silent majority'—and told me:

> People don't want us to have a voice because there are a lot of
> people amongst us who don't have the guts to speak up to ask
> these questions, so we are flooded with so many questions ... that
> should be answered by our leaders. That's why we keep exposing
> things that we think are not right. And when you start standing on
> someone's toe, you know they will react.

Since interviewing Benjamin, the stability of FSII and its principles has
been difficult to follow. In 2017, there were media reports that FSII
had expanded into an aligned political party, The People's Movement
(Tuni 2017). Though the Facebook group and movement were not limited

to young people, it was reported that the political party 'comprises mostly young tertiary students and people who initiated the Forum Solomon Islands International group' (Tuni 2017). Early in 2018, however, the FSII Facebook group was disbanded without official notice and there have been no further media mentions of The People's Movement.

Civic engagement in the online space

The popularity of the FSII Facebook page and its use by its members to critically question social, economic and political issues displayed the willingness of the Solomon Islands population—including diaspora outside the country and short-term migrants within—to engage in critical civic discussion if provided the opportunity. Rather than simply another example of how Pacific youth are creating their own spaces for civic engagement, FSII demonstrated how globalisation and technology are influencing new social dynamics within which active citizenship and critical conversations between marginalised groups and those in positions of authority are taking place. Although the youth in this online space were engaging in discussions in which they otherwise would not be able to participate, their deference to elders as authority figures to question and from whom to seek counsel is evidence that they were using the page to hybridise new forms of civic engagement with traditional values of respect and deference.

What is most notable about the success of the FSII Facebook page is that it existed in a context where critical civil society is scarcely visible. Compared with urban hubs in Fiji, particularly Suva, Solomon Islands does not have a highly visible critical civil society presence marked by public talks, demonstrations and figures known for their activist and social justice positions. Despite this, the page generated significant user engagement, particularly from young people. This indicates that limited engagement from youth and others in spaces of public discussion and decision-making is likely to reflect the limited opportunities to access such spaces, rather than apathy or a lack of willingness to engage with social, economic and political issues. This is a critical point to ponder in debates about the extent to which young people, in Oceania and beyond, are willing and able to participate in public discourse.

That the page has since been closed should not be read as a failure of FSII to embed long-term cultural change in relation to civic engagement in Solomon Islands. Rather, it is more accurate to view the cessation of FSII as an inherent risk of moderated internet-based discussion forums. The example of FSII's folding mirrored a similar trajectory of high engagement and sudden closure documented by Helen Morton Lee (2003: 292) of the Kava Bowl—an internet discussion forum aimed at Tongan diaspora communities that was active in the late 1990s. Further highlighting the volatility of tracking online environments, the Kava Bowl appears to have inspired more recent Pacific-focused social media platforms, such as the emergence in 2020 of the Auckland-based cross-platform Kava Bowl Media (Kava Bowl Media n.d.).

Like the case studies of emerging youth civic engagement discussed in the previous chapter, the example of FSII demonstrates the initiative of young people to participate in forms of civil society and decision-making processes in spaces where their exclusion has not already been socially embedded. In particular, FSII existed where the confluence of technological and cultural barriers had not acted to restrict youth engagement. Social media allows almost anyone with an internet connection to become actively involved in public discussions. In the offline, physical space, such participation would be severely restricted and frowned on. In the online space, however, such constraints are not as prevalent, allowing youth to demonstrate their willingness to be active citizens. Benjamin Afuga sees this as the area where FSII has the greatest potential to have a long-lasting impact on Solomon Islands culture, stating:

> Our role [in creating FSII] has given a voice to youth on issues that will affect them and their children. I believe the government has to be very, very accommodating in their approach to views on reforms and government programs. Otherwise, we will end up making laws for those who already died. Who are we going to blame? We will be blaming the graves.

Kleine (2013) has written of how it is virtually impossible for societies to resist and revert from technological advancements and the related increased reliance on material goods such as personal computers and mobile phones. The experience of globalisation in cultures and communities worldwide demonstrates that while the direction and pace of social change may vary in different contexts, there appears to be an inexorable spread of personal ICT in Oceania (Cave 2012). Acknowledging the inevitability of this uptake, it is nevertheless important to be aware of how youth engage with new technologies and communication platforms, as their use and deployment of such technology will influence ongoing practices of hybridisation and the indigenisation of 'modern' global influences within 'traditional' Pacific cultures.

Opportunity and threat

While the older generations in Oceania appear to still have some freedom in determining how much they will engage with the modernising components of society—maintaining their distance or engaging with these forces to varying degrees—it seems youth have less ability to do this. Advances in technology have spread the lure of economic and material gain as well as opportunities to inhabit individual identities free from the societal pressures of *kastom*. In Solomon Islands, Jourdan (1995: 211) noted of the groups of unemployed, undereducated youth known as *masta liu* that, '[m]ore than boredom, what the *liu* are avoiding is the inescapability of *kastom* and the control that their kin and members of older generations have over the young ones'. This complements the Fijian experience of youth seeing tradition as pivotal to one's identity but also inhibiting the development of human capital, as reported by Carling (2009: 70). Though these accounts were written some time ago, the discussions of Solomon Islander culture on FSII and the examples of young people incorporating tradition into their progressive politics discussed earlier in this chapter indicate that the desire to maintain cultural identity is strong for many Pacific youth. Usaia Moli addressed this issue with me when discussing the need to maintain connections to both iTaukei and Indo-Fijian cultures while embracing change:

> These are two unique cultures we all should be proud of, and we should also try and maintain as well for the sake of those who come after us, our children, to know where we're from. People thought that for a new direction to take place we need to forget about the past, but it doesn't have to be. You can change it and move on.

Within the conflict my informants identified between a wish to engage with modern, globalised cultures and a desire to maintain a link to traditional relationships and ways of living, a sense of uncertainty is created. Though developmental benefits such as increased access to safe water, medicines and knowledge that can assist with developmental problems are embraced, further stressors become apparent when such innovations are welcomed. These include increased involvement from state and regional authorities, which may not be trusted and may undermine local power structures; an increased lure for citizens to move from rural to urban areas for social and economic opportunities that carry risks; and the risks of increased poverty that come from a transition from basic and sustainable subsistence living to a market-oriented economy that diminishes established kinship, village or *mataqali*-based social support systems. Again, it must be noted that these challenges are not new. Both Fiji and Solomon Islands have been experiencing such pressures to varying degrees through migration, remittance practices and engagement with Western structures of human capital advancement, including plantation labour and the practice of influential families sending their children to domestic boarding schools or European education institutions. That these matters are still discussed by people in both countries indicates that they remain unresolved.

Compounding the challenge for youth to benefit from the positive changes brought about through modernity are the assumed threats felt by the older generations. Beyond the fear those in positions of authority have of losing their influence is a broader concern about Westernisation causing cultural erosion (Heron 2008: 89; Petras 1993)—based on the fear that the adoption of economic growth as the primary measure of development will result in a diminished sense of importance being placed on cultural values. The diminishment of cultural ideals may be both economic and social, such as the perceived tension between sociocentrism and individualism or between mass consumption and environmental sustainability. These concerns mirror those of dependency theories, which were explicitly concerned with the development industry's imposition of linear, static approaches to development in opposition to the 'traditional' cultures that limited their development (Grosfoguel 2000; Valenzuela and Valenzuela 1978), as promoted in Rostow's (1971) take-off approach to modernisation. Dakuvula's (1975: 15) assertion about development being an 'alien religious system', Wendt's (1976: 53) insistence that a return to pre-European contact living is impossible for Pacific peoples and Hau'ofa's (1983, 1985) cautionary warnings about the double-edged sword of modernity reinforce the fact that these concerns have been apparent in the Pacific for generations.

When combined, these fears of relinquishing authority and of cultural subsumption can act to inhibit societal and structural openness to youth participation and leadership. As discussed earlier, to deny youth engagement based on a fear of status hierarchies and culture being supplanted is misplaced. This is evident not only in the discrete practices of the youth who are maintaining and reimagining culture and tradition, as previously discussed, but also in the collective voice of the Pacific youth representatives at the second Pacific Youth Festival affirming that they hold their cultural identities dear and acknowledge a need to maintain indigenous values as globalisation brings new social, economic and developmental threats and opportunities (SPC 2009b). Mereani Rokotuibau, a regional development worker from Fiji, echoed this sentiment when discussing the need to maintain respect for culture while developing the capacity of Pacific young people. Reflecting comments that align concepts of hybridity, neotradition and indigenisation, Mereani stated:

> Empowerment needs to be packaged in such a way that it blends in with our existing structures, because it can be seen as doing harm to what exists in our culture and tradition, particularly in a village setting. For education and all that, we need to package it in such a way that it complements rather than [goes] against culture.

The speed with which globalisation is forcing hybridisation of 'traditional' and 'modern' cultures is creating further uncertainty for young people in terms of how they understand and express their cultural identity, as well as the roles they are allowed and expected to play in their communities. McMurray (2006: 5) argued more than a decade ago that the '[j]uxtaposition of traditional and modern cultures and values increases the level of uncertainty in young lives, and presents difficulties for young people and also for their adult carers'. Since then, there has been rapid growth in access to ICT, and the pace of globalisation has continued to increase. As Good (2019) writes of Tongan youth, social and economic uncertainty have become significant markers of the Pacific youth experience. Yet their ongoing structural minimisation means that many young Pacific people appear not to have the luxury of choosing their own pathways if these diverge from socially acceptable or ascribed roles and responsibilities. Likewise, the inevitability of globalisation means they also do not have the luxury of retreating from the forces of modernity. Encapsulating this difficulty, Salote Kaimacuata explains:

> For our young people, there is a lot of pressure to conform, to live up to the expectations of mums and dads. Also, our parents are bringing up children the way they were brought up in a different, new age. It is the dilemma between the old way of

> bringing up children while our children live in a new age. They are
> bombarded with information. They sound really clever, but the
> emotional maturity is yet to be developed. Just because you have
> a lot of information doesn't necessarily mean you're clever, doesn't
> necessarily mean you're wise.

Salote's comments about the dilemma for Pacific youth of maintaining traditional belief systems and customary practices while still preparing themselves to engage actively with contemporary global society are particularly poignant as they highlight the fact these issues are not new to Fijian society. Having lived, studied and worked outside the Pacific islands, Salote conveyed to me that since at least the 1990s she has been seen by some Fijians as embodying foreign ideals too much at times, through her work in various youth justice capacities. What distinguishes Salote's experience of straddling contemporary and traditional identities is that, unlike previous case study examples, she is not considered a youth. Further exemplifying the difficulty of navigating social roles and expectations, she explained to me that while she is criticised by some Fijians for her 'Western' ways, her children see her as representing 'traditional' values: 'To my children, I'm really old-fashioned and an ogre, but to my colleagues I'm not Fijian [because of a perceived Western approach to thinking] and I'm offended by that.'

The conflicting social expectations for youth to uphold tradition but also seek individual advancement through education and employment put them in a position to exert agency in relation to their identity, while simultaneously denying them the capacity and freedom to do so. Young people are socialised to consider their own needs as secondary to those of elders and the community, yet factors such as global economic forces and the reification in international development discourse of individual empowerment place pressure on youth to engage in self-development and seek to fulfil their individual capabilities. Good writes of empowerment that it is

> one of several terms circulating around the globe along the paths
> of development projects and foreign assistance, linking particular
> kinds of youthful action to idealized notions of liberal citizenship
> and individualized forms of agency. (2014: 222)

This is something that is clearly appealing to many youths, as evidenced by the continuing rural–urban migration trends discussed in the work of writers such as Jourdan (1995) and Woo and Corea (2009), and in the case study of Pesa's desires for employment, migration and status presented in Chapter Three. In contrast, however, are the actions of youth engaged in critical civil society who are actively working to shape their communities in ways they believe will lead to communal benefit in their communities, countries and cultures. As ideals of community and individualism are perceived to clash, this creates strains for youth in establishing their identities and fitting into their societies. Fenton Lutunatabua, who identifies more with a modern urban Fijian lifestyle than with any abstract notions of village-based traditionalism, articulated the complexities of developing an identity that balances sociocentric and individual values:

> If you come from the culture in the Pacific where you are not encouraged to elevate yourself above everyone else, that can be a little difficult to start thinking of yourself as the self.

Negotiating neotradition

Understanding the forms of youth participation in civic life requires an examination and interpretation of how young people engage with the ideas and practices of *kastom* and tradition. Here, again, it appears that the perceived clash between indigenous sociocentric world views of *kastom* and the more individualistic world views of modernised societies is vital to understanding young people's civic participation. The exponentially increased pace of social and economic change across the Pacific and globally in the past half-century appears to have created the conditions for a two-tiered approach to participation and civic engagement—one that is seen as traditional and is based on patience and passive observation, and one that is understood as being informed by greater access to information and communication and which emphasises individual capabilities and promotes individual identity.

The 'to be seen but not heard' approach to Pacific youth development and participation has been repeatedly referenced by Patrick Vakaoti in his work on Fijian youth citizenship practices. Vakaoti (2012: 3) notes, in research on how young people in Fiji participate as active citizens and demonstrate leadership, that in Fiji and across the Pacific young people occupy subordinate roles to adults and those in positions of authority. Vakaoti and Mishra (2010: 10) argue that '[t]his social status affects their participation in many facets of life'. Such subservience is encouraged in young Pacific people from childhood, with Carling (2009: 66) similarly noting the prevalence of this in her research into Fijian youth citizenship. The enculturation of passive participation from such a young age speaks to my contention of Pacific young people's structural minimisation: the roles of Pacific youth are systematically diminished through most of their formal and informal social interactions, with youth populations forced to wait to be invited into decision-making processes and institutions. For the youth and youth advocates whom I interviewed, a point of enduring frustration was the resistance from authority figures to youth occupying formal and informal positions of leadership.

Regardless of community attitudes, the reality is that youth generations will be the ones responsible for balancing aspects of traditional and modern cultures—creating their own 'neotraditional' cultures (Sahlins 2005). Young people are the ones who will lead their communities into new, hybrid understandings of what is culturally valuable and acceptable, as has been noted of Honiara, where the emerging urban middle class is driving a 'creolisation' of language and culture (Jourdan 1996, 2008) as well as of everyday ways of living (Moore 2015). These reconceptualisations of culture may be driven intentionally by an informed and capable youth populace—cognisant of the challenges, risks and opportunities inherent in such cultural changes—or they may emerge immanently in response to competing social and economic influences, leading to a hybrid social structure that will continue to change over time. Alternatively, such change may occur through a combination of intentional and immanent processes (Cowen and Shenton 1996), through which young people utilise foreign ideas, materials and interventions—such as by the international development community—to assist their reimagining of culture. This would be like the practices Jolly (1996) writes about of ni-Vanuatu women who have indigenised women's rights discourse to advocate for the prevention of violence against women while invoking notions of *kastom*.

Having the skills to navigate the forces of tradition and modernity is becoming an ever-more pressing issue for Pacific youth. Globalisation is resulting in increased precarity for young people that is best demonstrated by rural–urban migration. Through migratory practices, youth must engage in livelihood practices without the safety net of village subsistence farming while they straddle social roles as breadwinning remitters and subservient young people. Although Pacific youth are expected to uphold 'traditional' values, the social structures to support them in doing so have not kept pace with modern livelihood pressures. Vanuatu-based journalist

Dan McGarry (2014) noted this in a Pacific Institute of Public Policy blog, writing of the influence of diminished barriers to communication, information and transport and their impact on traditional Melanesian societies:

> Men and women both are no longer subject to the social and geographical confines of village life. Mobility and distance undermine traditions that have sustained Melanesian societies since time immemorial. The coercive or corrective power of community scrutiny recedes once it becomes possible to evade the villagers' gaze. The village's role as collective conscience has been eroded and, to date, nothing has arisen to take its place.

With recognition of the quickening pace of rural–urban migration in the Pacific, and particularly across Melanesia (see Kiddle 2016; Lindstrom and Jourdan 2017), this is an issue that is unlikely to abate. It is well established that young Pacific peoples are prepared to engage with the contemporary market economy and associated individual benefits, including material goods and increased independence. Rural–urban migration signals both the willingness of young people to leave their village contexts to seek financial gain and the increased social pressures to provide financial stability for themselves and their families. Jope Tarai, who has grown up in the peri-urban outskirts of Suva, outlined the combination of economic and employment opportunities driving such migration:

> We have high-rise buildings on this end and right next to that we have expanding squatter settlements—the majority of them young families within the youth category. That indicates that the youth population … in the Suva–Nausori corridor … are coming in to find financial and social security, access to better services and all that.

Despite technological advancements, economic pressures and increasing rural–urban migration, the fear of Pacific youth actively rejecting the maintenance of culture and tradition is at odds with their own practices and stated intentions. Indeed, Pacific youth voiced a clear commitment to maintaining their sense of identity through culture and enactments of tradition in the communiqué from the participants from 13 Pacific states who attended the second Pacific Youth Festival in Suva in 2009, including concerns about how '[t]he lack of focus on rural and outer island development increases incentives to move to urban areas and creates imbalance and disintegration of traditional values and practices' (SPC 2009b: 4). Such statements can appear superficial. Taken together with the examples of how youth are maintaining and reimagining culture in their progressive politics, however, these assertions go beyond platitudes about the connection young people feel to culture. They speak to specific practical areas where they feel culture is not being adequately supported at an institutional level and thus is at risk of deterioration. Jope sees this expression of youth connection to culture and the desire for its preservation as reflecting social norms driven by fear of the loss of identity and agency of Pacific peoples. While modernisation is seen to bring many benefits, it is also considered a threat to cultural purity. This supports the assertion of Sahlins, drawing on Jolly, that

> when Europeans change it is called 'progress', but when 'they' (the others) change, notably when they adopt some of our progressive attributes, it is a loss of their culture, some kind of adulteration. (Sahlins 2005: 45)

Jope argues that this sentiment is shared by some Pacific peoples (see also Pigg 1996: 178). As he told me:

> The colonial hangover does play a strong part in all of that. Over the years, people have taken it on … [and] a consequence of that has been 'us': this is our tradition; this is what we do; this is who we are. Everything that we have taken on from it—whether it be religion, whether it be the colonial hangover—everybody is boxed into their own community. Integration is, indirectly, highly discouraged … People are resistant, especially outside urban areas. They are resistant to these changes out of fear that they will lose something; that they will lose a bit of themselves—their identity.

It is worth noting again that such fears are not new, nor have they led to previous generations forgoing technological and accompanying cultural changes through their lifetimes. There are myriad ways such incorporation of foreign influences is strikingly apparent in both Fiji and Solomon Islands: the use of buses as a common mode of transport; the high levels of consumption of rice and instant noodles in rural and urban settings; the television sets that occupy pride of place in most village homes; even in the prevalence of Filipino soap operas I have witnessed being purchased from the DVD stores in Suva and Honiara—a practice remarked on in other Oceanic locations, such as by Good (2013) on the Tongan island of `Eua. The extent to which these practices reveal a willingness to embrace change as it occurs or the subversive power of technology to embed itself in people's lives regardless of their original wishes—which is the extension of the 'technologies of choice' theory (Kleine 2013)—is impossible to state with certainty. What is certain is that these practices clearly exemplify the contemporary hybridity of cultures in these societies.

For young people, their position between the ideas and practices of traditional and contemporary society is marked by further complications. As has already been discussed, youths are the ones most likely to engage in employment-motivated migration, both domestically and internationally. The urban and international areas to which they relocate are more exposed to global cultural and economic forces, so they are placed in a position of having to negotiate cultural hybridity with the real likelihood of a diminished close social network to help them through these processes. On top of this, as they begin to remit earnings back to family and clan, they embody two distinct positions, as subservient young person and as livelihood provider, which offer them greater authority at household and community levels. The tension of maintaining these twin facets of individual and communal identity was conveyed by Jope when he spoke of youth being given a greater voice as they contribute financially to the family yet still being expected to show deference in certain traditional settings. Interestingly, Jope continued by highlighting the fact that financial contributions do not elevate youth to an equal footing with adults, but rather grant them initial access to decision-making processes. Of the burden on urban-based youth to remit earnings, he stated:

> I have conversations with uncles within my age group who are frustrated with their own parents. Sometimes I get phone calls [requesting money] and I ask, 'How many cows do you people want to eat in a week?' It would be interesting to find out from Western Union the age group of people sending money back and forth. Obviously, they are young people.

As mentioned earlier in this chapter, an area of delineation between 'traditional' Pacific values and those perpetuated by Western market and development forces is in the value placed on the communal and the individual. As the forces of *kastom* and modernisation continue to be placed against and alongside one another, the impacts of sociocentric and individualistic approaches to civic participation will be shaped by the youth generation. As Good writes of Tongan youth:

> [D]espite their relatively low position in the status hierarchy that still determines the boundaries of social experience in Tonga, youth have become critical actors in the ways Tongan institutions and Tongan people think about and 'do' modernity. (2012: 18)

Unless communal, culturally agreed on approaches to participation that represent a hybridised future melding *kastom* and modernity are formally created, it is youth who will define what civic participation looks like through their practice of it, creating informal guidelines for later generations' engagement in similar spaces. In this way, the current youth generations are the ones who will indigenise foreign influences and create the neotraditions of tomorrow.

Comparing Fiji and Solomon Islands

With the pace of social change ever quickening globally—exponentially enhanced by developments in ICT—young people in Fiji and Solomon Islands face the same challenges in navigating tradition and modernity. The difference between the expectations of youths' participation within sociocentric and individualistic approaches is significant and challenging. If young people are not exposed to and included in decision-making processes from an early age, the lack of modelling will limit their understanding of how to negotiate such spaces. In villages and non-urban settings, this may not be problematic as there is the opportunity to learn through observation leading up to inclusion as one among many leaders often making decisions based in consultation and consensus. In urban and professional settings, however, these same young people are expected to understand the boundaries within which their participation takes place. The example of FSII, however, suggests that some of this slack may be taken up in the online space, where young people feel freer to openly seek the advice of their elders.

That perceived tensions between traditional and modern ways of living continue to be presented as problems by my informants demonstrates that they are yet to be resolved. Indeed, they may never be. Just as young people are perpetually discussed in terms of their waning morals and represented as embodying antisocial behaviours, discussions about social change are ongoing and harken back to an idealised past that may or may not have existed.

What I found more surprising in discussing these issues with my informants was how they actively engaged with notions of hybridity and indigenisation, even if they did not utilise these terms. This was evident through the statements of Andre Tipoki and Usaia Moli when they affirmed that engaging with new ideas does not mean having to disavow established practices and protocols, and Salote Kaimacuata and Mereani Rokotuibau, who called for young people to engage with traditional customs and expectations as a means of being granted access to discussions with those in positions of authority. More powerfully, an embrace of hybridity as a means of affirming culture, tradition and *kastom* was evident in the practices of various informants—Tura Lewai, Fenton Lutunatabua and Jope Tarai—who utilise cultural identity and values to ground their engagement with the forces of globalisation and modernisation. These actions are what affirm that a connection with and respect for tradition and culture go beyond rhetoric in the critical civil society spaces within which activist youth operate. Further, for as long as Pacific peoples speak of the challenges of maintaining tradition, it will remain a worthwhile site of investigation.

Conclusion

Beyond the impacts of a clash between indigenous and non-indigenous values and customs, the impacts of any such clash on the wellbeing of Pacific peoples, young and old alike, should not be overlooked. This includes considering how they shape understandings of what is cultural and 'traditional'. Culture is a means by which humans not only understand their lives, but also find meaning and purpose. Though shifts in cultural practices and beliefs about what is traditional have always incorporated foreign ideas and customs, the pace of globalisation means that the cooption of such ideas and customs is likely to occur similarly rapidly. The extent to which there is critical engagement with change is poised to determine the degree to which Pacific communities can negotiate such hybridity on terms favourable to them and their values. With heritage and cultural identity being expressed as of such personal and communal significance throughout the region, this is shaping as an important debate for Pacific people to engage in. Through this, the communities, countries and cultures of Oceania may be able to provide a counterpoint to the concept that 'development' is a homogenised cultural endpoint—one that assumes a Western form, based on principles of perpetual growth and individual merit-based advancement.

Pacific young people are uniquely poised to be affected by the competing social demands of sociocentric expectations and the individual and economic-focused demands of modernity. Older generations have had time to establish their societal roles and form their identities as the forces of globalisation and modernisation slowly entered Pacific societies. For youth, their futures and identities will largely be shaped by how they engage with and respond to the sweeping pace of social change, which is influenced significantly by progressions in the capability and accessibility of ICT. How Pacific youth navigate these changes will be determined, to a large extent, by the ways in which they utilise concepts of traditional knowledge and identity.

As I have repeatedly noted, Pacific youth currently experience significant minimisation of their participation, agency and capability. This is true at household levels in the determination of future livelihood prospects, at policy levels through the failure to reform institutions with poor records of developing young people as active citizens, and at the cultural level, where the role of youth is to be seen but not heard. In the context of the increasingly rapid impacts of modernisation on shaping individual and communal futures for the people of the Great Ocean States of the Pacific, this denial of youth participation is creating duopolistic environments of youth civic engagement. In physical spaces, Pacific youth engagement continues to be marginalised, and young people are not being mentored to become partners for today or leaders of tomorrow. In online spaces such as FSII, however, these same youth are asking questions of their leaders and forging space for their inclusion in decision-making processes.

The exclusion of youth from participation in some Pacific settings places them in a precarious position as far as shaping what will be viewed as traditional in coming generations while having limited access to the 'traditional' knowledge and decision-making forums that elders appear to wish them to inherit and uphold. As with the examples of emerging youth leaders discussed in Chapter Five, however, these young people are proving through alternative displays of active citizenship, including in online spaces, that they are interested in and connected to conceptions of how their societies should develop and function. Rather than lingering as adults-in-waiting, they are seizing opportunities to be actively engaged members of their communities, countries and cultures.

7

Pacific youth futures

We're always talking about resources, but … young people are our biggest resource.

— Usaia Moli, Fiji

In this monograph, I have investigated issues of youth livelihoods, leadership and civic engagement in Fiji and Solomon Islands through a lens that seeks to understand the challenges these young people face in increasing their livelihood opportunities and engaging critically as active citizens in their societies. This approach challenges deficit perspectives in researching youth populations, which have a disproportionate focus on the capacity of youth to engage in civil disobedience, unrest and even revolution. Instead, my approach aligns with recent literature from development organisations focusing on youth. This literature recognises the potential for young people to contribute as drivers of the economy, and to engage in civil society and political debates if provided with the appropriate skills and access to participation, but also acknowledges the risk of stalled developmental progress that is apparent in states that fail to provide such opportunities (for example, Curtain and Vakaoti 2011; Pruitt 2020; World Bank 2007). In echoes of the sentiment of Usaia Moli, young people are now being seen as a resource to be invested in and developed.

To engage in a rounded discussion that acknowledges the complexity and interconnectedness of the issues Fijian and Solomon Islander youth face, I apply a 'holistic livelihoods' approach that draws on this recent work by development organisations and the academic development literature. The holistic livelihoods approach marries work on basic needs (Maslow 1943) and capabilities (Sen 2003) with sentiments from the emerging adaptive school of development (Andrews et al. 2015; ODI 2014; TWP Community 2016). I acknowledge that development as a process and a goal mean different things to different communities. For the most disadvantaged and marginalised—those most in need of development assistance—the ongoing security of basic needs is of utmost importance. Beyond this, development is about having access to systems and structures that can promote the capacities of individuals and communities to, first, determine their own concepts of an ideal future, and then to achieve these. In this way, the roots of development may be universal, but its goals and processes can take multiple forms.

A holistic livelihoods approach to international development not only synthesises some of the pre-eminent approaches to development of recent decades; it also integrates what can be broadly understood as Western and Pacific notions of how development should be conceived and produced. As with other countries and regions labelled as 'developing', the Great Ocean States of the Pacific have strongly criticised development for reflecting Western values and institutions. Beginning with the independence movement of the 1960s and 1970s, these criticisms mirrored global concerns about dependency and appealed for Pacific development to be directed by Pacific peoples. Today, new models of development in the region are calling for a greater embrace of culture, identity and sustainability—a perspective that is reflected in contemporary national development strategies.

The holistic livelihoods approach offers a lens for understanding the multiple and complex factors that promote or inhibit the development of communities and individuals—including youth. It builds on established development theories and critiques, shaped by alternative development thinking, to acknowledge the significance of culture, context and history. Though discussions of development as a concept and a practice can be abstract, for disadvantaged and marginalised populations, the problems of development are real. It is within this reality that the discussion in these pages is grounded.

Issues of youth livelihoods, leadership and civic engagement in Fiji and Solomon Islands have been addressed in this book in two key ways. The first is an examination of established structures that promote an 'economic growth' approach to development—one that views education and employment from a livelihood security perspective. With most of my informants identifying unemployment as the most significant issue facing Fijian and Solomon Islander youth, I engage with questions about the purposes of education and employment in young people's lives and investigate the efficacy of the dominant systems and structures in achieving these ends.

The second key focus is on the social roles that young people are expected and allowed to play in their communities. Fijian and Solomon Islander youth are expected to be passive participants in their communities, fulfilling socially expected roles and obligations. Given the pressures associated with globalisation, increasing exposure to modernity, expectations of material gain and related matters such as migration from rural communities to urban centres, the social expectations of youth roles do not align with other expectations that they become skilled workers and breadwinners. Here, tensions between maintaining 'tradition' and embracing the 'modern' play out.

These two areas of focus merge in creating an understanding that the marginalisation of youth participation and active citizenship operates at the level of the household and village and permeates through the policies, programs and institutions of state. Formal education systems do not equip most young people to be prosperous and engaged citizens; these problems are compounded by social expectations of desirable pathways into white-collar employment even though this provides few opportunities. Though the impacts of the discrepancy between education and employment opportunities are much bemoaned by my informants and in various studies by Nilan and Tagicakiverata (Nilan et al. 2006; Tagicakiverata 2012; Tagicakiverata and Nilan 2018), interventions to improve the systems are piecemeal, reflecting the marginalised social status of youth through the minimised importance placed on the development of youth capabilities through formal institutions. Social commentator Jope Tarai of Fiji expressed frustration at the lack of progress in addressing youth issues over decades but noted that this frustration is motivating youth in critical civil society to push for structural change:

> The reason we are saying 'policy, policy, policy' is because this is the long run. Within a matter of years, we will have families and kids who will have to come back to the same things, and we don't want [that].

The result of the structural minimisation of youth is that opportunities for young people to realise their fullest potential are limited. Their ability to achieve self-actualisation through either the modern systems of education and employment or the traditional support structures is compromised. This not only limits the opportunities for youth self-actualisation at an individual level; it also has the potential to limit the future developmental opportunities of the communities and states of Oceania. Although I address youth issues from a strengths perspective, one Solomon Islander informant noted that even for those looking at youth from a security-focused, risk-management perspective, the implications of failing to provide opportunities for young people should be obvious. Reflecting on the Tensions at the turn of the century, they warned: '[W]hen youth issues are not addressed and young people are not engaged, look what happened to us.'

This chapter highlights some of the key contentions that have been discussed throughout this book. I begin by summarising the position of young people in Fiji and Solomon Islands and the impact of formal and informal social structures on their experiences. I then synthesise the core argument related to the mismatch between the livelihood opportunities available to Fijian and Solomon Islander youth and those they are trained and encouraged to seek; the ways in which these youth engage with civil society; how they are negotiating tradition and modernity in ways that reflect Pacific values, and how such practices may be imagined. I conclude the chapter by noting some of the areas where further research opportunities exist, before remarking that the youth of the Great Ocean States of the Pacific are the ones who will be largely responsible for determining what the developmental future looks like for their communities, countries and cultures. Although it is just as unfair and inaccurate to idealise youth as the developmental saviours of their communities, if only they realise their potential, as it is to demonise youth as an inherent social risk, the reality is they will eventually occupy the positions of power whether by invitation or natural attrition.

The structural minimisation of youth

The social positioning of Fijian and Solomon Islander youth is aptly captured in the phrase 'to be seen but not heard', offered by Tura Lewai. This is because their civic participation and the opportunities for the development of their human capital are marginalised so that not only do they have little or no opportunity to be fully engaged and active citizens, but also their role in their communities is premised on such marginalisation. That is, young people do not simply occupy a position where they *are* seen but not heard; they are actively encouraged *to be* seen but not heard.

The ramifications of this are wideranging and amount to the structural minimisation of Pacific youth. It begins with the marginalisation of active involvement in decision-making processes at the household and village levels, extending to inefficiencies in structures theoretically designed to promote youth capabilities. Rather than nurturing potential and preparing young people to achieve livelihood autonomy and develop as the future leaders of their communities, formal education and employment structures reinforce hierarchical relationships between youths and adults. As a result, young people in Fiji and Solomon Islands are not sufficiently equipped to take advantage of livelihood opportunities relevant to their countries' social and economic contexts.

The issue identified by my informants as being of most immediate concern for youth in Fiji, Solomon Islands and across wider Oceania is unemployment. This was echoed repeatedly through conversations I had with youth activists and advocates, as well as across each of the urban, peri-urban and rural communities in which I engaged in both countries. Allowing for the fact that several of my informants were representative stakeholders of specific demographics and interest groups—such as people with disabilities, LGBTIQ+ communities and climate change activists— these responses can be understood as representing a near-consensus belief that youth unemployment is the primary issue to understand and address for the improvement of youth livelihood, development and civic engagement opportunities in Fiji and Solomon Islands. Indeed, this research could very easily have kept a tight focus on how and why the employment sectors of Pacific states are failing to cater for their youth populations.

However, focusing only on youth unemployment would have failed to situate the issue within a broader perspective of the social, economic and cultural factors that compound the problem. Through this inquiry, the complexities of the political economy of youth were highlighted. Informants discussed recurrent issues underlying high rates of unemployment, including formal education failing to equip young people with the skills to avail themselves of a range of livelihood opportunities post schooling, and mismatches between the needs of the employment sector and the focus of curriculums, as well as a cultural environment in which critical inquiry is discouraged. The last tied in with other discussions about the means and meanings of the minimisation of youth participation and potential.

Youth in Fiji and Solomon Islands occupy a social position that is defined by a graduation from youthhood to adulthood through socially understood achievements and undertakings. This is largely based on cultural beliefs that youth can and should learn the ways of adulthood through observation and deference. As multiple informants—youths and adults alike—pointed out, young people are expected to bide their time and wait their turn to become active and engaged citizens, let alone leaders. Yet in the current context of increased rural–urban migration, exposure to global debates about politics, economics and civil society, and shared challenges related to issues such as climate change, 'traditional' understandings of the role of young people do not meet the 'modern' realities. The challenges that my informants identified as facing Pacific youth are not new. Unemployment, ineffective formal education and even debates about the tension between modernity and tradition are longstanding issues that have been remarked on for decades. That they remain at the forefront of the consciousness of those engaged in critical civil society suggests they are not being adequately addressed and/or are of little concern to people in positions of authority.

Youth livelihoods

The holistic livelihoods approach looks beyond the provision of basic needs, incorporating notions of agency, capability and civic engagement in its conception of how development can impact on young Pacific peoples. This does not ignore the importance of basic needs, however, with issues of creating livelihood pathways and providing for oneself also addressed. This is most evident in Chapters Two and Three, which explore the education and employment pathways Fijian and Solomon Islander youth follow and are expected to follow. Across both chapters, concerns emerged regarding the practical and theoretical purposes of formal education and employment, as well as a mismatch between the skills provided to young people through formal education structures and the opportunities available to them in the employment sector.

Issues related to the mismatch between the education and employment systems are not limited to livelihoods provision. In cultures where youth are considered adults-in-waiting, the desired education and employment pathways provide insight into cultural values as well as how young people engage—and are expected to engage—in their communities.

By investigating the pathways that youth are encouraged to follow, the pathways they intend to follow and the pathways they do follow, I have demonstrated that the structures implicitly intended to improve livelihood opportunities for Fijian and Solomon Islander youth are failing to adequately prepare them to take advantage of those opportunities to provide for their basic needs and potentially increase their economic and food security. Further, the limited autonomy these youths can exercise over their livelihood preferences is also made apparent.

Rather than providing a means for Pacific youth to establish their own livelihoods, agency and autonomy, the education and employment pathways for many are determined by authority figures such as parents and are influenced by social expectations. Statements from informants such as Roshika Deo from Fiji and Vince Nomae from Solomon Islands, quoted in Chapter Three, about the lack of alignment of skills acquired through formal education with employment opportunities support previous studies about the limits of youth agency and self-determination.

An intriguing phenomenon exists in young people being encouraged to migrate to urban hubs for livelihood opportunities and how such practices influence agency. Jope Tarai discussed with me how employment can act as a means of transitioning from youthhood to adulthood, though he also made clear that this process is gradual. For some young people, migration is regularly encouraged by parents and other authority figures with the intention of formal employment resulting in remittances. For others, as exemplified by the case study of Pesa in Chapter Three, the desire for migration is self-driven, connected to wishes for greater autonomy as well as the prospects of engaging in employment and starting a family, which are culturally significant markers of adulthood.

Youth civic engagement

Beyond the minimisation of their agency in determining their own livelihood pathways, for young people in the Great Ocean States of the Pacific, the space for active civic engagement is quite limited. Hierarchical cultures dictate that inclusion and participation in various decision-making processes are restricted. Adult men, particularly of chiefly lineage in Fiji and parts of Solomon Islands, occupy the highest rungs of such hierarchy. Factors relating to gender, ethnicity, sexuality and ability, among others, further dictate who is involved in community forums at various times. For Pacific youth, their social positioning as seen but not heard both represents and reinforces their lowly position in cultural hierarchies. By being exposed to the cultures of silence that exist in Fiji and Solomon Islands and discouraged from engaging in critical civil society practices, their possibilities for active civic engagement are minimised.

The denial of space for active civic engagement by youth was particularly noticeable when I sought examples of youth leaders from youth participants in my focus groups in both Fiji and Solomon Islands. That no group could readily identify a single example of someone who was considered both a leader and a youth speaks to multiple issues. Among these is the dichotomous relationship that exists between concepts of youthhood and concepts of leadership for Pacific peoples. There is also the issue of the limited capacity of many Pacific youth to engage critically with concepts that do not fit neatly within their world view. More significantly, the difficulty in identifying youth leaders demonstrated the lack of such leaders for Fijian and Solomon Islander youth communities. Though there is a smattering of young politicians and chiefs, their presence is limited.

Despite this, examples are ever present of young people in Fiji, Solomon Islands and across Oceania creating spaces for active and critical civic engagement. The case studies presented in Chapter Five of the Be the Change political campaign for the 2014 Fijian election and the Pacific Climate Warriors of 350 Pacific are evidence of the ways some young people refuse to have their participation marginalised. Notably, each of these communities engages in action and advocacy related to social justice issues. For Be the Change and 350 Pacific, by centring their civic engagement on youth, gender and sexual identity issues and on the climate crisis, respectively, they have become vocal and influential members of critical civil society by occupying the spaces of deliberation and decision-making that adults and those in positions of power have not yet fully claimed. These examples demonstrate that when Pacific youth are not actively excluded from civic engagement processes, some will willingly participate despite the cultures of silence that have informed their social and cultural growth. Again, however, it must be noted that these individuals are better understood as examples of 'positive deviance' (Andrews 2015), representing a minority of Pacific youth. Further, as in the discussions during focus groups regarding people who are both youths and leaders, it needs to be recognised that these examples are not widely recognised in their communities as exemplars of youth who are true community leaders. What is apparent through these examples is that while young people are regularly excluded from actively participating in decision-making processes and other civic engagement, they will embrace opportunities to participate when they arise.

Pressures of globalisation

Youth engagement in online spaces, and the use of ICT in general, is the most obvious example of the pace of social change in Pacific states through increased globalisation and the challenges this represents. Though cultures are constantly changing, the technological developments of recent decades have significantly increased the rate at which cultures are being exposed to new ideas, information and ways of living. As identified by West (2007), fears of change and of loss of status and authority act as primary causes globally of adults not engaging youth in participation—a situation mirrored in the Pacific, according to informants such as Salote Kaimacuata and Usaia Moli. The effects of globalisation and access to ICT are presenting new opportunities for Pacific youth to engage in displays of active citizenship, while also compounding perceptions of the potential for a loss of 'tradition'.

The challenge for adults and those in positions of authority appears to relate to how they can partner with Pacific youth in ways that reaffirm cultural values but are neither passive nor tokenistic. Informants made it clear in interviews that there are groups of adults who are fiercely resistant to change but there are also groups of young people who are not prepared to wait idly to be invited into decision-making spaces. In cultures with sociocentric values and lifestyles, significant challenges are presented by the spread of globalisation, neoliberal ideologies and the association of these with the lionisation of individualistic aspirations. Already, practices such as rural–urban migration have led to economics-driven decisions that disrupt traditional notions of how the family unit lives and operates. That young people can be physically disconnected from their families as urban-based breadwinners remitting earnings but still not considered fully adult provides one salient example.

The risk of cultures being revolutionised by individualistic youth who are disconnected from, and possibly disenchanted with, perceptions of tradition and *kastom* appears to be miniscule. The youth I interviewed expressed a strong sense of connection to their cultures and a desire to maintain traditional values in the ways they approach future developmental and other social changes. These young people reaffirmed the sentiments of the more than 300 youth who attended the last Pacific Youth Festival, held more than a decade ago. Tura Lewai's invocation of traditional sociocentric values to demonstrate how human rights can be indigenised by Fijians, rather than seen as a Western imposition, and 350 Pacific grounding its decision-making bodies in culturally significant terms provide just two salient examples of the practical ways emerging young leaders are maintaining a connection to tradition. Young people in the Pacific are creating their own hybridised versions of tradition—'neotraditions' (Sahlins 2005)—which reaffirm and reimagine their cultures in ways that correspond with contemporary social, political, economic and environmental realities.

Areas for future research

The research presented in this book covers a broad range of topics related to youth livelihoods and development issues in Fiji, Solomon Islands and the broader Oceanic region. The developmental and cultural challenges apparent in the formal and informal structures that are intended to promote the growth and advancement of youth—such as education, employment and civil society—have been explored to unearth how the structural minimisation of youth is impacting on their opportunities for self-actualisation and engagement with their communities, countries and cultures. This broad frame represents the complexity and interconnectedness of the factors that impact on the lived experiences of Fijian and Solomon Islander youth. Rather than being the final word on the livelihood, leadership and civic engagement challenges facing youth in Fiji, Solomon Islands and other areas of the Pacific, it is a contribution to the ongoing conversation within both development organisations and the academic literature.

From this research and other projects in which I have been involved while researching and writing this monograph, potential pathways for future research have emerged. As this book has provided an overview of youth livelihood, leadership and civic engagement issues, investigating the interconnectedness of matters relating to education, employment and civil society structures, scope exists for this to lead to further research into these individual areas, as well as how these structures interact in other locations. Further exploration may also be undertaken into differing and locally relevant conceptions of self-actualisation, such as *yalomatua* and *vakaturaga* in Fiji, which help to identify alternative structures and strategies for supporting young people's development. Given the depth and breadth of insight offered by the youth activists with whom I engaged, it is exciting to consider what insights may emerge through engaging with Pacific youth in other countries, including in the diaspora. It is also foreseeable that the influence of ICT will continue to shape how Pacific youth engage in civil society, so continued study in this area seems appropriate.

Ideally, similar research into youth livelihood and development issues would be led by interested young Pacific researchers. If Pacific peoples are to exercise sovereignty over their futures, research must surely engage indigenous visions and agenda-setting. It should also be noted that while I engaged with a diverse sample of informants, gaps existed—particularly in my attempts to engage Indo-Fijians in focus groups—so my informants should not be taken to represent whole communities. Further efforts to include various voices, including members of marginalised groups, should be made.

Another promising site for future research exists in following the implementation and outcomes of the National Youth Authority Bill legislated by the Government of Vanuatu in 2018. This legislation 'will see the establishment of a youth-led government advisory body that will have direct control over youth development services across the country' (Bryce 2018). As this initiative has no precedent or correlation in Oceania, it offers a fascinating case study for its impact on promoting active citizenship, as well as youth livelihood and leadership opportunities.

Pacific youth futures

It is my hope that this book contributes to an understanding of the social role of youth in Fiji and Solomon Islands, the livelihood pressures they face and the development structures that can promote or stymie their potential. By shining a light on how young people engage and are socially expected to engage with their communities, we can see that their civic engagement is informed by cultural rules about who can participate and in what settings. Though I have highlighted examples of young people creating spaces for their own displays of active citizenship, these are primarily related to emerging social and environmental issues where their exclusion is yet to be normalised. Moreover, the young people engaging in these spaces represent a small fraction of the total number of youths in each country.

Grounded in issues discussed by informants relating to flaws in formal education systems, entrenched unemployment and marginalised civic engagement, I have explored how these issues interact and placed them within a discussion of the local and global pressures of navigating concepts of tradition and modernity. This is not, however, a profile of a homogeneous category of 'youth'. Instead, I seek to provide a political and economic analysis of Fijian and Solomon Islander youth, highlighting the vast diversity of youth experiences within and across both countries. The experiences of my youth informants differ significantly, affected by matters including ethnicity, geography, gender, sexuality and physical ability. Even within these and other subcategories, the experiences of my informants are not universally representative.

Rather than trying to identify a single issue impinging on youth achieving their collective potential, I have explored how common issues are identified as problematic for youth. Kris Prasad of Fiji suggested that the acknowledgement of diversity and complexity in my research approach held the greatest promise for the potential long-term impact of this study. He stated:

> I like the fact that you are actually taking the time to talk to diverse people, so you'll probably end up with a very nuanced understanding of youth issues in Fiji and, from my perspective, not a lot of people in academia are able to do that. They may just come from outside and they may talk to some diverse people and they come up with a report but when you read the report you'll realise that this person barely scratched the surface.

Although I cannot claim to have captured all elements of diversity, by understanding the multiplicity of youth experiences and variation of access to opportunity, the complexities of youth livelihoods can be better appreciated. From this, more appropriate programs and policies targeted at young people can be enacted by governments, multilateral bodies and development organisations. Questions can be asked about the structural barriers that inhibit the potential for the self-actualisation of youth and better targeted initiatives can be put in place.

From an academic perspective, the holistic livelihoods lens offers a new approach to more comprehensively understanding international development issues. That development at a basic level is about putting food on one's table and keeping a roof over one's head is not a revolutionary idea, nor is it the case at a societal level that this is shaped by who has access to opportunities, who does not and why. Indeed, these concepts are well covered in established development approaches including basic needs, sustainable livelihoods and capabilities. The utility of the holistic livelihoods approach applied in this book is that it embraces the strengths of each of these methods to investigate the political, economic and cultural factors impacting on development at individual and societal levels. This approach is further informed by theories of adaptive development and complex adaptive systems that explicitly seek to understand local context and caution against the transplantation of findings from one situation to another.

Perhaps most importantly, this book adds to a small but growing literature on the everyday experiences and struggles faced by youth in Pacific communities. This includes research conducted by academics, civil society organisations and multilateral development organisations into youth development matters in individual countries and across the broader region. The 2019 publication of *Pacific Youth: Local and Global Futures*, edited by Helen Lee—the first edited volume in more than two decades looking at youth issues in Oceania—was a wonderful starting point for those looking to explore these issues further.

The documentation of Pacific youth experiences expands the ability of those living and working in Oceania to understand the structural barriers impeding youth livelihood and development opportunities and assist youth to develop their capabilities. Further, it provides an opportunity to open dialogue and explore these issues in greater depth. At a more practical level, the production of this research and related work allows for the voices of Pacific youth to be represented in ways that carry a sense of legitimacy, credibility and authority in discussions about youth livelihood and development policies and programs with people in positions of influence. This was a sentiment repeatedly expressed to me by informants when I asked what they would like to see result from this research.

Harry Olikwailafa, of Solomon Islands, spoke of the potential for research focused on young people to assist local governments to plan youth policies and programs. He said: 'To get the government informed to make good decisions in their policy direction, there should be research.' For Tura Lewai, of Fiji, the utility of the research lies in its very existence. This book adds to the academic and development literature focused on youth issues, providing insight and potentially provoking discussion among locals and foreigners engaged in the region. Tura stated:

> Research like yours will be able to create a wealth of information that—if you want to come into the Pacific, if you want to come into Fiji, if you want to work with young people—this is the body of research that is out there that can assist you.

This book discusses the limitations to youth achieving their potential in Fiji and Solomon Islands and identifies these limitations as structural. They are embedded in concepts of culture and reinforced through systems theoretically intended to improve youth capabilities, which are poorly revised when problems are identified. As my informants repeatedly emphasised, the expectations placed on youth to be deferential and humble result in systems that dictate their livelihood pathways, repeatedly fail to equip them to embrace social and economic opportunities and discourage critical thinking. More so, they limit the wider human and social capital development of Pacific societies. Multiple informants stressed to me the need for young people to be recognised as a resource in which to invest for the betterment of their communities and countries. Regional development worker Luisa Senibulu of Fiji remarked that '[y]outh are key to the development of communities, of countries, [and] the region'. Similarly, Tura Lewai stated: '[W]e need to be able to realise that the future of the Pacific, the future of Fiji, the future of any Pacific island lies in its young people.'

The current social, political and economic climates for Fijian and Solomon Islander youth are intriguing. They are culturally expected to occupy a marginalised role in the decision-making processes of their societies, yet they also constitute a disproportionately large percentage of their countries' populations. It is no exaggeration to state that the developmental futures of the Great Ocean States of the Pacific are to a great extent contingent on how their young people engage in their societies and develop as leaders.

The need to develop the active citizenship and leadership abilities of the young people of the Pacific has never been more pressing. Combined with the quickening pace of social, economic and political change brought by globalisation, the region is facing two concurrent existential crises. First, the climate crisis risks destabilising social, political and economic structures throughout the region, with displacement, increased risk of environmental disasters and associated livelihood insecurities presenting very real and present threats. Second, these risks are compounded by the health and economic impacts that COVID-19 will have in the world's most aid-dependent region. Their economic precarity and structural minimisation mean Pacific youth are positioned to disproportionately feel the negative impacts of these challenges, with limited capacity to help construct risk-reduction and mitigation responses. This is despite evidence that these young people are willing and able to address the complex challenges of social change. Reframing social perceptions of youth to view them as a resource in which to be invested has the potential to deepen the capacities of the Great Ocean States of the Pacific to envision and achieve alternative, self-determined developmental futures.

It is worth noting that despite the structural challenges youth in Fiji and Solomon Islands face, the outcomes are not fixed. Although the examples of robust engagement in critical civil society discussed in these pages may represent cases of positive deviance, they nonetheless illustrate that young people are adaptable and they do have a desire to engage actively in their societies. Rather than existing at the margins as adults-in-waiting, these young people are forging paths, striving to be partners for today, rather than waiting to be leaders of tomorrow.

Bibliography

350.org (n.d.) Website, 350.org, Boston, MA, available from: 350.org/.

350 Pacific (n.d.) *We Don't Normally Do This Here in Kiribati …*, 350 Pacific, available from: 350pacific.org/we-dont-normally-do-this-here-in-kiribati/.

350 Pacific (2016) *Pray for Our Pacific*, 350 Pacific, available from: 350pacific. org/prayforourpacific/.

Abbott, D. & Pollard, S. (2004) *Hardship and Poverty in the Pacific*, Asian Development Bank, Manila.

Alasia, S. (1997) *Party Politics and Government in Solomon Islands*, Discussion Paper 97/7, State, Society and Governance in Melanesia Program, The Australian National University, Canberra.

Ali, A. (1979) Girmit: The Indenture Experience in Fiji, *Bulletin of the Fiji Museum No. 5*, The Fiji Museum, Suva.

Allen, M. (2005) Greed and Grievance: The Role of Economic Agendas in the Conflict in Solomon Islands, *Pacific Economic Bulletin, 20*(2), 56–71.

Allen, M. (2012) Land, Identity and Conflict on Guadalcanal, Solomon Islands, *Australian Geographer, 43*(2), 163–180, doi.org/10.1080/00049182.2012.6 82294.

Allen, M. (2013) *Greed and Grievance: Ex-Militants' Perspectives on the Conflict in Solomon Islands, 1998–2003*, University of Hawai`i Press, Honolulu, doi.org/ 10.21313/hawaii/9780824838546.001.0001.

Allen, M. & Dinnen, S. (2015) Solomon Islands in Transition? *The Journal of Pacific History, 50*(4), 381–397.

Al-Momani, M. (2011) The Arab 'Youth Quake': Implications on Democratization and Stability, *Middle East Law and Governance, 3*, 159–170, doi.org/10.1163/ 187633711x591521.

Ambelye, I. (2019) Youth's Displaced Aggression in Rural Papua New Guinea, in H. Lee (ed.), *Pacific Youth: Local and Global Futures* (pp. 183–201), ANU Press, Canberra, doi.org/10.22459/PY.2019.08.

Anderson, L. (2011) Demystifying the Arab Spring, *Foreign Affairs, 90*(3), 2–7.

Andrews, M. (2015) Explaining Positive Deviance in Public Sector Reforms in Development, *World Development, 74*, 197–208, doi.org/10.1016/j.worlddev. 2015.04.017.

Andrews, M., Pritchett, L., Samji, S., & Woolcock, M. (2015) Building Capability by Delivering Results: Putting Problem-Driven Iterative Adaptation (PDIA) Principles into Practice, in A. Whaites, G. Teskey, S. Fyson, & E. Gonzalez (eds), *A Governance Practitioner's Notebook: Alternative Ideas and Approaches* (pp. 123–133), OECD, Paris.

Andrews, M., Pritchett, L., & Woolcock, M. (2012) *Escaping Capability Traps Through Problem-Driven Iterative Adaptation*, CGD Working Paper 299, Center for Global Development, Washington, DC, available from: www.cgdev.org/publication/escaping-capability-traps-through-problem-driven-iterative-adaptation-pdia-working-paper.

Armingeon, K. & Guthmann, K (2013) Democracy in Crisis? The Declining Support for National Democracy in European Countries, 2007–2011, *European Journal of Political Research, 53*(3), 423–442, doi.org/10.1111/1475-6765.12046.

Aumanu-Leong, C. (2021) Fashion and Social Media Drive Solomon Islands' New Thrift Industry, *Pacific Beat*, [ABC Radio Australia], 30 June, available from: www.abc.net.au/radio-australia/programs/pacificbeat/fashion-social-media-drive-solomon-islands-new-thrift-industry/13425648.

Australia Network News (2013) Fiji's Jobless Rate at its 'Highest Level': Union, *ABC News*, 15 May, available from: www.abc.net.au/news/2013-05-15/an-fiji-union-says-unemployment-at-highest-level/4691268.

Awan, M.S., Malik, N., Sarwar, H., & Waqas, M. (2011) Impact of Education on Poverty Reduction, *International Journal of Academic Research, 3*(1), 659–664, available from: mpra.ub.uni-muenchen.de/31826/.

Baba, K. (2014) Youth Mainstreaming in Pacific Development: Challenges and Opportunities, MA thesis, Victoria University of Wellington.

Bacalzo, D. (2019) Economic Changes and the Unequal Lives of Young People among the Wampar in Papua New Guinea, in H. Lee (ed.), *Pacific Youth: Local and Global Futures* (pp. 57–78), ANU Press, Canberra, doi.org/10.22459/PY.2019.03.

Ball, R., Beacroft, L., & Lindley, J. (2011) *Australia's Pacific Seasonal Worker Pilot Scheme: Managing vulnerabilities to exploitation*, Trends and Issues in Crime and Criminal Justice No. 432, Australian Institute of Criminology, Canberra.

Barrau, J. (1958) *Subsistence Agriculture in Melanesia*, South Pacific Commission, Honolulu.

Barrington, D.J., Sridharan, S., Saunders, S.G., Souter, R.T., Bartram, J., Shields, K.F., Meo., S., Kearton, A., & Hughes, R.K. (2016) Improving Community Health through Marketing Exchanges: A Participatory Action Research Study on Water, Sanitation, and Hygiene in Three Melanesian Countries, *Social Science & Medicine, 171*, 84–93, doi.org/10.1016/j.socscimed.2016.11.003.

Beehner, L. (2007) The Effects of 'Youth Bulge' on Civil Conflicts, *Backgrounder*, 13 April, Council on Foreign Relations, New York, available from: www.cfr.org/backgrounder/effects-youth-bulge-civil-conflicts.

Bennett, J. (2002) *Roots of conflict in Solomon Islands—Though much is taken, much abides: Legacies of tradition and colonialism*, Discussion Paper 5, State, Society and Governance in Melanesia Program, The Australian National University, Canberra.

Bennett, J.A. (1987) *Wealth of the Solomons: A History of the Pacific Archipelago, 1800–1978*, University of Hawai`i Press, Honolulu.

Benos, N. & Zotou, S. (2014) Education and Economic Growth: A Meta-Regression Analysis, *World Development, 64*, 669–689, doi.org/10.1016/j.worlddev.2014.06.034.

Berner, E. & Phillips, B. (2003) Left to their Own Devices? Community Self-Help between Alternative Development and Neoliberalism, *Community Development Journal, 40*(1), 17–29, doi.org/10.1093/cdj/bsi003.

Besnier, N. (2004) Diversity, Hierarchy, and Modernity in Pacific Island Communities, in A. Duranti (ed.), *A Companion to Linguistic Anthropology* (pp. 95–120), Blackwell Publishing, Malden, MA, doi.org/10.1002/9780470996522.ch5.

Besnier, N. (2011) *On the Edge of the Global*, Stanford University Press, Palo Alto, CA.

Bessant, J. (2004) Mixed Messages: Youth Participation and Democratic Practice, *Australian Journal of Political Science, 39*(2), 387–404, doi.org/10.1080/1036114042000238573.

Bhim, M. (2011) *Stifling Opposition: An Analysis of the Approach of the Fiji Government After the 2006 Coup*, Discussion Paper 2011/6, State, Society and Governance in Melanesia Program, The Australian National University, Canberra.

Biesta, G. (2006) What's the Point of Lifelong Learning if Lifelong Learning Has No Point? On the Democratic Deficit of Policies for Lifelong Learning, *European Educational Research Journal, 5*(3–4), 169–180, doi.org/10.2304/eerj.2006.5.3.169.

Biesta, G. (2009) Good Education in an Age of Measurement: On the Need to Reconnect with the Question of Purpose in Education, *Educational Assessment, Evaluation and Accountability, 21*(1), 33–46, doi.org/10.1007/s11092-008-9064-9.

Binns, M. (2015) Education in the Solomon Islands, [Blog], The Borgen Project, Tacoma, WA, available from: borgenproject.org/education-solomon-islands/.

Birdsall, N., Ross, D., & Sabot, R. (1995) Inequality and Growth Reconsidered: Lessons from East Asia, *The World Bank Economic Review, 9*(3), 477–508, doi.org/10.1093/wber/9.3.477.

Bole, F. (2009) Ministry Establishes the Fiji School of the Air, Press release, 14 September, Ministry of Education, National Heritage, Culture and Arts, Suva, available from: www.fiji.gov.fj/Media-Center/Press-Releases/Ministry-establishes-the-Fiji-School-of-the-Air.aspx.

Botvin, G.J. (1985) The Life Skills Training Program as a Health Promotion Strategy, *Special Services in the Schools, 1*(3), 9–13, doi.org/10.1300/J008v01n03_03.

Botvin, G.J., Eng, A., & Williams, C.L. (1980) Preventing the Onset of Cigarette Smoking through Life Skills Training, *Preventive Medicine, 9*, 135–143, doi.org/10.1016/0091-7435(80)90064-x.

Botvin, G.J. & Griffin, K.W. (2004) Life Skills Training: Empirical Findings and Future Directions, *Journal of Primary Prevention, 25*(2), 211–232, doi.org/10.1023/b:jopp.0000042391.58573.5b.

Boyle, M. (2018) Recruitment of Overseas Workers for Sugar Cane Farms, *FBC News*, 1 February, available from: www.fbc.com.fj/fiji/59304/recruitment-of-overseas-workers-for-sugar-cane-farms.

Bradshaw, T.K. (2007) Theories of Poverty and Anti-Poverty Programs in Community Development, *Community Development, 38*(1), 7–25, doi.org/10.1080/15575330709490182.

Braithwaite, J., Dinnen, S., Allen, M., Braithwaite, V., & Charlesworth, H. (2010) *Pillars and Shadows: Statebuilding as Peacebuilding in Solomon Islands*, ANU E Press, Canberra, doi.org/10.22459/ps.11.2010.

Brimacombe, T. (2017) Pacific Policy Pathways: Young Women Online and Offline, in M. Macintyre & C. Spark (eds), *Transformations of Gender in Melanesia* (pp. 141–162), ANU Press, Canberra, doi.org/10.22459/tgm.02.2017.06.

Brison, K.J. (2001) Crafting Sociocentric Selves in Religious Discourse in Rural Fiji, *Ethos, 29*(4), 453–474, doi.org/10.1525/eth.2001.29.4.453.

Brison, K.J. (2007) *Our Wealth is Loving Each Other: Self and Society in Fiji*, Lexington Books, Lanham, MD.

Brown, B.B. & Larson, R.W. (2002) The Kaleidoscope of Adolescence: Experiences of the World's Youth at the Beginning of the 21st Century, in B.B. Brown, R.W. Larson, & T.S. Saraswathi (eds), *The World's Youth: Adolescence in Eight Regions of the Globe* (pp. 1–20), Cambridge University Press, Cambridge, UK, doi.org/10.1017/cbo9780511613814.002.

Brown, R.P.C. (1997) Estimating Remittance Functions for Pacific Island Migrants, *World Development, 25*(4), 613–626, doi.org/10.1016/s0305-750x (96)00122-2.

Brownhill, S. (2009) The Dynamics of Participation: Modes of Governance and Increasing Participation in Planning, *Urban Policy and Research, 27*(4), 357–375, doi.org/10.1080/08111140903308842.

Bryce, B. (2018) National Youth Authority to Give a Voice to Young ni-Vanuatu People, *Pacific Beat*, [ABC Radio Australia], 19 June, available from: www. abc.net.au/radio-australia/programs/pacificbeat/van-youth-bill/9884822.

Bryer, T.A. (2010) Living Democracy in Theory and Practice: Getting Dirty in a Local Government Incorporation Process, *Public Administration and Management, 15*(1), 259–304.

Bugotu, F. (1986) Island Countries Ask, 'Education for What?', *Bulletin of the UNESCO Regional Office for Education in Asia and the Pacific, 27*(3), 41–50.

Burns McGrath, B. & Ka`ili, T.O. (2010), Creating Project Talanoa: A Culturally Based Community Health Program for U.S. Pacific Islander Adolescents, *Public Health Nursing, 27*(1), 17–24, doi.org/10.1111/j.1525-1446.2009.00822.x.

Campbell, I.C. (2008) Across the Threshold: Regime Change and Uncertainty in Tonga 2005–2007, *The Journal of Pacific History, 43*(1), 95–109, doi.org/ 10.1080/00223340802054719.

Caputo, V. (1995) Anthropology's Silent 'Others': A Consideration of Some Conceptual and Methodological Issues for the Study of Youth and Children's Cultures, in V. Amit-Talai & H. Wulff (eds), *Youth Cultures: A Cross-Cultural Perspective*, Routledge, London.

Carling, M. (2009) Maximizing Potential: The Citizenship Role of Young People in Fiji, MA thesis, School of Government, Development Studies and International Affairs, University of the South Pacific, Suva.

Carter, G. (2015) Establishing a Pacific Voice in the Climate Change Negotiations, in G. Fry & S. Tarte (eds), *The New Pacific Diplomacy* (pp. 205–220), ANU Press, Canberra, doi.org/10.22459/npd.12.2015.17.

Case, E. (2021) *Everything Ancient Was Once New: Indigenous Persistence from Hawai`i to Kahiki*, University of Hawai`i Press, Honolulu.

Cave, D. (2012) Digital Islands: How the Pacific's ICT Revolution is Transforming the Region, *Analyses*, 21 November, Lowy Institute, Sydney, available from: archive.lowyinstitute.org/publications/digital-islands-how-pacific-ict-revolution-transforming-region.

Cavu, P., Tagicakiverata, I., Naisilisili, S., & Rabici, V. (2009) Education and Training Needs of Rural Communities: A Situational Analysis of Selected Villages in Fourteen Provinces of Fiji, in R. Maclean & D. Wilson (eds), *International Handbook of Education for the Changing World of Work* (pp. 609–618), Springer, Dordrecht, Netherlands, doi.org/10.1007/978-1-4020-5281-1_40.

Chambers, R. & Conway, G.R. (1991) *Sustainable Rural Livelihoods: Practical Concepts for the 21st Century*, IDS Discussion Paper 296, Institute of Development Studies, Brighton, UK.

Chattier, P. (2016) Fiji's Roshika Deo: Outlier, Positive Deviant or Simply Feisty Feminist? [Blog], 1 February, Developmental Leadership Program, University of Birmingham, UK, available from: www.dlprog.org/opinions/fiji-s-roshika-deo-outlier-positive-deviant-or-simply-feisty-feminist.php.

Checkoway, B., Pothukuchi, K., & Finn, J. (1995) Youth Participation in Community Planning: What Are the Benefits? *Journal of Planning Education and Research, 14*(2), 134–139, doi.org/10.1177/0739456x9501400206.

Clark, G. (2003) Dumont d'Urville's Oceania, *The Journal of Pacific History, 38*(2), 155–161, doi.org/10.1080/0022334032000120503.

Clarke, D. & Azzopardi, P. (2017) *State of Pacific Youth 2017*, United Nations Population Fund, Suva.

Clemens, M., Graham, C., & Howes, S. (2014) *Skill Development and Regional Mobility: Lessons from the Australia–Pacific Technical College*, Discussion Paper 34, Development Policy Centre, The Australian National University, Canberra, doi.org/10.2139/ssrn.2439558.

Clemens, M. & Ogden, D. (2014) *Migration as a Strategy for Household Finance: A Research Agenda on Remittances, Payments, and Development*, CGD Working Paper No. 354, NYU Wagner Research Paper No. 2457148, Center for Global Development, Washington, DC, and New York University, New York, doi.org/10.2139/ssrn.2457148.

Cohen, J. (1997) Deliberation and Democratic Legitimacy, in J. Bohman & W. Rehg (eds), *Deliberative Democracy: Essays on Reason and Politics*, MIT Press, Cambridge, MA, doi.org/10.7551/mitpress/2324.003.0006.

Coleman, J. (1968) The Concept of Equality of Educational Opportunity, *Harvard Educational Review, 38*(1), 7–22, doi.org/10.17763/haer.38.1.m3770776577415m2.

Commonwealth of Nations (2020) Education in Solomon Islands, *Commonwealth Network*, Commonwealth of Nations, Cambridge, UK, available from: www.commonwealthofnations.org/sectors-solomon_islands/education/.

Connell, J. (2006) Migration, Dependency and Inequality in the Pacific: Old Wine in Bigger Bottles? (Part 2), in S. Firth (ed.), *Globalisation and Governance in the Pacific Islands* (pp. 81–106), ANU E Press, Canberra, doi.org/10.22459/ggpi.12.2006.05.

Connell, J. (2007) The Fiji Times and the Good Citizen: Constructing Modernity and Nationhood in Fiji, *The Contemporary Pacific, 19*(1), 85–109, doi.org/10.1353/cp.2007.0006.

Connell, J. (2010) From Blackbirds to Guestworkers in the South Pacific. *Plus ça change … ?*, *The Economic and Labour Relations Review, 20*(2), 111–122, doi.org/10.1177/103530461002000208.

Connell, J. (2011) Elephants in the Pacific? Pacific Urbanisation and its Discontents, *Asia Pacific Viewpoint, 52*(2), 121–135, doi.org/10.1111/j.1467-8373.2011.01445.x.

Connell, J. (2016) Greenland and the Pacific Islands: An Improbable Conjunction of Development Trajectories, *Island Studies Journal, 11*(2), 465–484.

Connell, J. & Corbett, J. (2016) Deterritorialisation: Reconceptualising Development in the Pacific Islands, *Global Society, 30*(4), 583–604, doi.org/10.1080/13600826.2016.1158701.

Connell, T., Carr, M., & Kirkwood, I. (2016) Newcastle Harbour Coal Blockade: Live Updates, *Newcastle Herald*, 8 May, available from: www.newcastleherald. com.au/story/3894106/newcastle-harbour-coal-blockade/.

Connors, A. & Barker, A. (2016) Papua New Guinea Shooting: Why Were Students Protesting against Peter O'Neill's Government? *ABC News*, 8 June, available from: www.abc.net.au/news/2016-06-08/papua-new-guinea-violence student-anger-at-oneill/7492874?nw=0.

Corbett, J. (2015) 'Everybody Knows Everybody': Practising Politics in the Pacific Islands, *Democratization, 22*(1), 51–72, doi.org/10.1080/13510347. 2013.811233.

Corcoran, P.B. & Koshy, K.C. (2010) The Pacific Way: Sustainability in Higher Education in the South Pacific Island Nations, *International Journal of Sustainability in Higher Education, 11*(2), 130–140, doi.org/10.1108/ 14676371011031856.

Cornwall, A. (2007) Buzzwords and Fuzzwords: Deconstructing Development Discourse, *Development in Practice, 17*(4–5), 471–484, doi.org/10.1080/ 09614520701469302.

Cornwall, A. & Brock, K. (2005) What Do Buzzwords Do for Development Policy? A Critical Look at 'Participation', 'Empowerment' and 'Poverty Reduction', *Third World Quarterly, 26*(7), 1043–1060, doi.org/10.1080/ 01436590500235603.

Cornwall, A. & Rivas, A.-M. (2015) From 'Gender Equality' and 'Women's Empowerment' to Global Justice: Reclaiming a Transformative Agenda for Gender and Development, *Third World Quarterly, 36*(2), 396–415, doi.org/ 10.1080/01436597.2015.1013341.

Cowen, M.P. & Shenton, R.W. (1996) *Doctrines of Development*, Routledge, New York.

Cox, J. (2017) Kindy and Grassroots Gender Transformations in Solomon Islands, in M. Macintyre & C. Spark (eds), *Transformations of Gender in Melanesia* (pp. 69–93), ANU Press, Canberra, doi.org/10.22459/tgm.02.2017.03.

Craney, A. (2019) Youth Leadership in Fiji and Solomon Islands: Creating Opportunities for Civic Engagement, in H. Lee (ed.), *Pacific Youth: Local and Global Futures* (pp. 137–158), ANU Press, Canberra, doi.org/10.22459/ PY.2019.06.

Craney, A. (2021a) Fault Lines for Unrest in the Pacific: Youth, Livelihoods and Land Rights in Driving and Mitigating Conflict, *Asia Pacific Viewpoint*, 18 June [Online first], doi.org/10.1111/apv.12311.

Craney, A. (2021b) Seeking a Panacea: Attempts to Address the Failings of Fiji and Solomon Islands Formal Education in Preparing Young People for Livelihood Opportunities, *The Contemporary Pacific, 33*(2), 338–362.

Cremin, P. & Nakabugo, M.G. (2012) Education, Development and Poverty Reduction: A Literature Critique, *International Journal of Educational Development, 32*, 499–506, doi.org/10.1016/j.ijedudev.2012.02.015.

Crocombe, R. (1975) Seeking a Pacific Way, in S. Tupouniua, R. Crocombe, & C. Slatter (eds), *The Pacific Way: Social Issues in National Development* (pp. 1–6), South Pacific Social Sciences Association, Suva.

Curtain, R. (2006) For Poor Countries' Youth, Dashed Hopes Signal Danger Ahead, *Current History, 105*(695), 435–440, doi.org/10.1525/curh.2006. 105.695.435.

Curtain, R., Dornan, M., Doyle, J., & Howes, S. (2016) *Labour Mobility: The Ten Billion Dollar Prize*, The World Bank, Canberra.

Curtain, R. & Vakaoti, P. (2011) *The State of Pacific Youth 2011: Opportunities and Obstacles*, UNICEF Pacific and Pacific Community, Suva.

Dakuvula, J. (1975) Rituals of Planning and Realities of Development, in S. Tupouniua, R. Crocombe, & C. Slatter (eds), *The Pacific Way: Social Issues in National Development* (pp. 15–17), South Pacific Social Sciences Association, Suva.

D'Arcy, P. (2014) The Chinese Pacifics: A Brief Historical Review, *The Journal of Pacific History, 49*(4), 396–420.

de Haan, L. & Zoomers, A. (2005) Exploring the Frontier of Livelihoods Research, *Development and Change, 36*(1), 27–47, doi.org/10.1111/j.0012-155x.2005. 00401.x.

de Tocqueville, A. (1947) *Democracy in America: A New Translation by Arthur Goldhammer*, Library of America, New York.

Diamond, L. (1994) Toward Democratic Consolidation, *Journal of Democracy, 5*(3), 4–17.

Diamond, L. (2015) Facing Up to the Democratic Recession, *Journal of Democracy, 26*(1), 141–155.

Dinnen, S. (2012) The Solomon Islands—RAMSI, Transition and Future Prospects, *Security Challenges, 8*(4), 61–71.

Domingo, P., O'Neil, T., & Foresti, M. (2014) Women's Participation in Peace and Security: Normative Ends, Political Means, *ODI Briefing, 88*(1), 1–6.

Dornan, M. & Pryke, J. (2017) Foreign Aid to the Pacific: Trends and Developments in the Twenty-First Century, *Asia & the Pacific Policy Studies,* *4*(3), 386–404, doi.org/10.1002/app5.185.

Downs, A. (1957) *An Economic Theory of Democracy*, Harper, New York.

Duncan, R. (2014) Reflections on Constraints to Growth in Pacific Island Countries, Keynote address, 2014 Pacific Update, The Australian National University, Canberra, 16–17 June, available from: devpolicy.org/reflections-on-constraints-to-growth-in-pacific-island-countries-20140626/?utm_source=Devpolicy&utm_campaign=4c7c26d90e-Devpolicy_News__June_27_2014&utm_medium=email&utm_term=0_082b498f84-4c7c26d90e-312043489.

Duncan, R. & Voigt-Graf, C. (2008) *Labour Market Scenarios for the Asian Decent Work Decade in the Pacific Island Countries*, ILO Asia-Pacific Working Paper Series, International Labour Organization, Bangkok.

Easterly, W. (2006) *The White Man's Burden: Why the West's Efforts to Aid the Rest Have Done So Much Ill and So Little Good*, Penguin, New York.

Ecumenical Council for Research, Education and Advocacy (ECREA) (2002) *Listening to Youth*, Ecumenical Council for Research, Education and Advocacy, Suva.

Englund, H. & Leach, J. (2000) Ethnography and the Meta-Narratives of Modernity, *Current Anthropology, 41*, 225–248, doi.org/10.2307/3596698.

Escobar, A. (1992) Imagining a Post-Development Era? Critical Thought, Development and Social Movements, *Social Text, 10*(31), 20–56.

Escobar, A. (2000) Beyond the Search for a Paradigm? Post-Development and Beyond, *Development, 43*(4), 11–14, doi.org/10.1057/palgrave.development.1110188.

Esteva, G. (2010) Development, in W. Sachs (ed.), *The Development Dictionary: A Guide to Knowledge as Power* (2nd edn), Zed Books, London.

Esteva, G. & Prakash, M.S. (1998) Beyond Development, What? *Development in Practice, 8*(3), 280–296.

Evans, D. (2016) *Hard Work: Youth Employment Programming in Honiara, Solomon Islands*, Discussion Paper 2016/7, State, Society and Governance in Melanesia Program, The Australian National University, Canberra.

Evans, D. (2019) 'Things Still Fall Apart': A Political Economy Analysis of State–Youth Engagement in Honiara, Solomon Islands, in H. Lee (ed.), *Pacific Youth: Local and Global Futures* (pp. 79–109), ANU Press, Canberra, doi.org/10.22459/PY.2019.04.

Evershed, N., Liu, R., & Livsey, A. (2016) Are You Reflected in the New Parliament? *The Guardian*, 31 August, available from: www.theguardian.com/australia-news/datablog/ng-interactive/2016/aug/31/are-you-reflected-in-the-new-parliament-diversity-survey-of-australian-politics.

Fanon, F. (1967) *The Wretched of the Earth*, Penguin, Harmondsworth, UK.

Farrar, D. (2017) The 52nd New Zealand Parliament Demographics, *Kiwiblog*, [Wellington], 9 October, available from: www.kiwiblog.co.nz/2017/10/the_52nd_new_zealand_parliament_demographics.html.

Fearon, J.D. & Laitin, D.D. (2003) Ethnicity, Insurgency, and Civil War, *American Political Science Review, 97*(1), 75–90.

Ferguson, J. (1994) The Anti-Politics Machine: 'Development' and Bureaucratic Power in Lesotho, *The Ecologist, 24*(5), 176–181.

Fiji Bureau of Statistics (FBoS) (2018) 2017 Population and Housing Census: Release 1—Age, Sex, Geography and Economic Activity, *Statistical News*, 5 January, Fiji Bureau of Statistics, Suva, available from: www.statsfiji.gov.fj/statistics/2007-census-of-population-and-housing.

Fiji Bureau of Statistics (FBoS) (2020) Annual Paid Employment Statistics 2018, *Statistical News*, No. 4, 28 January, Fiji Bureau of Statistics, Suva, available from: www.statsfiji.gov.fj/index.php/statistics/social-statistics/employment-statistics44.

Fiji Bureau of Statistics (FBoS) (2021a) 2007 Population Size and Growth by Ethnicity and Geographic Sector, *Census of Population and Housing*, Fiji Bureau of Statistics, Suva, available from: www.statsfiji.gov.fj/statistics/2007-census-of-population-and-housing.

Fiji Bureau of Statistics (FBoS) (2021b) Provisional No. of Paid Employment by Salary and Wage—2014, *Employment Statistics*, Fiji Bureau of Statistics, Suva, available from: www.statsfiji.gov.fj/statistics/social-statistics/employment-statistics44.

The Fijian Government (n.d.) *Young Entrepreneurship Scheme*, Ministry of Industry, Trade and Tourism, Suva, available from: yes.gov.fj/.

The Fijian Government (2012) *Situational Analysis of Youths in Fiji 2011*, Ministry of Youth and Sports, Suva.

The Fijian Government (2015) *Policy on Tuition Fee Free Grant for Primary and Secondary Schools*, Ministry of Education, Heritage and Arts, Suva.

Firth, S. (2012) Reflections on Fiji Since Independence, *The Round Table: The Commonwealth Journal of International Affairs, 101*(6), 575–583, doi.org/10.1080/00358533.2012.749098.

Firth, S. (2018) Instability in the Pacific Islands: A Status Report, *Analyses*, 4 June, Lowy Institute, Sydney.

Fletcher, G., Brimacombe, T., & Roche, C. (2016) *Power, Politics and Coalitions in the Pacific: Lessons from Collective Action on Gender and Power*, Research Paper 42, Pacific Women, Suva, and Developmental Leadership Program, Birmingham, UK.

Fletcher, J., Parkhill, F., Fa`aofi, A., Taleni, L.T., & O'Regan, B. (2009) Pasifika Students: Teachers and Parents Voice their Perceptions of What Provides Supports and Barriers to Pasifika Students' Achievements in Literacy and Learning, *Teaching and Teacher Education, 25*, 24–33, doi.org/10.1016/j.tate.2008.06.002.

Fox, C.E. (1967) *The Story of the Solomons*, DOM Publications, Taroaniara, Solomon Islands.

Fraenkel, J. (2015) An Analysis of Provincial, Urban and Ethnic Loyalties in Fiji's 2014 Election, *The Journal of Pacific History, 50*(1), 38–53, doi.org/10.1080/00223344.2015.1013598.

Fraenkel, J. (2019a) The Politics of Riots in the Solomon Islands, *East Asia Forum*, 30 April, available from: www.eastasiaforum.org/2019/04/30/the-politics-of-riots-in-the-solomon-islands/.

Fraenkel, J. (2019b) Postcolonial Political Institutions in the South Pacific Islands: A Survey, in S. Firth & V. Naidu (eds), *Understanding Oceania: Celebrating the University of the South Pacific and its Collaboration with The Australian National University* (pp. 127–151), ANU Press, Canberra, doi.org/10.22459/uo.2019.07.

Fraenkel, J. & Firth, S. (2009a) The Enigmas of Fiji's Good Governance Coup, in S. Firth, J. Fraenkel, & B.V. Lal (eds), *The 2006 Military Takeover in Fiji: A Coup to End All Coups?* (pp. 3–17), ANU E Press, Canberra, doi.org/10.22459/mtf.04.2009.01.

Fraenkel, J. & Firth, S. (2009b) Fiji's Coup Syndrome, in S. Firth, J. Fraenkel, & B.V. Lal (eds), *The 2006 Military Takeover in Fiji: A Coup to End All Coups?* (pp. 449–458), ANU E Press, Canberra, doi.org/10.22459/mtf.04.2009.31.

Frank, A.G. (1970) The Development of Underdevelopment, in R.F. Rhodes (ed.), *Imperialism and Underdevelopment* (pp. 4–17), Monthly Review Press, New York.

Frank, A.G. (1972) *Lumpenbourgeoisie Lumpendevelopment: Dependence, Class, and Politics in Latin America*, Monthly Review Press, New York.

Frank, K.I. (2006) The Potential of Youth Participation in Planning, *Journal of Planning Literature, 20*(4), 351–371, doi.org/10.1177/0885412205286016.

Fry, G. (1981) Regionalism and International Politics of the South Pacific, *Pacific Affairs, 54*(3), 455–484, doi.org/10.2307/2756789.

Fukuda-Parr, S. (2003) The Human Development Paradigm: Operationalizing Sen's Ideas on Capabilities, *Feminist Economics, 9*(2–3), 301–317, doi.org/10.1080/1354570022000077980.

Fukuyama, F. (2001) Social Capital, Civil Society and Development, *Third World Quarterly, 22*(1), 7–20.

Fuller, G. & Pitts, F.R. (1990) Youth Cohorts and Political Unrest in South Korea, *Political Geography Quarterly, 9*(1), 9–22, doi.org/10.1016/0260-9827(90)90003-s.

Fussell, E. & Greene, M.E. (2002) Demographic Trends Affecting Youth around the World, in B.B. Brown, R.W. Larson, & T.S. Saraswathi (eds), *The World's Youth: Adolescence in Eight Regions of the Globe* (pp. 21–60), Cambridge University Press, Cambridge, UK, doi.org/10.1017/cbo9780511613814.003.

Gallagher, M. (2008) Foucault, Power and Participation, *International Journal of Children's Rights, 16*(3), 395–406.

Garcia Canclini, N. (1995) *Hybrid Cultures: Strategies for Entering and Leaving Modernity*, Translated by C.L. Chiappari & S.L. Lopez, University of Minnesota Press, Minneapolis, doi.org/10.1016/s0261-3050(97)83599-1.

Gaye, M. & Diallo, F. (1997) Community Participation in the Management of the Urban Environment in Rufisque (Senegal), *Environment and Urbanization, 9*(1), 9–29, doi.org/10.1177/095624789700900110.

Gegeo, D.W. (2001) Cultural Rupture and Indigeneity: The Challenge of (Re)visioning 'Place' in the Pacific, *The Contemporary Pacific, 13*(2), 491–507, doi.org/10.1353/cp.2001.0052.

Gell-Mann, M. (1992) Complexity and Complex Adaptive Systems, in J.A. Hawkins & M. Gell-Mann (eds), *The Evolution of Human Languages* (pp. 3–18), Santa Fe Institute Studies in the Sciences of Complexity No. 11, Addison-Wesley, Redwood City, CA.

Geraghty, P. (1983) *The History of the Fijian Languages*, University of Hawai`i Press, Honolulu.

Geraghty, P. (2005) The Ivolavosa and the Codification of Fijian, *Directions: Journal of Educational Studies, 27*(1), 77–94.

Gibson, J. & McKenzie, D. (2009) *The Microeconomic Determinants of Emigration and Return Migration of the Best and Brightest: Evidence from the Pacific*, IZA Discussion Paper No. 3926, Institute of Labor Economics, Bonn, doi.org/ 10.1016/j.jdeveco.2009.11.002.

Gibson, J. & McKenzie, D. (2014) The Development Impact of a Best Practice Seasonal Worker Policy, *The Review of Economics and Statistics, 96*(2): 229–243, doi.org/10.1162/rest_a_00383.

Gibson, J., McKenzie, D., & Rohorua, H. (2008) *How Pro-Poor is the Selection of Seasonal Migrant Workers from Tonga Under New Zealand's Recognised Seasonal Employer (RSE) Program?* Discussion Paper 07/08, Centre for Research and Analysis of Migration, University College London, doi.org/10.1596/1813-9450-4698.

Goddard, M. (2010) *Justice Delivered Locally: Solomon Islands*, Justice for the Poor, The World Bank, Washington, DC.

Goldstone, J.A. (2002) Population and Security: How Demographic Change Can Lead to Violent Conflict, *Journal of International Affairs, 56*(1), 3–21.

Golombeck, S.B. (2006) Children as Citizens, *Journal of Community Practice, 14*(1), 11–30.

Good, M.K. (2012) Modern Moralities, Moral Modernities: Ambivalence and Change Among Youth in Tonga, PhD thesis, University of Arizona, Tucson.

Good, M.K. (2013) Filipino Film Lovers, *Anthropology Now, 5*(3), 41–51.

Good, M.K. (2014) The Fokisi and the Fakaleiti, in K. Alexeyeff & N. Besnier (eds), *Gender on the Edge: Transgender, Gay, and Other Pacific Islanders*, University of Hawai`i Press, Honolulu, doi.org/10.21313/hawaii/9780824838829.003. 0010

Good, M.K. (2019) Flexibility, Possibility and the Paradoxes of the Present: Tongan Youth Moving into the Future, in H. Lee (ed.), *Pacific Youth: Local and Global Futures* (pp. 33–55), ANU Press, Canberra, doi.org/10.22459/PY.2019.02.

Gounder, N. & Prasad, B. (2013) *Economic Growth, Investment, Confidence and Poverty Reduction in Fiji: Semi-rational Exuberance?* Development Policy Centre Discussion Paper 31, Crawford School of Public Policy, The Australian National University, Canberra, doi.org/10.2139/ssrn.2327382.

Government of Solomon Islands (2002) *Solomon Islands Human Development Report 2002: Building a Nation*, Mark Otter for Government of Solomon Islands, Brisbane.

Government of Solomon Islands (2010) *National Youth Policy 2010–2015*, Government of Solomon Islands, Honiara.

Government of Solomon Islands (2011) *2009 Population and Housing Census: Report on Migration and Urbanisation*, Government of Solomon Islands, Honiara.

Government of Solomon Islands (2016) *National Education Action Plan 2016–2020*, Ministry of Education and Human Resource Development, Solomon Islands Government, Honiara, available from: www.mehrd.gov.sb/documents?view=download&format=raw&fileId=1560.

Government of Solomon Islands (2017) *National Youth Policy 2017–2030*, Government of Solomon Islands, Honiara.

Grosfoguel, R. (2000) Developmentalism, Modernity, and Dependency Theory in Latin America, *Nepantla: Views from South, 1*(2), 347–374.

Guendelman, S. & Perez-Itriago, A. (1987) Migration Tradeoffs: Men's Experiences with Seasonal Lifestyles, *The International Migration Review, 21*(3), 709–727, doi.org/10.1177/019791838702100314.

Gupte, J., te Lintelo, D., & Barnett, I. (2014) Understanding 'Urban Youth' and the Challenges they Face in Sub-Saharan Africa: Unemployment, Food Insecurity and Violent Crime, *Evidence Report No. 81: Addressing and Mitigating Violence*, Institute of Development Studies, Brighton, UK.

Halapua, S. (2000) *Talanoa Process: The Case of Fiji*, East–West Center, Honolulu.

Halapua, S. (2013) Talanoa in Building Democracy and Governance, Paper prepared for the Conference of Future Leaders of the Pacific, Pago Pago, American Samoa, 4–7 February, available from: talanoa.org/Home_files/Talanoa%20in%20Building%20Democracy%20and%20Governance.pdf.

Haley, B.D. & Wilcoxon, L.R. (1997) Anthropology and the Making of Chumash Tradition, *Current Anthropology, 38*(5), 761–794, doi.org/10.1086/204667.

Haley, N. (2008) *Strengthening Civil Society to Build Demand for Better Governance in the Pacific: Literature Review and Analysis of Good Practice and Lessons Learned*, Discussion Paper No. 7, State Society and Governance in Melanesia Program, The Australian National University, Canberra.

Hameiri, S. (2007) The Trouble with RAMSI: Reexamining the Roots of Conflict in Solomon Islands, *The Contemporary Pacific, 19*(2), 409–441, doi.org/ 10.1353/cp.2007.0052.

Hanushek, E.A. (2016) Will More Higher Education Improve Economic Growth? *Oxford Review of Economic Policy, 32*(4), 538–552, doi.org/10.1093/oxrep/ grw025.

Hanushek, E.A. & Woessmann, L. (2007) *The Role of Education Quality in Economic Growth*, Policy Research Working Paper No. 4122, The World Bank, Washington, DC, available from: openknowledge.worldbank.org/ handle/10986/7154.

Harris, A. (2006) Introduction: Critical Perspectives on Child and Youth Participation in Australia and New Zealand/Aotearoa, *Children, Youth and Environments, 16*(2), 220–230.

Harris, A., Wyn, J., & Younes, S. (2010) Beyond Apathetic or Activist Youth: 'Ordinary' Young People and Contemporary Forms of Participation, *Young, 18*(9), 9–32, doi.org/10.1177/110330880901800103.

Harsch, E. (2016) Blowing the Same Trumpet? Pluralist Protest in Burkina Faso, *Social Movement Studies, 15*(2), 231–238, doi.org/10.1080/14742837.2016. 1144052.

Hart, R. (1992) *Children's Participation: From Tokenism to Citizenship*, Innocenti Essays No. 4, UNICEF International Child Development Centre, Florence.

Hau`ofa, E. (1983) *Tales of the Tikongs*, University of Hawai`i Press, Honolulu.

Hau`ofa, E. (1985) The Future of Our Past, in R.C. Kiste & R.A. Herr (eds), *The Pacific Islands in the year 2000* (pp. 151–169), Working Paper Series, Pacific Islands Studies Program, Center for Asian and Pacific Studies, University of Hawai`i at Manoa, available from: hdl.handle.net/10125/15522.

Hau`ofa, E. (1994) Our Sea of Islands, *The Contemporary Pacific, 6*(1), 148–161.

Hau`ofa, E. (1998) The Ocean in Us, *The Contemporary Pacific, 10*(2), 392–410.

Hayward-Jones, J. (2012) Fiji Ends Public Emergency Regulations, *The Interpreter*, 5 January, available from: www.lowyinstitute.org/the-interpreter/fiji-ends-public-emergency-regulations.

Hendrixson, A. (2004) *Angry Young Men, Veiled Young Women: Constructing a New Population Threat*, Briefing 34, The Corner House, Dorset, UK.

Herd, G.P. (2011) The Arab Spring: Challenges, Obstacles and Dilemmas, *Connections: The Quarterly Journal, 10*(4), 103–120, doi.org/10.11610/connections.10.4.07.

Heron, T. (2008) Globalization, Neoliberalism and the Exercise of Human Agency, *International Journal of Politics, Culture and Society, 20*, 85–101.

Herzfeld, M. (2001) *Anthropology: Theoretical Practice in Culture and Society*, Blackwell Publishers, Oxford.

Hess, S. (2006) Strathern's Melanesian 'Dividual' and the Christian 'Individual': A Perspective from Vanua Lava, Vanuatu, *Oceania, 76*(3), 285–296, doi.org/10.1002/j.1834-4461.2006.tb03058.x.

Hicks, N. & Streeten, P. (1979) Indicators of Development: The Search for a Basic Needs Yardstick, *World Development, 7*(6), 567–580, doi.org/10.1016/0305-750x(79)90093-7.

Hill, H. (2001) Non-Formal Education as an Important Strategy for Youth Empowerment, *Development Bulletin, 56*, 18–20.

Holmberg, A. (2016) *The Price of Conflict, the Prospect of Peace: Virtual Reality in Honiara, Solomon Islands*, 28 September, [Video], The World Bank, Washington, DC, available from: www.worldbank.org/en/news/video/2016/09/28/the-price-of-conflict-the-prospect-of-peace-virtual-reality-in-honiara-solomon-islands.

Honiara City Council (n.d.) School Fees, [Online], Honiara City Council, Honiara, available from: honiaracitycouncil.com/index.php/education-and-recreation-2/hcc-schools-parents-2/school-fees-2/.

Honwana, A. (2014) 'Waithood': Youth Transitions and Social Change, in D. Foeken, T. Dietz, L. de Haan, & L. Johnson (eds), *Development and Equity* (pp. 28–40), Brill Publishers, Leiden, Netherlands, doi.org/10.1163/9789004269729_004.

Hopwood, B., Mellor, M., & O'Brien, G. (2005) Sustainable Development: Mapping Different Approaches, *Sustainable Development, 13*, 38–52, doi.org/10.1002/sd.244.

Howe, K.R. (1979) Pacific Islands History in the 1980s: New Directions or Monograph Myopia? *Pacific Studies, 3*(1), 81–90.

Hudson, D., Mcloughlin, C., Marquette, H., & Roche, C. (2018) *Inside the Black Box of Political Will: 10 Years of Findings from the Developmental Leadership Program*, Developmental Leadership Program, Birmingham, UK.

Hughes, H. (2003) *Aid Has Failed the Pacific*, Issue Analysis No. 33, The Centre for Independent Studies, Sydney.

Hummelbrunner, R. & Jones, H. (2013) *A Guide for Managing in the Face of Complexity*, Working Paper, Overseas Development Institute, London.

Hunt, D. (2007) Hunting the Blackbirder: Ross Lewin and the Royal Navy, *The Journal of Pacific History, 42*(1), 37–53, doi.org/10.1080/0022334070 1286826.

Illich, I. (1968) To Hell with Good Intentions, Paper presented to Conference on InterAmerican Student Projects, Cuernavaca, Mexico, 20 April.

International Labour Organization (ILO) (2016a) *Fiji Labour Market Update*, International Labour Organization, Suva.

International Labour Organization (ILO) (2016b) *World Employment and Social Outlook for Youth 2016: In Which Countries is it Hardest for Young People to Find Work in 2016?* [Online], International Labour Organization, Geneva, available from: www.ilo.org/global/about-the-ilo/multimedia/maps-and-charts/enhanced/WCMS_514559/lang--en/index.htm.

Internet World Stats (2021) *Internet World Stats: Usage and Population Statistics*, [Online], available from: www.internetworldstats.com/stats.htm.

Jacobson, T.L. (2016) Amartya Sen's Capabilities Approach and Communication for Development and Social Change, *Journal of Communication, 66*, 789–810, doi.org/10.1111/jcom.12252.

Jakimow, T. (2012) A Site for the Empowerment of Women? The Clash of Patriarchal Values and Development Norms in a Family-Based NGO, *Ethnography, 13*(2), 213–235, doi.org/10.1177/1466138111420507.

Jayaweera, S. & Morioka, K. (2008) *Giving South Pacific Youth a Voice: Youth Development through Participation*, The World Bank, Suva.

Jeffrey, C. (2010) Timepass: Youth, Class, and Time among Unemployed Young Men in India, *Journal of the American Ethnological Society, 37*(3), 465–481, doi.org/10.1111/j.1548-1425.2010.01266.x.

John, A. (2015) Sore: Moves to Deregister FSII an Option, *Solomon Star*, [Honiara], accessed from: www.solomonstarnews.com/news/national/8059-sore-moves-to-deregister-fsii-an-option [page discontinued].

Johnson, C. (1982) *MITI and the Japanese Miracle*, Stanford University Press, Stanford, CA.

Johnson, C. (1999) The Developmental State: Odyssey of a Concept, in M. Woo-Cummings (ed.), *The Developmental State* (pp. 32–60), Cornell University Press, Ithaca, NY.

Jolly, M. (1994) Hierarchy and Encompassment: Rank, Gender and Place in Vanuatu and Fiji, *History and Anthropology*, 7(1–4), 133–167, doi.org/10.1080/02757206.1994.9960843.

Jolly, M. (1996) 'Woman Ikat Raet Long Human Raet O No?' Women's Rights, Human Rights and Domestic Violence in Vanuatu, *Feminist Review*, 52, 169–190, doi.org/10.2307/1395780.

Jourdan, C. (1995) Masta Liu, in V. Amit-Talai & H. Wulff (eds), *Youth Cultures: A Cross-Cultural Perspective*, Routledge, London.

Jourdan, C. (1996) Where Have All the Cultures Gone? Sociocultural Creolisation in the Solomon Islands, in J. Friedman and J. Carrier (eds), *Melanesian Modernities*, Lund University Press, Lund, Sweden.

Jourdan, C. (2008) Language Repertoires and the Middle-Class in the Solomon Islands, in M. Meyerfoff & N. Nagy (eds), *Social Lives in Language: Sociolinguistic and Multilingual Language Communities* (pp. 43–67), John Benjamin Publishing Company, Amsterdam, doi.org/10.1075/impact.24.07jou.

Jumeau, R. (2013) Small Island Developing States, Large Ocean States, Paper presented to Expert Group Meeting on Oceans, Seas and Sustainable Development: Implementation and Follow-Up to Rio+20, United Nations, New York, 18–19 April.

Kabutaulaka, T.T. (2001) *Beyond Ethnicity: The Political Economy of the Guadalcanal Crisis in Solomon Islands*, Working Paper 1/2001, State, Society and Governance in Melanesia Program, The Australian National University, Canberra.

Kaiku, P. (2017) Re-Thinking the Youth Bulge Theory in Melanesia, *Contemporary PNG Studies: DWU Research Journal*, 26, 1–14.

Kava Bowl Media (n.d.) Pacific Stories for the World, Webpage, available from: kavabowlmedia.com/.

Keen, M. & Barbara, J. (2015) *Pacific Urbanisation: Changing Times*, In Brief 2015/64, State, Society and Governance in Melanesia Program, The Australian National University, Canberra.

Keesing, R.M. (1982) Kastom and Anticolonialism on Malaita: 'Culture' as Political Symbol, *Mankind, 13*(4), 357–373, doi.org/10.1111/j.1835-9310.1982. tb01000.x.

Kidd, S. (2012) *Poverty, Vulnerability and Social Protection in the Pacific: The Role of Social Transfers*, Pacific Social Protection Series, Australian Agency for International Development, Canberra.

Kiddle, L. (2010) Contemporary Urban Squatting in Fiji: Recent Trends, Intervention and a Potential Policy Framework, *Fijian Studies, 8*(1), 83–98.

Kiddle, L. (2011) Informal Settlers, Perceived Security of Tenure and Housing Consolidation: Case Studies from Urban Fiji, PhD thesis, Victoria University of Wellington.

Kiddle, L. (2016) The Pacific Urban Forum: Challenges and Lessons for Land Governance, Paper presented to FIG Working Week: Recovery from Disaster, International Federation of Surveyors, Christchurch, New Zealand, 2–6 May.

Klarman, M.J. (1994) Brown, Racial Change, and the Civil Rights Movement, *Virginia Law Review, 80*(1), 7–150, doi.org/10.2307/1073592.

Klasen, S. & Lamanna, F. (2009) The Impact of Gender Inequality in Education and Employment on Economic Growth: New Evidence for a Panel of Countries, *Feminist Economics, 15*(3), 91–132, doi.org/10.1080/13545700902893106.

Kleine, D. (2010) ICT4What?—Using the Choice Framework to Operationalise the Capability Approach to Development, *Journal of International Development, 22*(5), 674–692, doi.org/10.1002/jid.1719.

Kleine, D. (2013) *Technologies of Choice? ICTs, Development, and the Capabilities Approach*, MIT Press, Cambridge, MA.

Krantz, L. (2001) *The Sustainable Livelihood Approach to Poverty Reduction: An Introduction*, Swedish International Development Cooperation Agency, Stockholm.

Kuhn, R. (2012) On the Role of Human Development in the Arab Spring, *Population and Development Review, 38*(4), 649–683, doi.org/10.1111/ j.1728-4457.2012.00531.x.

Kumar, K. (2018) Fiji Has a General Unemployment Rate of 4.5%: Usamate, *FBC News*, 2 September, available from: www.fbcnews.com.fj/news/fiji-has-a-general-unemployment-rate-of-4-5-usamate/.

Lal, B.V. (2002) In George Speight's Shadow: Fiji General Elections of 2001, *The Journal of Pacific History, 37*(1), 87–101, doi.org/10.1080/0022334 0220139298.

Lal, B.V. (2009) 'Anxiety, Uncertainty and Fear in Our Land': Fiji's Road to Military Coup, 2006, in S. Firth, J. Fraenkel, & B.V. Lal (eds), *The 2006 Military Takeover in Fiji: A Coup to End All Coups?* (pp. 21–41), ANU E Press, Canberra, doi.org/10.22459/mtf.04.2009.02.

Lal, B.V. (2015) *Historical Dictionary of Fiji*, Rowman & Littlefield, Lanham, MD.

Lal, B.V. (2016) Fiji Indians and the Fiji General Elections of 2014: Between a Rock and a Hard Place and a Few Other Spots in Between, in S. Ratuva & S. Lawson (eds), *The People Have Spoken: The 2014 Elections in Fiji* (pp. 59–82), ANU Press, Canberra, doi.org/10.22459/tphs.03.2016.04.

Lawson, S. & Hagan Lawson, E. (2015) *Chiefly Leadership in Fiji: Past, Present, and Future*, Discussion Paper No. 5, State, Society and Governance in Melanesia Program, The Australian National University, Canberra.

Lee, H. (2011) Rethinking Transnationalism through the Second Generation, *The Australian Journal of Anthropology, 22*(3), 295–313, doi.org/10.1111/ j.1757-6547.2011.00150.x.

Lee, H. (2017) CEDAW Smokescreens: Gender Politics in Contemporary Tonga, *The Contemporary Pacific, 29*(1), 66–90, doi.org/10.1353/cp.2017.0003.

Lee, H. (2019a) The New Nobility: Tonga's Young Traditional Leaders, in H. Lee (ed.), *Pacific Youth: Local and Global Futures* (pp. 111–136), ANU Press, Canberra, doi.org/10.22459/py.2019.05.

Lee, H. (ed.) (2019b) *Pacific Youth: Local and Global Futures*, ANU Press, Canberra, doi.org/10.22459/PY.2019.

Lee, H. & Craney, A. (2019) Pacific Youth: Local and Global, in H. Lee (ed.), *Pacific Youth: Local and Global Futures* (pp. 1–31), ANU Press, Canberra, doi.org/10.22459/PY.2019.01.

Leftwich, A. (1994) Governance, the State and the Politics of Development, *Development and Change, 25*(2), 363–386.

Leftwich, A. (1995) Bringing Politics Back In: Towards a Model of the Developmental State, *Journal of Development Studies, 31*(3), 400–427, doi.org/10.1080/00220389508422370.

Leftwich, A. (2011) *Thinking and Working Politically: What Does it Mean? Why is it Important? And How Do You Do It?* DLP Discussion Paper, Developmental Leadership Program, Birmingham, UK.

Levitt, P. & Merry, S. (2009) Vernacularization on the Ground: Local Uses of Global Women's Rights in Peru, China, India and the United States, *Global Networks, 9*(4), 441–461, doi.org/10.1111/j.1471-0374.2009.00263.x.

Liloqula, R. (2000) Understanding the Conflict in Solomon Islands as a Practical Means to Peacemaking, *Development Bulletin, 53*, 41–43.

Lindstrom, L. & Jourdan, C. (2017) Urban Melanesia, *Journal de la Société des Océanistes*, (144–145), 5–22, doi.org/10.4000/jso.7848.

Lusby, S. (2017) Securitisation, Development and the Invisibility of Gender, in M. Macintyre & C. Spark (eds), *Transformations of Gender in Melanesia* (pp. 23–43), ANU Press, Canberra, doi.org/10.22459/tgm.02.2017.01.

McDonald, D. & Kyloh, D. (2015) *Evaluation of the Youth@Work Program: Solomon Islands 2012–2015*, Pacific Leadership Program, Suva.

MacDonald, L., Fishkin, B., & Witzel, D. (2014) *Citizen Voice in a Globalized World*, CGD Policy Paper 045, Center for Global Development, Washington, DC.

MacFarlane, K. (2018) Education, Sufficiency, and the Relational Egalitarian Ideal, *Journal of Applied Philosophy, 35*(4), 759–774, doi.org/10.1111/japp.12260.

McGarry, D. (2014) Honour is Respectable, *Pacific Politics*, 25 June 2014, accessed from: pacificpolicy.org/2014/06/honour-is-respectable/ [page discontinued].

McGavin, K. (2014) Being 'Nesian': Pacific Islander Identity in Australia, *The Contemporary Pacific, 26*(1), 126–154, doi.org/10.1353/cp.2014.0013.

Macintyre, M. (2017) Introduction: Flux and Change in Melanesian Gender Relations, in M. Macintyre & C. Spark (eds), *Transformations of Gender in Melanesia* (pp. 1–21), ANU Press, Canberra, doi.org/10.22459/TGM.02.2017.

MacKenzie, R. & Forde, C. (2009) The Rhetoric of the 'Good Worker' Versus the Realities of Employers' Use and the Experiences of Migrant Workers, *Work, Employment and Society, 23*(1), 142–159, doi.org/10.1177/0950017008099783.

McKillop, C. (2017) Shocking Exploitation of Workers Prompts Renewed Calls for National Crackdown on Dodgy Labour Hire Companies, *ABC Rural*, 29 March, available from: www.abc.net.au/news/rural/2017-03-28/growers-call-for-national-crackdown-on-worker-exploitation/8394252.

McLaverty, P. (2002) Civil Society and Democracy, *Contemporary Politics, 8*(4), 303–318, doi.org/10.1080/13569770216068.

McLeod, A. (2007) *Literature Review of Leadership Models in the Pacific*, Targeted Research Papers for AusAID, State, Society and Governance in Melanesia Program, The Australian National University, Canberra.

McLeod, A. (2015) *Women's Leadership in the Pacific*, Developmental Leadership Program, Birmingham, UK.

McMurray, C. (2006) Young People's Participation in the Pacific: Facilitating Factors and Lessons Learned, Paper presented to Children's Rights and Culture in the Pacific Seminar, Suva, 30 October.

Madden, R. (2017) *Being Ethnographic: A Guide to the Theory and Practice of Ethnography*, 2nd edn, Sage, London.

Madraiwiwi, J. (2015) The Fijian Elections of 2014: Returning to Democracy … ?, *The Journal of Pacific History, 50*(1), 54–60, doi.org/10.1080/0022334 4.2015.1016255.

Maebiru, R. (2013) Young People Creating the Future Today: Youth Development in the Pacific, in D. Hegarty & D. Tryon (eds), *Politics, Development and Security in Oceania* (pp. 147–151), ANU E Press, Canberra, doi.org/10.22459/pdso.04.2013.11.

Mahiri, I. (1998) Comparing Transect Walks with Experts and Local People, *PLA Notes,* (31), 4–8, International Institute for Environment and Development, London.

Makuwira, J. (2018) Power and Development in Practice: NGOs and the Development Agenda Setting, *Development in Practice, 28*(3), 422–431, doi.org/10.1080/09614524.2018.1433816.

Mara, K. (1997) *The Pacific Way: A Memoir*, University of Hawai`i Press, Honolulu.

Maron, N. & Connell, J. (2008) Back to Nukunuku: Employment, Identity and Return Migration in Tonga, *Asia Pacific Viewpoint, 49*(2), 168–184, doi.org/10.1111/j.1467-8373.2008.00368.x.

Martin, K. (2007) Your Own *Buai* You Must Buy: The Ideology of Possessive Individualism in Papua New Guinea, *Anthropological Forum, 17*(3), 285–298, doi.org/10.1080/00664670701637743.

Maslow, A.H. (1943) A Theory of Human Motivation, *Psychological Review, 50*(4), 370–396.

Mausio, A. (2003) Melanesia in Review: Issues and Events—Fiji, *The Contemporary Pacific, 15*(2), 440–447, doi.org/10.1353/cp.2003.0049.

Mecartney, S. & Connell, J. (2017) Urban Melanesia: The Challenges of Managing Land, Modernity and Tradition, in S. McDonnell, M.G. Allen, & C. Filer (eds), *Kastom, Property and Ideology: Land Transformations in Melanesia* (pp. 57–84), ANU Press, Canberra, doi.org/10.22459/kpi.03.2017.02.

Mellor, T. & Jabes, J. (2004) *Governance in the Pacific: Focus for Action 2005–2009*, Asian Development Bank, Manila.

Merchant, J. (2013) Troubled Youth: Risk, Individualisation and Social Structure, in J. Kearney & C. Donovan (eds), *Constructing Risky Identities in Policy and Practice* (pp. 91–105), Palgrave Macmillan, Hampshire, UK, doi.org/10.1057/9781137276087_6.

Merry, S. (2006) Transnational Human Rights and Local Activism: Mapping the Middle, *American Anthropologist, 108*(1), 38–51, doi.org/10.1525/aa.2006.108.1.38.

Milkman, R., Luce, S., & Lewis, P. (2013) *Changing the Subject: A Bottom-Up Account of Occupy Wall Street in New York City*, The Murphy Institute, Columbia University, New York.

Mishra-Vakaoti, V. (2013) The Experience of Schooling and Discontinuing Schooling in Fiji, PhD thesis, The Australian National University, Canberra.

Mitchell, J. (2011) 'Operation Restore Public Hope': Youth and the Magic of Modernity in Vanuatu, *Oceania, 81*(1), 36–50, doi.org/10.1002/j.1834-4461.2011.tb00092.x.

Moghadam, V.M. (2013) What is Democracy? Promises and Perils of the Arab Spring, *Current Sociology, 61*(4), 393–408, doi.org/10.1177/0011392113479739.

Mohanty, M. (2011) Informal Social Protection and Social Development in Pacific Island Countries: Role of NGOs and Civil Society, *Asia-Pacific Development Journal, 18*(2), 25–56, doi.org/10.18356/7ed1f44a-en.

Moller, H. (1968) Youth as a Force in the Modern World, *Comparative Studies in Society and History, 10*(3), 237–260.

Moore, C. (2015) Honiara: Arrival City and Pacific Hybrid Living Space, *The Journal of Pacific History, 50*(4), 419–436, doi.org10.1080/00223344. 2015.1110869.

Morgan, M. (2005) *Cultures of Dominance: Institutional and Cultural Influences on Parliamentary Politics in Melanesia*, Discussion Paper 2, State, Society and Governance in Melanesia Program, The Australian National University, Canberra.

Morton, H. (1996) *Becoming Tongan: An Ethnography of Childhood*, University of Hawai`i Press, Honolulu.

Morton Lee, H. (2003) *Tongans Overseas: Between Two Shores*, University of Hawai`i Press, Honolulu.

Moser, C. (1993) *Gender Planning and Development: Theory, Practice & Training*, Routledge, London.

Moynagh, M. (1981) *Brown or White? A History of the Fiji Sugar Industry, 1873–1973*, The Australian National University, Canberra.

Munro, D. (1993) The Pacific Islands Labour Trade: Approaches, Methodologies, Debates, *Slavery and Abolition, 14*(2), 87–108, doi.org/10.1080/014403993 08575099.

Munro, J. (2017) Gender Struggles of Educated Men in the Papuan Highlands, in M. Macintyre & C. Spark (eds), *Transformations of Gender in Melanesia* (pp. 45–67), ANU Press, Canberra, doi.org/10.22459/tgm.02.2017.02.

Muttarak, R. & Lutz, W. (2014) Is Education a Key to Reducing Vulnerability to Natural Disasters and Hence Unavoidable Climate Change? *Ecology and Society, 19*(1), 42, doi.org/10.5751/es-06476-190142.

Mutua, M. (2001) Savages, Victims, and Saviors: The Metaphor of Human Rights, *Harvard International Law Journal, 42*(1), 201–245.

Naidu, V. (2003) Modernisation and Development in the South Pacific, in A. Jowitt & T. Newton Cain (eds), *Passage of Change: Law, Society and Governance in the Pacific* (pp. 5–31), Pandanus Books, Canberra.

Naidu, V. (2013) *Fiji: The Challenges and Opportunities of Diversity*, Minority Rights Group International, London.

Nankani, G., Page, J., & Judge, L. (2005) Human Rights and Poverty Reduction Strategies: Moving Towards Convergence? in P. Alston & M. Robinson (eds), *Human Rights and Development: Towards Mutual Reinforcement*, Oxford University Press, Oxford, UK, doi.org/10.1093/acprof:oso/9780199284627. 003.0018.

Narayan, U. (1998) Essence of Culture and a Sense of History: A Feminist Critique of Cultural Essentialism, *Challenges to Philosophy, 13*(2), 86–106, doi.org/10.1111/j.1527-2001.1998.tb01227.x.

Narayan, V. (2018) There is No Data Available Based on Ethnicity from the 2017 Census—AG, *FijiVillage*, [Online], 6 March, available from: fijivillage.com/ news-feature/There-is-no-data-available-based-on-ethnicity-from-the-2017-Census---AG-k29sr5/.

Narsey, W. (2012) Fijians, I-Taukei, Indians and Indo-Fijians: Name Changes by Military Decree, *Narsey on Fiji—Fighting Censorship*, [Online], 18 March, available from: narseyonfiji.wordpress.com/2012/03/18/fijians-i-taukei-indians-and-indo-fijians-name-changes-by-military-decree/.

National Employment Centre (NEC) (2021) National Employment Centre, [Online], Ministry of Employment, Productivity and Industrial Relations, Suva, available from: web.archive.org/web/20200127120703/http://www.nec. gov.fj/.

Naupa, A. (2016) Watch this Space: The Pacific's Great Ocean States, *Griffith Asia Insights*, [Blog], 8 June, Griffith University, Brisbane, available from: blogs. griffith.edu.au/asiainsights/watch-this-space-the-pacifics-great-ocean-states/.

Ncube, M., Anyanwu, J.C., & Hausken, K. (2013) *Inequality, Economic Growth, and Poverty in the Middle East and North Africa*, Working Paper No. 19, African Development Bank Group, Tunis, doi.org/10.1111/1467-8268.12103.

Nederveen Pieterse, J. (1998) My Paradigm or Yours? Alternative Development, Post-Development, Reflexive Development, *Development and Change, 29*(2), 343–373, doi.org/10.1111/1467-7660.00081.

Nelson, P.J. & Dorsey, E. (2003) At the *Nexus* of Human Rights and Development: New Methods and Strategies of Global NGOs, *World Development, 31*(12), 2013–2026, doi.org/10.1016/j.worlddev.2003.06.009.

Nem Singh, J. & Ovadia, J.S. (2018) The Theory and Practice of Building Developmental States in the Global South, *Third World Quarterly, 39*(6), 1033–1055, doi.org/10.1080/01436597.2018.1455143.

Nilan, P. (2007) Fijian Female Youth: School-to-Work/Career Transitions, Paper presented to Public Sociologies: Lessons and Trans-Tasman Comparisons, Australian Sociological Association and Sociological Association of Aotearoa New Zealand Joint Conference, Auckland, 4–7 December.

Nilan, P. (2009) Indigenous Fijian Female Pupils and Career Choice: Explaining Generational Gender Reproduction, *Asia Pacific Journal of Education, 29*(1), 29–43, doi.org/10.1080/02188790802655031.

Nilan, P., Cavu, P., Tagicakiverata, I., & Hazelman, E. (2006) White-Collar Work: Career Ambitions of Fiji Final Year School Students, *International Education Journal, 7*(7), 895–905.

Noble, C., Pereira, N., & Saune, N. (2011) *Urban Youth in the Pacific: Increasing Resilience and Reducing Risk for Involvement in Crime and Violence*, UNDP Pacific Centre, Suva.

Nussbaum, M.C. (2003) Capabilities as Fundamental Entitlements: Sen and Social Justice, *Feminist Economics, 9*(2–3), 33–59, doi.org/10.1080/135457 0022000077926.

Oakeshott, D. (2021) 'Just Something in History': Classroom Knowledge and Refusals to Teach the Tension in Solomon Islands, *The Contemporary Pacific, 33*(2), 386–408.

Oakeshott, D. & Allen, M. (2015) *Schooling as a 'Stepping-stone to National Consciousness' in Solomon Islands: The Last Twenty Years*, Discussion Paper 2015/8, State, Society and Governance in Melanesia Program, The Australian National University, Canberra.

O'Kane, C. (2003) *Exploring Concepts: Children and Young People as Citizens*, Save the Children, Kathmandu.

Okin, S.M. (1998) Feminism: Women's Human Rights, and Cultural Differences, *Border Crossings: Multicultural and Postcolonial Feminist Challenges to Philosophy, 13*(2), 32–52.

Organisation for Economic Co-operation and Development (OECD) (2016) *States of Fragility 2016: Understanding Violence*, OECD Publishing, Paris.

Overseas Development Institute (ODI) (2014) *Doing Development Differently*, Overseas Development Institute, London, accessed from: www.odi.org/ projects/2857-doing-development-differently [page discontinued]; available from: odi.org/en/publications/doing-development-differently-two-years-on-what-have-we-done/.

Owen, D. (1996) Dilemmas and Opportunities for the Young Active Citizen, *Youth Studies Australia, 15*(1), 20–23.

Pacific Community (SPC) (2009a) *Mapping the Youth Challenge: The Youth Challenge in the Pacific Region*, Pacific Community, Noumea.

Pacific Community (SPC) (2009b) *The Suva Declaration from the 2nd Pacific Youth Festival: Actioning the Youth Agenda*, Pacific Community, Suva.

Pacific Islands Forum Secretariat (PIFS) (n.d.) Youth, [Online], Pacific Islands Forum Secretariat, Suva, accessed from: www.forumsec.org/pages.cfm/news room/documents-publications/youth.html [page discontinued].

Pacific Islands Forum Secretariat (PIFS) (2012) *Pacific Plan Annual Progress Report 2012*, Pacific Islands Forum Secretariat, Suva.

Pacific Islands Forum Secretariat (PIFS) (2013) *Pacific Plan Annual Progress Report 2013*, Pacific Islands Forum Secretariat, Suva.

Pacific Women in Politics (PacWIP) (2012–21) National Women MPs, [Online], Pacific Women in Politics, Suva, available from: www.pacwip.org/women-mps/national-women-mps/.

Packard, A. (2014) *Coal Ships Stopped. The Warriors Have Risen!* 20 October, 350 Pacific, Suva, available from: world.350.org/pacificwarriors/2014/10/20/coal-ships-stopped-the-warriors-have-risen/.

Palet, L.S. (2014) Roshika Deo: Fiji's Feminist Voice, *OZY*, 29 September, available from: www.ozy.com/the-new-and-the-next/roshika-deo-fijis-feminist-voice/34034/

Parke, A. (2014) *Degei's Descendants: Spirits, Place and People in Pre-Cession Fiji*, ANU Press, Canberra, doi.org/10.22459/TA41.08.2014.

Perrottet, A. & Robie, D. (2011) Pacific Media Freedom 2011: A Status Report, *Pacific Journalism Review, 17*(2), 148–186, doi.org/10.24135/pjr.v17i2.356.

Petras, J. (1993) Cultural Imperialism in the Late 20th Century, *Journal of Contemporary Asia, 23*(2), 139–148, doi.org/10.1080/00472339380000091.

Pharr, S.J., Putnam, R., & Dalton, R.J. (2000) Trouble in the Advanced Democracies? A Quarter-Century of Declining Confidence, *Journal of Democracy, 11*(2), 5–23.

Phillips, T. & Keen, M. (2016) *Sharing the City: Urban Growth and Governance in Suva, Fiji*, Discussion Paper 2016/6, State, Society and Governance in Melanesia Program, The Australian National University, Canberra.

Pigg, S.L. (1996) The Credible and the Credulous: The Question of 'Villagers' Beliefs' in Nepal, *Cultural Anthropology, 11*(2), 160–201, doi.org/10.1525/can.1996.11.2.02a00020.

Pinkney, R. (2003) *Democracy in the 3rd World* (3rd edn), Lynne Rienner Publishers, London.

Post, R.C. & Rosenblum, N.L. (2002) Introduction, in N.L. Rosenblum & R.C. Post (eds), *Civil Society and Government* (pp. 1–25), Princeton University Press, Princeton, NJ.

Prasad, B.C. (2012a) Fiji Economy: Muddling Through, *The Round Table: The Commonwealth Journal of International Affairs, 101*(6), 557–573, doi.org/10.1080/00358533.2012.749096.

Prasad, B.C. (2012b) *Why Fiji is not the 'Mauritius' of the Pacific? Lessons for Small Island Nations in the Pacific*, Development Policy Centre Discussion Paper No. 23, Crawford School of Public Policy, The Australian National University, Canberra, doi.org/10.2139/ssrn.2141800.

Prasad, S. (2017) Governance Paradoxes and Pathways in Pacific Island Countries, *Pacific Dynamics, 1*(2), 325–339.

Protzko, J. & Schooler, J.W. (2019) Kids These Days: Why the Youth of Today Seem Lacking, *Science Advances, 5*(10), eaav5916, doi.org/10.1126/sciadv.aav5916.

Pruitt, L. (2020) Rethinking Youth Bulge Theory in Policy and Scholarship: Incorporating Critical Gender Analysis, *International Affairs, 96*(3), 711–728, doi.org/10.1093/ia/iiaa012.

Psacharopoulos, G. & Woodhall, M. (1985) *Education for Development: An Analysis of Investment Choice*, Oxford University Press for The World Bank, New York.

Puna, H. (2015) Thinking 'Outside the Rocks': Reimagining the Pacific, in G. Fry & S. Tarte (eds), *The New Pacific Diplomacy* (pp. 285–289), ANU Press, Canberra, doi.org/10.22459/NPD.12.2015.

Putnam, R. (1995) Bowling Alone: America's Declining Social Capital, *Journal of Democracy, 6*(1), 65–78, doi.org/10.1353/jod.1995.0002.

Quain, B. (1948) *Fijian Village*, University of Chicago Press, Chicago.

Radio New Zealand (RNZ) (2019) Skill Shortage: Fiji Hiring Tile Layers from Asia, *Radio New Zealand*, 29 October, available from: www.rnz.co.nz/international/pacific-news/401991/skill-shortage-fiji-hiring-tile-layers-from-asia.

Rapid Employment Project (REP) (2019) Rapid Employment Project, [Online], The World Bank, Washington, DC, available from: projects.worldbank.org/ P114987/rapid-employment-project?lang=en.

Ratuva, S. (2019) *Contested Terrain: Reconceptualising Security in the Pacific*, ANU Press, Canberra, doi.org/10.22459/ct.2019.

Rauch, A. & Frese, M. (2012) Born to Be An Entrepreneur? Revisiting the Personality Approach to Entrepreneurship, in J.R. Baum, M. Frese, & R.A. Baron (eds), *The Psychology of Entrepreneurship*, Psychology Press, New York, doi.org/10.4324/9781315750989.

Ravuvu, A.D. (1983) *Vaka i Taukei: The Fijian Way of Life*, Institute of Pacific Studies, University of the South Pacific, Suva.

Ravuvu, A.D. (1988) *Development or Dependence: The Pattern of Change in a Fijian Village*, Institute of Pacific Studies and the Fiji Extension Centre, University of the South Pacific, Suva.

Ravuvu, A.D. (1991) *The Facade of Democracy: Fijian Struggles for Political Control 1830–1987*, Reader Publishing House, Suva.

Reed, C., Southwell, A., Healy, M., & Stafford, N. (2011) *Final Evaluation of the Pacific Seasonal Worker Pilot Scheme*, Department of Education, Employment and Workplace Relations, Canberra, accessed from: docs. employment.gov.au/system/files/doc/other/pswps_-_final_evaluation_report. pdf [page discontinued]; available from: hdl.voced.edu.au/10707/445175.

Regan, A.J. (2003) Constitutions as Limits on the State in Melanesia: Comparative Perspectives on Constitutionalism, Participation and Civil Society, in A. Jowitt & T. Newton Cain (eds), *Passage of Change: Law, Society and Governance in the Pacific* (pp. 305–328), Pandanus Books, Canberra, doi.org/10.22459/pc. 11.2010.15.

Reilly, B. (2004) State Functioning and State Failure in the South Pacific, *Australian Journal of International Affairs, 58*(4), 479–493, doi.org/10.1080/ 1035771042000304742.

Ride, A. (2019) Riots in Solomon Islands: The Day After, *Australian Outlook*, 26 December, Australian Institute of International Affairs, Canberra, available from: www.internationalaffairs.org.au/australianoutlook/riots-solomon-islands-day-after/.

Rittel, H.W.J. & Webber, M.M. (1973) Dilemmas in a General Theory of Planning, *Policy Sciences, 4*, 155–169, doi.org/10.1007/bf01405730.

Robarts Ferguson, A.J. (2019) Entrepreneurship and Social Action among Youth in American Samoa, in H. Lee (ed.), *Pacific Youth: Local and Global Futures* (pp. 159–181), ANU Press, Canberra, doi.org/10.22459/PY.2019.07.

Robbins, J. (2007) Afterword: Possessive Individualism and Cultural Change in the Western Pacific, *Anthropological Forum, 17*(3), 299–308, doi.org/10.1080/00664670701637750.

Roberts, K. (2003) Change and Continuity in Youth Transitions in Eastern Europe: Lessons for Western Sociology, *The Sociological Review, 51*(4), 484–505, doi.org/10.1111/j.1467-954x.2003.00432.x.

Robertson, R. (2012) Cooking the Goose: Fiji's Coup Culture Contextualised, *The Round Table: The Commonwealth Journal of International Affairs, 101*(6), 509–519, doi.org/10.1080/00358533.2012.749095.

Rogaly, B. (1998) Workers on the Move: Seasonal Migration and Changing Social Relations in Rural India, *Gender & Development, 6*(1), 21–29, doi.org/10.1080/741922628.

Rosaldo, R. (1995) Foreword, in N. Garcia Canclini (ed.), *Hybrid Cultures: Strategies for Entering and Leaving Modernity*, University of Minnesota Press, Minneapolis.

Rostow, W.W. (1959) The Stages of Economic Growth, *The Economic History Review, 12*(1), 1–16.

Rostow, W.W. (1971) *Politics and the Stages of Growth*, Cambridge University Press, Cambridge, UK.

Sahlins, M. (1963) Poor Man, Rich Man, Big-Man, Chief: Political Types in Melanesia and Polynesia, *Comparative Studies in Society and History, 5*(3), 285–303, doi.org/10.1017/s0010417500001729.

Sahlins, M. (1999) What Is Anthropological Enlightenment? Some Lessons of the Twentieth Century, *Annual Review of Anthropology, 28*, i–xxiii, doi.org/10.1146/annurev.anthro.28.1.0.

Sahlins, M. (2005) On the Anthropology of Modernity, Or, Some Triumphs of Culture over Despondency Theory, in A. Hooper (ed.), *Culture and Sustainable Development in the Pacific* (pp. 44–61) (3rd edn), ANU E Press, Canberra, doi.org/10.22459/csdp.04.2005.03.

Sanga, K., Reynolds, M., Paulsen, I., Spratt, R., & Maneipuri, J. (2018) A Tok Stori about Tok Stori: Melanesian Relationality in Action as Research, Leadership and Scholarship, *Global Comparative Education, 2*(1), 3–19, doi.org/10.26686/wgtn.12838157.

Saraswathi, T.S. & Larson, R.W. (2002) Adolescence in Global Perspective: An Agenda for Social Policy, in B.B. Brown, R.W. Larson, & T.S. Saraswathi (eds), *The World's Youth: Adolescence in Eight Regions of the Globe* (pp. 344–362), Cambridge University Press, Cambridge, UK, doi.org/10.1017/cbo9780 511613814.012.

Schmaljohann, M. & Prizzon, A. (2014) *The Age of Choice: Fiji and Vanuatu in the New Aid Landscape*, Overseas Development Institute, London.

Scholte, J.A. (2002) Civil Society and Democracy in Global Governance, *Global Governance, 8*(3), 281–304.

Scoones, I. (2009) Livelihoods Perspectives and Rural Development, *The Journal of Peasant Studies, 36*(1), 171–196, doi.org/10.1080/03066150902820503.

Seah, C.M. (1983) Youth and Female Unemployment and Underemployment in the ESCAP Region, *Southeast Asian Journal of Social Science, 11*(1), 1–31, doi.org/10.1163/080382483x00013.

Sen, A. (1999) *Development as Freedom*, Oxford University Press, New York.

Sen, A. (2003) Development as Capability Expansion, in S. Fukuda-Parr & A.K.S. Kumar (eds), *Readings in Human Development: Concepts, Measures and Policies for a Development Paradigm* (pp. 3–16), Oxford University Press, New York.

Sharma, U., Forlin, C., Sprunt, B., & Merumeru, L. (2016) Identifying Disability-Inclusive Indicators Currently Employed to Monitor and Evaluate Education in the Pacific Island Countries, *Cogent Education, 3*, 1–17, doi.org/ 10.1080/2331186x.2016.1170754.

Singh, S. & Prakash, S. (2006) Politics, Democracy and the Media: Case Studies in Fiji, Tonga and the Solomon Islands, *Pacific Journalism Review, 12*(2), 67–85, doi.org/10.24135/pjr.v12i2.863.

Slatter, C. (2006) Treading Water in Rapids? Non-Governmental Organisations and Resistance to Neo-Liberalism in Pacific Island States, in S. Firth (ed.), *Globalisation and Governance in the Pacific Islands* (pp. 23–42), ANU E Press, Canberra, doi.org/10.22459/ggpi.12.2006.02.

Smith, K. (2012) From Dividual and Individual Selves to Porous Subjects, *The Australian Journal of Anthropology, 23*, 50–64, doi.org/10.1111/j.1757-6547.2012.00167.x.

Sogavare, M. (2016) Prime Minister Manasseh Sogavare on the Occasion of the Closing of the PIDF Pre-Summit, Paper presented at the 2016 Pacific Islands Development Forum Leaders' Summit, Honiara, 12–13 July.

Solomon Islands National Statistics Office (SINSO) (2011) *Report on 2009 Solomon Islands Population and Housing Census: Basic Tables and Census Description. Volume 1*, SINSO, Ministry of Finance and Treasury, Honiara, available from: www.statistics.gov.sb/statistics/demographic-statistics/census.

Solomon Islands National Statistics Office (SINSO) (2012) Solomon Islands Population and Housing Census 2009: Basic Tables and Census Description, *Statistical Bulletin No: 6/2012*, Government of Solomon Islands, Honiara.

Solomon Islands National Statistics Office (SINSO) (2020) *Provisional Count: 2019 National Population and Housing Census*, Census Release: 1/2020, 16 November, 2019 Census Project Office, SINSO, Ministry of Finance and Treasury, Honiara, available from: www.statistics.gov.sb/images/Solomon Files/Social-and-Demography-Statistics/2019_National_Population_and_Housing_Census/Provisional_Count-2019_Census_Result.pdf.

Solomon Islands National University (SINU) (2021) Website, Solomon Islands National University, Honiara, available from: www.sinu.edu.sb/.

Solomon Islands Truth and Reconciliation Commission (2012) *Solomon Islands Truth and Reconciliation Commission Final Report: Confronting the Truth for a Better Solomon Islands*, Solomon Islands Truth and Reconciliation Commission, Honiara.

Solomon Times (2009) Launch of Fee Free Education, *Solomon Times*, [Honiara], 16 January, available from: www.solomontimes.com/news/launch-of-fee-free-education/3406.

South Pacific Tourism Organisation (SPTO) (2017) *Annual Review of Visitor Arrivals in Pacific Island Countries*, South Pacific Tourism Organisation, Suva.

Spark, C., Cox, J., & Corbett, J. (2019) Gender, Political Representation and Symbolic Capital: How Some Women Politicians Succeed, *Third World Quarterly, 40*(7), 1227–1245, doi.org/10.1080/01436597.2019.1604132.

Storey, D. (2005) *Urban Governance in Pacific Island Countries: Advancing an Overdue Agenda*, Discussion Paper 7, State, Society and Governance in Melanesia Program, The Australian National University, Canberra.

Strathern, M. (1988) *The Gender of the Gift*, University of California Press, Berkeley, CA.

Sukarieh, M. & Tannock, S. (2017) The Global Securitisation of Youth, *Third World Quarterly, 39*(5), 854–870, doi.org/10.1080/01436597.2017.1369038.

Sumner, A. & Tezanos Vazquez, S. (2014) *How Has the Developing World Changed Since the Late 1990s? A Dynamic and Multidimensional Taxonomy of Developing Countries*, CGD Working Paper 375, Center for Global Development, Washington, DC, doi.org/10.2139/ssrn.2476558.

Taft, J.K. & Gordon, H.R. (2011) Rethinking Youth Political Socialization: Teenage Activists Talk Back, *Youth & Society, 43*(4), 1499–1527, doi.org/10.1177/0044118x10386087.

Taft, J.K. & Gordon, H.R. (2013) Youth Activists, Youth Councils and Constrained Democracy, *Education, Citizenship and Social Literature, 8*(1), 87–100, doi.org/10.1177/1746197913475765.

Tagicakiverata, I. (2012) TVET in Fiji: Attitudes, Perceptions and Discourses, PhD thesis, University of Newcastle, Newcastle, NSW.

Tagicakiverata, I. & Nilan, P. (2018) Veivosaki-Yaga: A Culturally Appropriate Indigenous Research Method in Fiji, *International Journal of Qualitative Studies in Education, 31*(6), 545–556, doi.org/10.1080/09518398.2017.1422293.

Tarai, J. (2015) *To Regulate or Not: Fiji's Social Media*, In Brief 2015/53, State, Society and Governance in Melanesia Program, The Australian National University, Canberra.

Tarai, J. (2016) Re-Thinking the Fijian Man, [Video], *TEDxSuva*, 31 May, available from: www.youtube.com/watch?v=qh_ClbaSVTs.

Tarai, J. (2017) God is Dead! *Fijian Scholar: Thoughts, Questions, Issues ...*, [Blog], 4 March, available from: jopetarai.wordpress.com/2017/03/04/god-is-dead/.

Tarte, S. (2009) Reflections on Fiji's 'Coup Culture', in S. Firth, J. Fraenkel, & B.V. Lal (eds), *The 2006 Military Takeover in Fiji: A Coup to End All Coups?* (pp. 409–414), ANU E Press, Canberra, doi.org/10.22459/mtf.04.2009.27.

Tavola, H. (1991) *Secondary Education in Fiji: A Key to the Future*, Institute of Pacific Studies, University of the South Pacific, Suva.

Taylor, M. (2018) *Know Our Ocean—An Opinion-Editorial by Meg Taylor, DBE on World Oceans Day*, Pacific Islands Forum Secretariat, Suva, available from: www.forumsec.org/know-our-ocean-an-opinion-editorial-by-meg-taylor-dbe-on-world-oceans-day/.

Teaiwa, T. (1996) Review, E. Waddell, V. Naidu, & E. Hau`ofa (eds), 'A New Oceania: Rediscovering Our Sea of Islands', *The Contemporary Pacific, 8*(1), 214–217.

Teaiwa, T. (2005) The Classroom as a Metaphorical Canoe: Cooperative Learning in Pacific Studies, *WINHEC: International Journal of Indigenous Education Scholarship, 1*, 38–48.

Teaiwa, T. (2006) On Analogies: Rethinking the Pacific in a Global Context, *The Contemporary Pacific, 18*(1), 71–87, doi.org/10.1353/cp.2005.0105.

The Solomons News Drum (1976) Master Lius Move in on the Potato Market, *The Solomon News Drum*, [Honiara], 12 November, p. 3.

Thomas, N. (1989) The Force of Ethnology: Origins and Significance of the Melanesia/Polynesia Division, *Current Anthropology, 30*(1), 27–41.

Thomas, P. (2001) Introduction: Involving Young People in Development, *Development Bulletin, 56*, 4–6.

Thurbon, E. & Weiss, E. (2016) The Developmental State in the Late Twentieth Century, in E.S. Reinert, J. Ghosh, & R. Kattel (eds), *Handbook of Alternative Theories of Economic Development* (pp. 637–650), Edward Elgar, Cheltenham, UK, doi.org/10.4337/9781782544685.00041.

Titifanue, J., Kant, R., Finau, G., & Tarai, J. (2017) Climate Change Advocacy in the Pacific: The Role of Information and Communication Technologies, *Pacific Journalism Review, 23*(1), 133–149, doi.org/10.24135/pjr.v23i1.105.

Torres, S. (2003) *Black, White, and in Color: Television and Black Civil Rights*, Princeton University Press, Princeton, NJ.

Tryon, D. (2009) Linguistic Encounter and Responses in the South Pacific, in M. Jolly, S. Tcherkezoff, & D. Tryon (eds), *Oceanic Encounters: Exchange, Desire, Violence* (pp. 37–55), ANU E Press, Canberra, doi.org/10.22459/oe.07.2009.02.

Tuimaleali`ifano, M. (2007) Indigenous Title Disputes: What they Meant for the 2006 Election, in J. Fraenkel & S. Firth (eds), *From Election to Coup in Fiji: The 2006 Campaign and its Aftermath* (pp. 261–271), ANU E Press, Canberra, doi.org/10.22459/FECF.06.2007.20.

Tuinamuana, K. (2007) Reconstructing Dominant Paradigms of Teacher Education: Possibilities for Pedagogical Transformation in Fiji, *Asia-Pacific Journal of Teacher Education, 35*(2), 111–127, doi.org/10.1080/1359866070 1268544.

Tuni, K. (2017) FSII-Aligned Political Party 'The People's Movement' Set for 2019 Elections, *SIBC Online*, 27 September, available from: www.sibconline.com.sb/fsii-aligned-political-party-the-peoples-movement-set-for-2019-elections/.

Two Fishes (2018) Citizen, Know Thyself, [Audio], *SoundCloud*, available from: soundcloud.com/twofishesshow/02-citizen-know-thyself.

TWP Community (2016) *The Case for Thinking and Working Politically: The Implications of 'Doing Development Differently'*, ECDPM, Maastricht, Netherlands, available from: ecdpm.org/wp-content/uploads/Case-Thinking-Working-Politically.pdf.

Ul Haq, M. (1981) Foreword, in P. Streeten, S.J. Burki, M. Ul Haq, N. Hicks, & F. Stewart (eds), *First Things First: Meeting Basic Human Needs in Developing Countries* (pp. vii–x), The World Bank & Oxford University Press, New York.

United Nations (UN) (1948) *Universal Declaration of Human Rights*, United Nations General Assembly, New York, available from: www.un.org/en/about-us/universal-declaration-of-human-rights.

United Nations Children's Fund (UNICEF Pacific), Secretariat of the Pacific Community, Noumea, and United Nations Population Fund (Office for the Pacific) (2005) *The State of Pacific Youth 2005*, UNICEF Pacific, Suva, available from: linkasea.pbworks.com/f/UNICEF+State+of+Pacific+youth_2005.pdf.

United Nations Department of Economic and Social Affairs (UN DESA) (n.d.[a]) Country Profile: Fiji, *UNdata*, [Online database], available from: data.un.org/en/iso/fj.html.

United Nations Department of Economic and Social Affairs (UN DESA) (n.d.[b]) Country Profile: Solomon Islands, *UNdata*, [Online database], available from: data.un.org/en/iso/sb.html.

United Nations Development Programme (UNDP) (2020) *Human Development Report 2020: The Next Frontier—Human Development and the Anthropocene*, United Nations Development Programme, New York, doi.org/10.18356/9789210055161.

United Nations Economic and Social Council (ECOSOC) (2007) *Participatory Governance and Citizens' Engagement in Policy Development, Service Delivery and Budgeting: Note by the Secretariat*, United Nations Economic and Social Council, New York, available from: digitallibrary.un.org/record/593485?ln=en.

United Nations Human Settlements Programme (UN-Habitat) (2015) *Urbanization and Climate Change in Small Island Developing States*, UN-Habitat, Nairobi, available from: unhabitat.org/sites/default/files/download-manager-files/SIDS_Updated.pdf.

United Nations Population Fund (UNFPA) (2005) *The Case for Investing in Young People as Part of a National Poverty Reduction Strategy*, United Nations Population Fund, New York, available from: www.unfpa.org/sites/default/files/pub-pdf/case_youngpeople_eng.pdf.

UN Women (2008) *UNiTE by 2030 to End Violence against Women Campaign*, UN Women, New York.

Urdal, H. (2004) *The Devil in the Demographics: The Effect of Youth Bulges on Domestic Armed Conflict, 1950–2000*, Social Development Papers No. 14, The World Bank, Washington, DC.

Urdal, H. (2006) A Clash of Generations? Youth Bulges and Political Violence, *International Studies Quarterly, 50*, 607–629, doi.org/10.1111/j.1468-2478. 2006.00416.x.

Uvin, P. (2007) From the Right to Development to the Rights-Based Approach: How 'Human Rights' Entered Development, *Development in Practice, 17*(4–5), 597–606, doi.org/10.1080/09614520701469617.

Vaioleti, T.M. (2006) Talanoa Research Methodology: A Developing Position on Pacific Research, *Waikato Journal of Education, 12*, 21–34, doi.org/10.15663/wje.v12i1.296.

Vakaoti, P. (2009) Researching Street-Frequenting Young People in Suva: Ethical Considerations and their Impacts, *Children's Geographies, 7*(4), 435–450, doi.org/10.1080/14733280903234493.

Vakaoti, P. (2012) *Mapping the Landscape of Young People's Participation in Fiji*, Discussion Paper 6, State, Society and Governance in Melanesia Program, The Australian National University, Canberra.

Vakaoti, P. (2013) Young People's Participation in Fiji: Merits, Challenges and the Way Forward, *Asia Pacific Viewpoint, 54*(1), 77–90, doi.org/10.1111/apv.12003.

Vakaoti, P. (2014) *Young People and Democratic Participation in Fiji*, Citizens' Constitutional Forum, Suva.

Vakaoti, P. (2016) Fiji Elections and the Youth Vote—Token or Active Citizenship? in S. Ratuva & S. Lawson (eds), *The People Have Spoken: The 2014 Elections in Fiji* (pp. 157–175), ANU Press, Canberra, doi.org/10.22459/tphs.03.2016.08.

Vakaoti, P. (2017) Young People's Participation in Fiji: Understanding Conceptualizations and Experiences, *Journal of Youth Studies, 20*(6), 697–712, doi.org/10.1080/13676261.206.1260695.

Vakaoti, P. (2018) *Street-Frequenting Young People in Fiji: Theory and Practice*, Palgrave Macmillan, Cham, Switzerland, doi.org/10.1007/978-3-319-63079-3.

Vakaoti, P. & Mishra, V. (2010) *An Exploration of Youth Leadership Models in Fiji*, Pacific Leadership Program, Suva.

Valenzuela, J.S. & Valenzuela, A. (1978) Modernization and Dependency: Alternative Perspectives in the Study of Latin America, *Comparative Politics, 10*(4), 535–557, doi.org/10.2307/421571.

van der Berg, S., Burger, C., Burger, R., de Vos, M., du Rand, G., Gustafsson, M., Moses, E., Shepherd, D.L., Spaull, N., van Broekhuizen, H., & von Fintel, D. (2011) *Low Quality Education as a Poverty Trap*, Stellenbosch Economic Working Papers No. 25/2011, Department of Economics and the Bureau for Economic Research, University of Stellenbosch, Stellenbosch, South Africa, doi.org/10.2139/ssrn.2973766.

van Fossen, A. (2018) Passport Sales: How Island Microstates Use Strategic Management to Organise the New Economic Citizenship Industry, *Island Studies Journal, 13*(1), 285–300, doi.org/10.24043/isj.30.

van Meijl, T. (2001) Contesting Traditional Culture in Post-Colonial Maori Society: On the Tension between Culture and Identity, *Paideuma: Mitteilungen zur Kulturkunde, 47*, 129–145.

Vella, L. (2014) *Translating Transitional Justice: The Solomon Islands Truth and Reconciliation Commission*, Discussion Paper 2014/2, State, Society and Governance in Melanesia Program, The Australian National University, Canberra.

Veramu, J. (1992) *Let's Do it Our Way: A Case Study of Participatory Education in a Rural Fijian School and Community*, Institute of Pacific Studies of the University of the South Pacific, Suva.

Wainwright, E. (2003) *Our Failing Neighbour: Australia and the Future of Solomon Islands*, Australian Strategic Policy Institute, Canberra.

Ware, H. (2004) Pacific Instability and Youth Bulges: The Devil in the Demography and the Economy, Paper presented to 12th Biennial Conference of the Australian Population Association, Canberra, 15–17 September.

Watson-Gegeo, K.A. & Gegeo, D.W. (1992) Schooling, Knowledge, and Power: Social Transformation in the Solomon Islands, *Anthropology & Education Quarterly, 23*(1), 10–29, doi.org/10.1525/aeq.1992.23.1.05x1101i.

Wee, C.J.W.-L. (1996) The 'Clash' of Civilizations? Or an Emerging 'East Asian Modernity'? *SOJOURN: Journal of Social Issues in Southeast Asia, 11*(2), 211–230, doi.org/10.1355/sj11-2b.

Wendt, A. (1976) Towards a New Oceania, *Mana Review, 1*(1), 49–60.

West, A. (2007) Power Relationships and Adult Resistance to Children's Participation, *Children, Youth and Environments, 17*(1), 123–135.

White, C.M. (2007) Schooling in Fiji, in C. Campbell & G. Sherrington (eds), *Going to School in Oceania* (pp. 79–132), Greenwood Press, CT.

White, R. & Wyn, J. (2013) *Youth and Society* (3rd edn), Oxford University Press, Melbourne.

Willans, F. & Prasad, R. (2021) From Hindustani to (Fiji) Hindi and Back to Fiji Baat? Metalinguistic Reconstructions of the National Variety of Hindi in Fiji, *The Journal of Pacific History, 56*(2), 101–118, doi.org/10.1080/00223344. 2021.1914456.

Wilson, K. (2013) *Wan laki aelan*? Diverse Development Strategies on Aniwa, Vanuatu, *Asia Pacific Viewpoint, 54*(2), 246–263, doi.org/10.1111/apv.12012.

Winter, J.P. & Eyal, C.H. (1981) Agenda Setting for the Civil Rights Issue, *Public Opinion Quarterly, 45*, 376–383, doi.org/10.1086/268671.

Wong, K.F. (2003) Empowerment as a Panacea for Poverty: Old Wine in New Bottles? Reflections on the World Bank's Conception of Power, *Progress in Development Studies, 3*(4), 307–322, doi.org/10.1191/1464993403ps067oa.

Woo, S. & Corea, R. (2009) *Pacific Youth Literature Review*, The World Bank, Suva.

Wood, T. (2014), *Understanding Electoral Politics in Solomon Islands*, Centre for Democratic Institutions Discussion Paper 2014/02, The Australian National University, Canberra.

Woods, D. (1992) Civil Society in Europe and Africa: Limiting State Power through a Public Sphere, *African Studies Review, 35*(2), 77–100, doi.org/ 10.2307/524871.

World Bank (2007) *World Development Report 2007: Development and the Next Generation*, The World Bank, Washington, DC, doi.org/10.1596/978-0-8213-6541-0.

World Bank (2011) *Republic of Fiji: Poverty Trends, Profiles and Small Area Estimation (Poverty Maps) in Republic of Fiji (2003–2009)*, The World Bank, Suva.

World Bank (2015) Changing Lives through Urban Employment in Solomon Islands' Capital, *News*, 11 December, The World Bank, Honiara, available from: www.worldbank.org/en/news/feature/2015/12/11/changing-lives-through-urban-employment-in-solomon-islands-capital.

World Bank (2021a) Unemployment, Youth Total (% of Total Labor Force Ages 15–24) (Modeled ILO Estimate)—Fiji, *ILOSTAT Database*, [Online], The World Bank, Washington, DC, available from: data.worldbank.org/indicator/SL.UEM.1524.ZS?locations=FJ.

World Bank (2021b) Unemployment, Youth Total (% of Total Labor Force Ages 15–24) (Modeled ILO Estimate)—Solomon Islands, *ILOSTAT Database*, [Online], The World Bank, Washington, DC, available from: data.worldbank.org/indicator/SL.UEM.1524.ZS?locations=SB.

Wyn, J. (1995) V: 'Youth' and Citizenship, *Critical Studies in Education, 36*(2), 45–63.

Yongzheng, Y. (2014) In Search of a Pacific Model of Growth, *Devpolicy Blog*, 17 July, Development Policy Centre, The Australian National University, Canberra, available from: devpolicy.org/in-search-of-a-pacific-model-of-growth-20140717/?utm_source=Devpolicy&utm_campaign=92a72cb2de-Devpolicy_News__July_25_2014&utm_medium=email&utm_term=0_082b498f84-92a72cb2de-312043489.

Youth Co:Lab (2021) *How Young Entrepreneurs in Asia-Pacific Responded to COVID-19*, Report, 2 June, United Nations Development Programme, New York.

Youth@Work (n.d.) Youth at Work Solomon Islands, *Facebook*, available from: www.facebook.com/youthatworksolomonislands.

Zhang, T. & Minxia, Z. (2006) Universalizing Nine-Year Compulsory Education for Poverty Reduction in Rural China, *International Review of Education, 52*(3–4), 261–286, doi.org/10.1007/s11159-006-0011-z.

Zorn, J.G. (2003a) Custom Then and Now: The Changing Melanesian Family, in A. Jowitt & T. Newton Cain (eds), *Passage of Change: Law, Society and Governance in the Pacific* (pp. 95–123), Pandanus Books, Canberra, doi.org/10.22459/pc.11.2010.05.

Zorn, J.G. (2003b) Issues in Contemporary Customary Law: Women and the Law, in A. Jowitt & T. Newton Cain (eds), *Passage of Change: Law, Society and Governance in the Pacific* (pp. 125–142), Pandanus Books, Canberra, doi.org/10.22459/pc.11.2010.06.

www.ingramcontent.com/pod-product-compliance
Lightning Source LLC
Chambersburg PA
CBHW040151270326
41926CB00079B/4630